Country Boys
and
Merchant Princes

Wall Street, 1850. COURTESY ENO COLLECTION, PRINTS DIVISION, THE NEW YORK PUBLIC LIBRARY, ASTOR, LENOX AND TILDEN FOUNDATIONS.

Country Boys and Merchant Princes

THE SOCIAL CONTROL OF YOUNG MEN

IN NEW YORK

Allan Stanley Horlick

Lewisburg

BUCKNELL UNIVERSITY PRESS
London: **ASSOCIATED UNIVERSITY PRESSES**

© 1975 by Associated University Press, Inc.

Associated University Presses, Inc.
Cranbury, New Jersey 08512

Associated University Presses
108 New Bond Street
London W1Y OQX, England

Library of Congress Cataloging in Publication Data

Horlick, Allan Stanley, 1941-
    Country boys and merchant princes.

    Bibliography: p.
    1. Merchants—New York (City)—History. 2. Occupational mobility
—New York (City)—History. 3. New York (City)—Social conditions. I.
Title.
HF3163.N7H66   301.44'42'097471   73-2887
ISBN 0-8387-1361-0

To Mary

Contents

Acknowledgments 9

Introduction 11

PART I: THE SETTING 23

1 The Growth of New York 25

2 Making Sense of Change 45

PART II: PROBLEMS 65

3 The Rise of William E. Dodge 67

4 A Passing Tradition 83

5 A Tale of Two Clerks 106

  a. William Hoffman 106

  b. Edward N. Tailer, Jr. 121

PART III: THE SEARCH FOR SOLUTIONS 145

6 Advice to Young Men 147

7 The Need for Institutions 179

8 Phrenology 210

9 The Founding of the YMCA 226

10 Institutions: Reservoirs of Character 244

Selected Bibliography 267

Index 274

Acknowledgments

In the course of preparing this book I have assumed many debts. The following deserve special thanks: James B. Gilbert, by his presence on the Teachers College faculty in 1968-69, helped me to gain access not only to the Columbia University and Barnard College libraries, where I did most of my writing, but also to the T.C. gymnasium, where I was able to release some of the tension built up during a day's work; Arthur Breton, then of the New-York Historical Society, led me to the Hoffman and Tailer diaries; and Virginia Downes, then of the YMCA Historical Library, offered me cheerful conversation and rare freedom in searching through the materials in her care. I am most indebted to William R. Taylor, now of the State University of New York at Stony Brook. The criticisms he made of the first draft of the study helped me to clarify the argument and make explicit many points I had overlooked. More important was the role he played in teaching me some of the most significant lessons I have learned about the nature of historical thinking. The excitement this teaching generated has been an essential part of whatever continuing, sustained interest I have had in doing historical work.

At a later stage of writing I received advice and encouragement from Paul H. Mattingly, Lawrence Cremin, Berenice M. Fisher, and

Donald M. Scott. Miss Fisher generously offered thorough and thoughtful criticism, from which I have benefited greatly even when I have not followed her suggestions. Mr. Scott provided me with especially provoking commments and this book is better as a result. Naturally none of the above are responsible for the stubbornness with which I have pursued certain lines of argument and neglected others, even when tactical considerations counseled otherwise.

Introduction

By the late 1840s and 1850s the New York mercantile community was the wealthiest and most powerful in the nation. The port around which it had grown had secured its dominance over its rivals; its future prosperity for decades to come was assured. Yet the merchants, bankers, and manufacturers, whose living depended in one way or another on the prosperity of the port, could not look with unalloyed pleasure on its growth. For the forces which made this development possible also presented them with problems that seemed to threaten the gains in wealth, power, and prestige they had won.

The growth of New York's port took place at a time when many kinds of rural employment were vanishing and when the proportion of young people in the population was greater than it had been since the nation's founding. The result was an unparalleled movement of young people, especially young men, to the cities where they might be most likely to find work.[1] New York, for a number of reasons

1. This conclusion is suggested by the demographic data in James Potter, "Demographic Factors in American Population Before 1860," Lecture to Economic History Workshop, University of Wisconsin, May 1965; Yasukichi Yasuba, *Birth Rates of the White Population in the United States. 1800-1860* (Baltimore, 1932), p. 141; and William B. Whiteside, "The Boston YMCA and Community Need: A Century's Evolution, 1851-1951" (Ph.D. diss., Harvard University, 1951), pp. 14-16.

(some of which will be discussed in chapter 1), was the obvious destination for many of them; in the decades before the Civil War its growth rate was one of the highest in the nation.

Many of the leading members of the New York community, especially its businessmen, were profoundly troubled by this influx. In sermons, speeches, books, and the magazine and newspaper articles that they addressed to young men, they revealed a great deal of unsettled thinking about the threat the young arrivals from rural districts posed to established traditions of mercantile and social practice. Very quickly merchants realized that young men of such numbers and from such backgrounds could not easily be integrated into mercantile life by the system that had ushered them into commerce a generation earlier.

This system, by which merchants of an older generation had been recruited and trained to assume their present professional and social stations, amounted to a combination of custom and habit that had evolved informally over decades of practice. Although these traditions lacked the legal force of apprentice agreements in the artisan and mechanical trades, they often had the same consequences for the daily life of the young men involved: their education and social preparation would revolve almost completely around their work. When New York's mercantile community was small and close-knit by ties of family and social background, a young man's initiation into mercantile practice was also part of his initiation into a social class. Indeed, in this early period of the nineteenth century the distinctions between a man's social and business life were probably less sharp than they are today. Men who lived in, or very near to, their places of business were social neighbors as well as business acquaintances.

This apprenticelike system began to falter under the combined need for added employees created by the port's growth and the pressure created by increasing numbers of petitioners for situations. Established merchants began to realize that the set of practices they had been using to initiate young men into the mercantile profession and class could not be used to pick out far larger numbers of young men for other lower-level positions in their countinghouses. The arrangements that had performed selection and education services for a community that was compact and whose members were familiar with one another could not perform them for a community that began to expand as rapidly as that of mid-century New York. Merchants knew these functions had to be carried out by some social agency: they clearly needed larger numbers of reliable employees to keep pace with their expanding operations. Yet, they feared that the entry of newcomers, if not carefully supervised and properly superintended, would lead to profound business and social dislocations. They feared that the integrity of their profession (and their profits), in addition to their association with the city's most respected social echelons, would be undermined. If the mercantile community could not control access to all of its positions, then it might become infiltrated by young men with no love for its traditions and no stake in maintaining its social prerogatives. The behavior of young men without these allegiances might be dangerously hard to anticipate.

By controlling access, merchants could both safeguard their own position and regularize the unpredictable behavior they attributed to newcomers. What they needed was some way of directing petitioners into the channels where they would be most useful. Filling vacant elite positions was a minor problem; family and close business ties could still be counted on to provide the talent needed, even if the chosen youths, as we will see, appeared more refractory than earlier. More important was the problem of finding a body of reliable employees to work at less demanding but increasingly more numerous tasks. If young men who would never be very mobile could be made to assimilate the values and ideals of those who would, they might remain loyal and hard working without growing anxious about leaving the modest stations they occupied. Unfortunately, agencies that could be pressed into this work were not abundant. No simple, obvious solution seemed to present itself. Merchants and other community leaders would have to try whatever was at hand and hope a satisfactory solution could be found before too much damage to longstanding business and social practice resulted. Yet the "damage" was perhaps inevitable: their own actions—expanding profitable commercial investments and moving accumulated capital into railroads, real estate, manufacturing, banking, and insurance—had created the problems they found so difficult to deal with.

This study is an attempt to show how the old set of practices broke down and to describe the way merchants sought replacements to carry out the necessary channeling functions it once performed. The period in which these developments took place, roughly the three decades before the Civil War, was one of experimenting with, one of groping for—of trying out and discarding—viable forms or vehicles that could exercise the functions merchants felt essential to maintaining the integrity of their profession and to securing a reliable body of employees. Merchants in this period began to fear that the social prestige of their profession was slipping and that its membership, once socially homogeneous, was being overrun by those of lower social standing.

Unfortunately, the erosion of status and the inundation by unrestrained youth did not seem easily curtailed. The society that merchants surveyed for solutions appeared to be barren of stable institutional forms that could be used as substitutes for the older and dysfunctional forms of apprenticeship. The traditional channels by which they selected, recruited, and trained their workforce had seemingly vanished.[2] Merchants now had no reliable way of finding "worthy" subordinates, and young men seeking jobs had no reliable way of knowing how they might find work. Meetings that later proved beneficial to both groups seemed accidental and random. The old apprenticeship system had regularized contacts between merchants and aspiring clerks; it had enabled both groups to know how to seek one another out and had given each an idea of what to expect from the other. Merchants knew what kind of young men they would be hiring and young men knew what kind of work and conditions they would find when they took positions. By the 1840s and 1850s this certainty, this set of expectations had broken down: the traditional channels that had guided a few young men to high positions and had guided others—not so talented or well connected—to secure, if less influential, careers in the mercantile community were rapidly disappearing.

Merchants and other community leaders dimly aware of what was happening cast around for agencies that would enable them to reestablish the control of social mobility they once felt rested exclusively

2. Even for the sons of well-established merchants, as the career of Edward N. Tailer, Jr. (see chap. 5) shows, these channels were proving unworkable.

in their hands. Their view of this process had always been implicit in the way apprenticeship operated in practice. But by the 1840s, now that the process began to diverge sharply from the way they hoped it operated, it was expressed more directly and hortatively. A need for articulation that did not often appear when customary arrangements could be taken for granted now became overwhelming. Not only did merchants and the writers who shared their point of view *describe* more explicitly the way young men moved in society. Increasingly they employed their efforts to *prescribe* the way young men should move in society. If the young came to understand the special version of the mobility process that merchants elaborated, the restless, uncalculated drive imputed to them could be slowed.

Some idea of the dimensions of the problem merchants saw themselves confronting can be obtained from examining the wealth of literature that in one way or another revealed this new stance. The sudden appearance of this literature in the decades before the Civil War strongly suggests an effort to deal with social and institutional changes that merchants were unprepared for. By demonstrating their surprise and bewilderment and by describing the discomfort merchants experienced, it is possible to show how the quality of their expression—and hence their feelings—differs from writing about the same subject at an earlier or later date. By recognizing this difference, by paying attention to the ways and forms in which people express themselves, the historian often has a way to get from the piece of expression—whether a sermon, magazine article, or novel—to the society that produced it. He has a way to define how that society has changed. It goes without saying that the historian must be careful about the connections he sees and the hypotheses he draws from such analysis, but he is justified in assuming that a relationship exists between a piece of writing and the time in which it was written. No matter how singular or exceptional a piece of writing may appear, if its author expects people to read it, he will write in a language that, by its assumptions and phrasing, can be used to locate it in a particular time and place. If this is a truism, it is one that is too often forgotten. Such writings as popular novels, sermons, diaries, and books of advice may often be the only tangible clues to the changes occurring at a particular time, especially a time of such institutional disarray as the 1840s and 1850s. Historians who are interested in describing such changes should not overlook these valuable and often readily available sources.

Many social and cultural historians have been attracted to this period because of its obvious ferment and innovation. With an occupationally trained eye for what is new, they have not failed to notice the appearance of new political rhetoric, new correctional and educational arrangements, a new effort to define national character, new artistic and architectural forms, and new kinds of didactic literature.[3] They have noted, in short, an effort by mid-nineteenth-century Americans to find new ways of conceptualizing—and of rooting institutionally—their national life.

As I studied the growth of urban life in this period, I too was struck by the appearance of new ways of talking and acting. I was struck by the new ways writers began talking about cities, by the way they talked about the dangers certain to befall young men flocking there, by the new kinds of advice (with its special emphases on character and mercantile careers) they offered and the new benevolent organizations they supported to assist the newcomers.

In trying to explain these developments I came to see them also as efforts at conceptualization and institutionalization. They seemed to be efforts to order, to make sense out of, to regularize and normalize an urban environment that was passing out of control. But unlike some historians of this period, I felt that the beginnings of an adequate explanation of the responses I had located required an attempt to connect them with specific changes in the life of the community. The earlier attempts to explain the rise and proliferation of new rhetorical or institutional forms too often relied simply on a broad notion of "unsettled social change" or some effort Americans made to "understand" change.[4]

3. See the work of Marvin Meyers, *The Jacksonian Persuasion* (Stanford, Calif., 1957); David J. Rothman, *The Discovery of the Asylum* (Boston, 1971); Michael Katz, *The Irony of Early School Reform* (Cambridge, Mass., 1968); Neil Harris, *The Artist in American Society* (New York, 1966); William R. Taylor, *Cavalier and Yankee* (New York, 1961); and Arthur M. Schlesinger, *Learning How to Behave* (New York, 1947).

4. For these two examples, see respectively Schlesinger, p. 19, and Rothman, p. 58.

In one recent account, the rise of asylums and penitentiaries in this period is ultimately accounted for by the failure of Americans to fit their *"perception* of nineteenth century society as mobile and fluid into an eighteenth century *definition* of a well-ordered community." Its author, in explaining why medical superintendents of insane asylums were convinced "that their society lacked all elements of fixity and cohesion," feels the difficulty was that they "judged" their society "by a nostalgic *image* of the eighteenth century." Their main problem, he says, *"was that they still adhered to the precepts of traditional social theory, to the ideas that they had inherited from the colonial period."*[5]

Apart from the lack of evidence offered to support his view, there are other difficulties with the author's position. One is that he sees no need to push the explanation beyond the disparity he notes between two distinct perceptions of the eighteenth and mid-nineteenth centuries. He seems to rely on that alone to provide explanatory power instead of continuing to ask how these perceptions can be used to suggest something about the societies they are meant to characterize.[6] Second, his tendency to seek explanations in a mental realm of conceptual images divorced from actual social experience encourages him to construct lines of reasoning for his protagonists which, though logical, may be far from accurate. In his discussion of the way reformers came to an environmental theory of crime, he says:

> Thinking that an orderly society had to be a fixed one, they judged the discrepancies between traditional postulates and present reality as promoting deviant behavior. Not having evolved an alternative to the colonial vision of society, they looked back both with envy and discomfort.[7]

Not only does this kind of explanation impose a degree of rationality

5. Rothman, pp. 70 and 127. (italics mine)
6. Questions are immediately suggested by Americans' characterization of colonial society. For example, a statement such as, "By these colonial standards men were to take their rank in the hierarchy, know their place in society and not compete to change positions" seems to offer a fruitful way to get at *nineteenth*-century anxiety about social mobility. *Ibid.*, p. 127.
7. *Ibid.*, p. 69.

on men that they do not possess (and hence prevents us from seeing the real complexities in their search for answers), but it also diverts our attention from looking at the interaction of men and their society as a way of understanding their behavior.[8] We are given, in other words, little way to see how, by what steps (or even if) the Americans involved came to their solutions by wrestling with problems connected to the roles they played and the positions they occupied in that society. Although the author's intention is "to place America's discovery of the asylum in a social context," he does not seem to get beyond characterizing it in vague and insubstantial terms such as the "open, freewheeling and disordered life of the community."[9] Because he finds his explanations by looking, in the last analysis, away from the society itself, he does not think to relate the images of social life he finds to actual social changes. In noting the picture Americans developed of a society filled with "a myriad of temptations," he characteristically explains it as a consequence of their adherence to a colonial *conception* of order instead of closely examining the various parts of the picture to learn something specific about those who devised it.[10] The cumulative effect is to divert us from the social processes that most need examination and, indeed, from the notion of process itself.

By contrast what I have tried to do in explaining broadly similar kinds of responses (books of advice—for young men instead of mothers, and agencies to regulate conduct—the YMCA for example instead of penitentiaries) is to use the language and form of the responses as a way to approach the process by which men take account of and try to respond to actual changes around them. I have tried to show how an expression of their fears and anxieties either in language or action can be used to suggest the specific changes that inform it.

In particular I have focused on one change that affected the lives

8. It is almost as if the tightness of the reasoning the author offers reinforces his tendency to look away from the society: if the conclusion follows inexorably from the premises as his formulation suggests, then it might occur to any nineteenth-century American regardless of social position.

9. *Ibid.*, pp. xviii and 210.

10. *Ibid.*, p. 70.

of young men and mercantile leaders in New York. I decided to focus on New York because of the unique extent to which its social life was dominated by commerce. I felt that the rapid development of its port facilities, the intensity of its mercantile activity, the degree to which social standing and influence resided in mercantile hands, unmatched in other cities, would intensify the quality and quantity of reflection occasioned by the problems that merchants and those sharing their interests were forced to deal with. Because New York's commercial problems touched so wide a part of the population, I felt they would generate the widest variety of speculation and thereby reflect more sides of the changes men of trade were confronting. Whether or not I have succeeded depends not on the nature or value of the sources but on how well I have been able to use them.

Country Boys
and
Merchant Princes

PART I

The Setting

1

The Growth of New York

New York merchants who reached middle age in the 1840s and 1850s came to maturity in a city undergoing its most rapid expansion. From an increase of 28 percent between 1810 and 1820, its population grew at a rate averaging close to 60 percent for the next four decades.[1] It is necessary to understand the reasons for this growth and its effects on the physical size of the city before the specific problems it caused for the mercantile community can be appreciated.

In 1818, the year one of the city's most prominent mid-century merchants, William E. Dodge, took his first clerkship, New York still resembled a small, uncrowded town. It received its water supply from wells scattered in various parts of the city. It had no sewers. Householders disposed of garbage and ashes by shoveling them to the middle of the street for removal by the city authorities twice a

1. George Rogers Taylor, "The Beginnings of Mass Transportation in Urban America: Part I," *The Smithsonian Journal of History* 1, no. 2 (1966): 36.

week. Light was by oil[2] and transportation was generally by foot. Before 1820 the city was still sparsely settled above City Hall; above Fourteenth Street there were only isolated farms and country houses.[3] Many merchants and bankers lived above their places of business, often with their apprentices or clerks, and those who maintained separate residences had only a short walk to the business district. From their homes on the lower West Side, in Greenwich Street and lower Broadway, it was just a few blocks east to Wall Street and the wharves on the East River.

The community was compact. Distances in city guidebooks were given in miles, the unit most helpful to people on foot, and New Yorkers found it possible to make up to forty calls on friends and relatives in a single New Year's Day.[4]

Beginning in the 1820s, New York's population began to grow at the rate it would sustain into the 1860s. But because the settled area increased in most places less than one-half mile above its limit in 1820,[5] the increase in population meant little to most New Yorkers. Only when the coming of mass transit in the 1830s allowed the increasingly congested city to spread northward did they realize how much New York City had changed. In the 1820s most people still lived under two miles from City Hall, even though the population was over 200,000 by the end of the decade. During this period New Yorkers could see the city as a small village, not because they were familiar with most of its inhabitants but because it was still possible for an hour's walk to bring them within reach of any part of it.

The census of new buildings that James Hardie undertook in 1825 reveals how imperfectly New York's growth in the 1820s was perceived. It also reveals the contrast between New Yorkers who could still view the city's growth with complacency and ease and those who, in the following decades, could confront it only with expres-

2. Henry Wysham Lanier, *A Century of Banking in New York. 1822-1922* (New York, 1922), p. 15.

3. *Ibid.*, p. 25. See also Bayrd Still, *Mirror for Gotham: New York as Seen by Contemporaries from Dtuch Days to the Present* (New York, 1956), p. 78.

4. See the New Year's Day entries in *The Diary of Philip Hone, 1828-1851,* ed. Allan Nevins (New York, 1935).

5. Taylor, "Beginnings of Mass Transportation," p. 37.

sions of alarm and disorientation. Hardie, born in Scotland in 1760, emigrated to the United States some time before 1784. After attending Columbia College, he was often employed by the city in such capacities as secretary for the Board of Health, assistant City Inspector, and a transcriber of manuscript laws for the Common Council.[6]

For reasons that are unclear—though one historian suggests that a wager among friends prompted him[7]—Hardie decided to "put an end to the controversy . . . concerning the number of houses, which had been built in this city, during the year 1824."[8] He intended to compile a list of all newly erected buildings and arrange them according to height and materials used. As Hardie tells us in the pamphlet he published presenting his results—he hoped that its sale would amply compensate his efforts and expenses—he "carefully traversed every street, lane and alley from the Bowery to the utmost limits of the Lamp and Water Districts" to make the "enumeration" as accurate as possible (p. 3).

He anticipated that two groups of citizens would question his results: "those who did not believe that our number of new buildings exceeded five or six hundred" and "those who entertained the idea that they amounted to 3000 and upwards." Hardie admitted that he had been a member of the second faction and explained why they quickly should have seen that their guess was in error. First, the number of workmen and the amount of materials necessary to put up so many buildings would have made the task impossible. Second, and decisive, was the population increase that so great a number of buildings would reflect. Hardie said that he and others who had made the same guess should have realized that nine tenths of the new structures would be built in the upper wards of the city and that all of them would house two families each. "If we suppose," he said, "that in each family, between parents, children, servants, relations, apprentices and boarders, there are six persons (and the supposition is not extravagant) we would have twelve persons in each house, and

6. Lawrence B. Romaine, "Talk of the Town: New York City, January, 1825," *Bulletin of the New York Public Library* 63, no. 4 (1959): 175-79.

7. *Ibid.*, p. 176.

8. James Hardie, *A Census of the New Buildings Erected in this City, in the Year 1824 . . .* (New York, 1825), p. 3.

in our 3000 new houses, an additional population of 36,000 inhabitants. *Would not this,"* he asked, *"make a snug little city of itself?"* (pp. 3-4; original italics). Hardie supposed that if the city continued to grow at the same rate for the next twenty years it would have as many inhabitants as London or Paris. But, he said, such extrapolations were unnecessary; New York was growing fast enough. "By telling the precise truth, it will be found, that New York encreases [sic] in population, in a degree of rapidity, perhaps unparalleled in history. We have therefore no occasion for exaggeration" (p. 4).

After these reflections Hardie presented an alphabetical list of streets and the number of new buildings he had found in each. His total came to 1,624: 720 were of brick or stone, 503 had brick fronts, 401 were of wood; 49 had one story, 1298 had two, 328 three, and 49 four or more (p. 12). The growth of the city had been substantial; New York, he noted, was clearly changing very rapidly. The speculation that the growth had created—and which in part prompted his undertaking—testified that the changes had been noticed by many New Yorkers. But the disparity of their estimates indicated how difficult it was for most people to judge accurately just what the rate was; Hardie's figure came as a surprise to both bodies of opinion he had defined. As Hardie reported it, people had felt that the city's growth had been either slight or enormous. His results proved that both guesses had been far from correct.

As significant as the imprecision with which Hardie's results were foreseen in understanding how New Yorkers saw the growth of their city during this period was the enthusiasm with which he undertook the project. It never seemed to occur to him that the operation might be more than a one-man job. Romaine, the historian who followed his movements, submits that this was the case; Hardie, he says, worked alone.[9] Despite New York's huge growth and substantial size (the growth rate was 64 percent during the decade 1820-30; the population was more than 150,000), Hardie apparently never considered that the city was too large for his plan to be undertaken without assistance. In discussing the project in the preface in his booklet, he never hinted that the job might be difficult or fraught with obstacles

9. Romaine, "Talk of the Town," p. 183.

requiring methods more sophisticated than the simple plan he intended to follow. He never seemed to doubt that he could easily recognize all the buildings that had gone up during the year, that he would not mistake any that were actually a few years old for new ones. He seemed to take for granted that he was so familiar with all areas of the city that he would have no difficulty distinguishing new buildings from older ones.[10] It is this assumption that sets him off from later New Yorkers. For Hardie, New York was easily traversed and its buildings easily catalogued. The city Hardie had investigated was still considered easy to comprehend.

Even though he recognized that New York was growing rapidly, he did not seem alarmed or unsettled. He welcomed the opportunity to speculate on the direction this growth would take. Hardie felt it was obvious that in the area between City Hall and the Battery, from the East to the Hudson Rivers, the number of new "dwelling-houses" could not be increased. New buildings might be substituted for old ones torn down. But, he reasoned, because the lower part of the city had so great an "eligibility for the extension of trade and commerce," razed dwelling-houses would rapidly be replaced by banks, insurance offices, countinghouses, and storage areas for merchandise. Many merchants, he noted, who did business in the area had already moved their places of residence up Broadway and Greenwich Street "and in other healthy and more retired situations." For this reason, Hardie was certain that the number of inhabitants in the business quarter would diminish rather than grow. Additional population would settle uptown:

> Our increase must . . . take place, in that part of the city, which lies above the City Hall, between which, and Kingsbridge [the northern end of Manhattan], there is vacant ground sufficient for the erection of more houses than would make a city as large as any of which we have authentic record in history. (p. 18)

By 1845 five-sixths of New York's population, he said, would be above City Hall. This calculation was reasonably accurate, but one of the conclusions he drew from it, though logical, was not. Hardie

10. Hardie, *Census of New Buildings,* pp. 3-4.

prophesied that City Hall, which would then be at one extremity of the city instead of at its center, as it had been, would have to be rebuilt further uptown. Only then could city authorities stave off complaints that those who had business at City Hall "have too far to travel to the seat of Justice, which ought, as far as possible, be brought to everyman's door" (p. 19). Hardie was able to imagine how fast the population would increase (though this did not shake his confidence that New York was still the easily comprehensible unit of his earlier years), but was apparently unable to imagine the technological and industrial changes that would provide some degree of mass transit and thereby make the removal of City Hall unnecessary.

Later New Yorkers, living amidst these technological developments, would view the city far differently. To them New York's alteration would appear too cataclysmic to be seen as complacently as James Hardie saw it. While the city grew at no faster rate—indeed during the decade 1830-40 the rate was only 54 percent compared to 64 percent during 1820-30—growth was more visible as New York began to spread out. The difficulties involved in getting from one part of the city to another became more evident, and the fact that there were separate neighborhoods for rich and poor and separate areas devoted to work and domestic life more obvious.

As Hardie had foreseen, the downtown section of New York was more and more given over to the business operations tied to the growing port. With its natural advantages, its early dominance in European importing, its profits from the "cotton triangle" trade and then finally its control of the enormous hinterland afforded by the opening of the Erie Canal, New York after 1815 firmly established its commercial superiority over rival cities.[11] For good reasons, as Amos Hawley has shown, population and wealth tend to gather at breaks or interruptions in transportation routes.[12] New York's control of the trade routes from Europe, the South, and the West made it such a point of intersection. Goods from the South or West had to be put on vessels going overseas. Those from Europe had to be put on

11. Robert Greenhalgh Albion, *The Rise of New York Port, 1815-1860* (New York, 1939), p. 10.

12. Amos Hawley, *Human Ecology: A Theory of Community Structure* (New York, 1950), pp. 242-43.

carriers going South or inland. Until exchanges were completed or transportation appropriate to new destinations arranged, goods had to be stored. Facilities for their handling and transfer had to be provided. Buildings for the repair and maintenance of transporting vehicles and office space for administrative work were also necessary. All this required a large work force of varied talents (pp. 242-43).

The area around South Street, Wall Street, and Pearl Street was devoted to handling the commercial needs that developed. South Street was the most directly maritime; shipowners, ship brokers, and ship agents populated its countinghouses. Insurance companies and banking houses centered on Wall Street. And the merchandizing community that handled the goods shippers carried grew up close by. The offices of importers, commission merchants, auctioneers, and jobbers who specialized in dry goods, flour, and hardware lined the street surrounding the port. From Pearl Street, an 1852 survey said, they had quickly spread to William, Broad, Pine, Cedar, Liberty, Water, and Front Streets. In addition, retailers kept pushing up Broadway and Nassau Street, establishing their stores where the city's plushest residences once stood.[13]

Industry added to the increasing mercantile specialization that accompanied the port's growth. With the availability of coal and the development of steam engines in the 1840s, manufacturing plants began to appear more widely in New York, especially those associated with the large East River shipbuilding yards and steamboat industry.[14] Advances in the steam industry also led to the development of railroad lines, which enabled New York to retain its commercial dominance over Boston, Philadelphia, and Baltimore. In 1853 the New York Central opened rail service between Buffalo and Albany and was able to make connections with railroads from New York and Boston and with the Hudson River steamboats. And, by 1850, the Hudson River Railroad had made connections upriver as far as Poughkeepsie.[15] These extensions of New York's transporta-

13. Albion, *The Rise of New York Port,* pp. 266-82.

14. Taylor, "Beginnings of Mass Transportation," p. 39 and Albion, *The Rise of New York Port,* pp. 148, 287-311.

15. Robert Ernst, *Immigrant Life in New York City, 1825-1863* (New York, 1949), p. 15.

tion network solidified the gains and expanded the need for faciliites and manpower that water travel had originally brought to the city.

The effect of this manufacturing and commercial activity on New York's physical development was vast. The business section was pushed further from the water's downtown edge. Banks, counting-houses, markets, exchanges, factories, warehouses, lumber yards, and taverns increasingly crowded out the old residential dwellings of the area.[16] As downtown land increased in value because of its importance for business sites, established families—like that of Philip Hone, as we will see— profited by moving elsewhere, generally uptown. Here, on land less accessible to the major intercommunity transportation routes, relatively cheap plots were available.[17] The working classes, whose labor was needed in the business district and who could not afford the time or money it took to use the limited mass transportation facilities, were forced to crowd into districts near their work. These areas close to business and industry were high in value and deteriorated in condition. Owners of the land held it in the hope that it would soon be put to more intensive commercial uses; they were reluctant to spend heavily for maintenance or new residential construction. This factor, in addition to the proximity of these areas to the noise and filth caused by the traffic, business, and industry nearby, gave the districts on the lower West Side and near East Side a low rental for family use. The Third Ward on the lower West Side along Greenwich Street, once the location of fine homes and families, became the home of Irish and German immigrants in the 1840s and 1850s.[18] Soon afterward it became the site of the rows of warehouses that still line its upper portions.

The near East Side, the area just behind the present Foley Square courthouses, was also relegated to working-class and immigrant use by these and other factors. The district was close to the East River shore, an area that had been preempted by shipyards and ironworks servicing the steamboat industry as far north as Fourteenth Street.

16. Taylor, "Beginnings of Mass Transportation," p. 39.
17. Hawley, *Human Ecology,* p. 276.
18. George Rogers Taylor, "The Beginnings of Mass Transportation in Urban America: Part II, *"The Smithsonian Journal of History* 1, no. 3 (1966): 51; Hawley, *Human Ecology,* p. 281; Ernst, *Immigrant Life,* p. 39.

This virtually made certain that areas adjacent to it would never be put to residential use by the middle and upper classes. But these areas would probably not have been put to such use even if this was not the case. The district was the former site of the Collect Pond, around whose soggy perimeter slaughterhouses and tanneries had flourished. And although the Pond had been filled and many of the cattle-processing plants shut down, the poor who had gathered there remained on the marshy fill. Rents were predictably the lowest in the city and the area was only a short walk away from work on docks and in warehouses nearby. In the 1820s and 1830s, Irish immigrants occupying old dilapidated buildings or flimsy dwellings they had put up themselves with local materials were already giving the area—called the Five Points—its notorious reputation.[19] For reasons we will explore in the next chapter, the chaos, viciousness, and criminality of the area were generally overemphasized. But poverty, as one historian noted, was certainly widespread and the congestion in squalid, fetid garrets and cellars did little to alleviate tensions that might lead to riot and violence.[20]

Those better off were naturally able to avoid this kind of crowding. The introduction of the omnibus in the late 1820s, the commuter railroads and steam ferries of the 1830s and 1840s and the enormous growth of the horsecars or street railways of the 1850s enabled those who could afford the fare and the delay to push the settled portion of New York outward.[21] Those who did so, at first moved up the West Side—partly, one suspects, to avoid traveling to and from work through areas like the Five Points. Fashionable areas on the East Side developed later. In 1830 Grammercy Park was still a swamp and not until 1847 was Madison Square cleared for settlement.[22]

19. Alvin F. Harlow, *Old Bowery Days* (New York, 1931), pp. 90, 127-28.

20. Ernst, *Immigrant Life,* p. 39. See also Lynn H. Lees, "Patterns of Lower-Class Life: Irish Slum Communities in Nineteenth-Century London," in Stephan Thernstrom and Richard Sennett, eds. *Nineteenth Century Cities* (New Haven, 1969), p. 383, for an argument countering the view that slum life was in fact chaotic or socially deteriorated.

21. See Taylor, "Mass Transportation: Part II."

22. Harry James Carman, *The Street Surface Railway Franchises of New York City* (New York, 1919), p. 13.

One way to gauge the rapid expansion of the city is to look at the number of wards added to New York after the introduction of mass transportation. Between 1850 and 1853 four wards between Twenty-sixth Street and Eighty-sixth Street were added to the city. Together they added 115,440 people. By 1855 the six wards above Fourteenth Street—the practical boundary of the walking city (it was just under two miles to City Hall)—accounted for 194,678 inhabitants, or 30 percent of the total population of New York. By contrast, in 1825, the the last census year before mass transit became a factor, there were no wards above Fourteenth Street. Between 1808 and 1825 the number of wards comprising New York City remained—though their population increased markedly—the same. But in the next thirty years the number of wards steadily increased, so that by 1855 eleven new ones had been added.[23]

One result of these developments was the partitioning of New York into separate residential districts. Even an inefficient system of mass transit enabled some of those who could pay the tariff to move northward and build elegant homes. Yet, because of its relatively high cost and inefficiency, it did not really disperse the congestion in the wards adjacent to the business district, especially on the East Side. By 1860 more than half of New York's 813,669 population still crowded below Fourteenth Street.[24]

Philip Hone was one of those wealthy enough to move uptown. For many years before 1821 he had been one of New York's most successful merchants, and he was still one of its most prominent citizens. His initiation into commercial affairs began when, at the age of sixteen, he started helping in his brother's auction house. Within three years he had become a partner and for over twenty years thereafter worked tirelessly and methodically in a business where risks, as Allan Nevins tells us, were virtually nonexistent.[25]

In 1821 Hone retired and devoted his time to acquiring the education and culture he had never obtained formally (accumulating a sub-

23. See chart in Ernst, *Immigrant Life,* p. 191.
24. Taylor, "Mass Transportation: Part II," p. 52.
25. *The Diary of Philip Hone,* p. ix. Also see Albion, pp. 276-80, for an account of the importance of the auction system in this period.

stantial library and art collection in the process), to travel, and to politics. In 1823 and 1824 he was elected assistant alderman and in 1825-26 served a one-year term as mayor. Much of his time was also consumed in social affairs; he was considered a member of the city's most elite and aristocratic circles and spent many hours entertaining and being entertained by New York's patrician class. Hone was also an active philanthropist. He was one of the leading patrons of the Mercantile Library Association and helped build Clinton Hall which, after 1832, housed it. He was a trustee of Columbia College and the Bloomingdale Asylum, and a governor of the New York Hosptial.

After his retirement he continued making wise investments (as in the Delaware and Hudson coal mines and canal), but the depressions of 1834 and 1837 forced him to live in a reduced manner. Despite these reverses he was able, in 1837-38, to abandon his home opposite City Hall Park and move his family to a new house, eighteen blocks north. Here on the corner of Broadway and Great Jones Street he continued to be served by a contingent of coachmen, cook, errand boy, and maids, and to maintain a barouche, two carriage horses, and a saddle horse.[26]

Men like Hone, by virtue of their social and political contacts and their ties to commerce—the lifeblood of the city—stood at the center of life in New York.[27] Because of this position they were perhaps as sensitive to change as any group in the city. Change was a fact of life they could not ignore. It was with them every day in the form of market fluctuations and business competition. It was with them socially as they witnessed the constant struggle for status and position among their contemporaries. They speculated in land and superintended the business operations that resulted in the relocation of hundreds of families, including their own. Sometimes they witnessed these changes approvingly, but other times they did not. Hard-won economic and social gains could be overturned in a day. And the population growth that presented them with opportunities to profit

26. *The Diary of Philop Hone,* pp. ix-xvii.
27. See Douglas T. Miller, *Jacksonian Aristocracy: Class and Democracy in New York, 1830-1860* (New York, 1967), p. 59 and Still, p. 133 for an idea of the centrality of commerce to New York life.

also represented a challenge to their social and occupational security: the immigrants and native young men who gained a foothold in New York were soon seeking entry to the merchants' professional and social circles. When change so directly affected one's own life, it was difficult to avoid thinking about its sources and consequences.

Philip Hone was no exception. In the diary he kept during the 1830s and 1840s, he left a record of his attempt to come to grips with the forces changing his world. Here he assessed the advantages and disadvantages of new technological advances, like steamships and railroads, reflected on the swiftness and violence of the city's expansion, and speculated on the growing divisions between New York's rich and poor. To Hone and others, New York was changing beyond recognition; the city he described at the beginning of his diary was a very different place from the one he described at the end. After a walk one April afternoon in 1846, he realized that he "knew no more about New York as it now is than the hermit of Saba. Such a mass of busy population, such noises of 'armorers closing rivets up,' such creaking of blocks, such pulling of ropes and such caulking of seams!"[28] Unlike James Hardie, who seemed so familiar with all parts of New York, Hone recognized that he had become a provincial in his own city.

As Hardie had predicted, business emporiums expanded in lower Broadway and crowded out family residences. Hone's own home became worth too much not to sell. In 1836 he deeded it to Elijah Boardman for a $35,000 profit. He had held the property only fifteen years. The new owner planned to turn the lower story into shops; the upper story was to become part of the American Hotel. Hone regretted being "turned out of doors." "But," he said, "$60,000 [Boardman's price] is a great deal of money." Many of those he knew found themselves in a similar situation:

> Almost everyone downtown is in the same predicament, for all the dwelling houses are to be converted into stores. We are tempted with prices so exhorbitantly [sic] high that none can resist, and the old downtown burgomasters, who have fixed to one spot all their lives, will be seen during the next summer in flocks, marching

28. *The Diary of Philip Hone*, p. 761.

reluctantly north to pitch their tents in places which, in their time, were orchards, cornfields, or morasses a pretty smart distance from town and a journey to which was formerly an affair of some moment, and required preparation beforehand, but which constitutes at this time the most fashionable quarter of New York. (p. 202)

It is noteworthy that Hone considered these changes in terms of the new distances they created and the travel time and preparation they occasioned. He was being forced to think of the city as a place covering a growing area whose various sections were no longer easily accessible to one another.

Hone also was agitated by the haste, disarray, and disruption with which removal was carried out. His diary was littered with entries about old buildings razed and the new ones that seemed to take their place almost overnight. So quickly did this process occur that Hone could think of no better way to describe it than to liken the change to a great natural cataclysm:

The pulling down of houses and stores in the lower parts of the city is awful. Brickbrats, rafters, and slates are showering down in every direction. There is no safety on the sidewalks, and the head must be saved at the expense of dirtying the boots. In Wall Street, besides the great Exchange, which occupies with huge blocks of granite a few acres of the highway of merchants there is the beautiful New Bank of the United States opposite, still obstructing the walk. Besides which four banks . . . are in progress of destruction; it looks like the ruin occasioned by an earthquake. (pp. 394-95)

Everywhere buildings seemed to be coming down, streets seemed to be filled with litter and debris, and pedestrians seemed to be nervously scurrying from place to place. New York was a place dominated by the "spirit of pulling down and building." It appeared to be a place that was never at rest, never quiet or at peace, never finished. "The whole of New York, he said, "is rebuilt about once in ten years" (p. 395).

Hone was most upset by the carelessness of builders, whose shoddy work often led to serious accidents. "Everything in New York has been rising for some time past," he said, "but nothing falls but the new houses.'' With land so valuable and rents so high, contractors did not make the effort to give new edifices the stability they required. Just the day before, he noted on one occasion, between ten and eleven in the morning the granite front and party wall of a range of new buildings on Fulton Street collapsed. And today he said, fixing the time precisely at a quarter past one, ''the large and unfinished granite building belonging to the Messrs. Josephs came down with a crash like that of an earthquake.''[29]

Not all change, Hone agreed, was bad. He recognized that developments in steam and coal technology, for example, could be put to beneficial uses. But his sense of awe was muted by his predilection for dwelling on the disastrous consequences their power could unleash. In places the diary reads like a catalogue of steamboat, railroad, and mining disasters.[30] In recounting the catastrophes, the viollence and the uncontrolled force that the new advances represented were constantly in his mind. He admitted that the potential of steam energy was enormous. ''This powerful agent which regulates just now the affairs of the world,'' he said, ''is all potent for good and for evil.'' But it appeared to Hone that its tendency toward destruction outweighed its advantages at the present time.

> [It] has become a substitute for war in the philosophical plan of keeping down the superabundance of the human race, and thinning off the excessive population of which political economists have from time to time expressed so much dread. Scarcely a day passes that we do not hear of some steamboat being blown up . . . or of a locomotive running off the railroad and thus bringing many to an unexpected termination of their journey.[31] [elipsis in Nevins edition]

There is much in the diary to indicate that Hone often wished he could turn the clock back to a time before these intrusions existed. One summer weekend in 1831, Hone went to visit the Delaware and Hudson mines, in which he had invested. As Allan Nevins excerpts his retelling of the trip, Hone seemed more gratified inspecting the

29. *Ibid.*, p. 246. See also p. 896.
30. See, for example, *ibid.*, pp. 334, 599, 656, 753.
31. *Ibid.*, p. 598. See also pp. 203, 261.

site on Sunday, when it was at rest, than he might have been had he
seen it at work earning him a dividend.

> The rattling of cars, the explosion of gunpowder, and the clanking
> of pickaxes, is now as still as the tomb of the Capulets, and the
> miners who were yesterday begrimed with coal and looked like
> citizens of the nether world, are seen this morning on their way to
> church clean and well dressed, with long coats and gilt buttons,
> high shirt collars and brooches in their bosoms. (p. 45)

The unusual quiet of the collieries or the clean and, as Hone described it, almost elegant dress of the workers on their way to
church—a picture as far as posssible from the "nether world" they
ordinarily inhabited—barely identified the area with the activity that
characterized it. On another occasion the following spring, Hone was
dismayed to discover that Paterson, New Jersey, had diverged
sharply from the fine rural retreat it used to be. "Green trees have
given place to brown stone walls, and the singing of birds to the
everlasting noise of spinning jennies and power looms" (p. 62). The
natural and peaceful were rapidly giving way to the unnatural and
discordant forces of industrialism.

His reading habits were one more indication of his feelings of loss.
Sir Walter Scott was his favorite (he filled almost thirty pages of his
diary with extracts from Lockhart's *Scott*), and he also enjoyed
Prescott's histories (from which he again copied out long passages)
and the nostalgic novels of his friend John Pendleton Kennedy (he
called *Horse-Shoe Robinson,* a historical romance about the Revolutionary War, "the best American story I have ever read") (pp.
291, 326, 179). Perhaps in these works he thought he could find
some evidence of the traditions of chivalry and gentlemanly conduct
that appeared to be passing from the New York scene. Instead of
cherishing and preserving a record of the men who had kept these
practices alive, New Yorkers now seemed eager only to eliminate
any trace of their existence. "Overturn, overturn, overturn!" wrote
Hone, "is the maxim of New York. The very bones of our ancestors
are not permitted to lie quiet a quarter of a century, and one generation of men seem studious to remove all relics of those which pre-
ceeded [*sic*] them (p. 730).

Hone's feeling that his environment was dangerously unstable, that it was changing with a catastrophic swiftness practically impossible to keep track of, and that it was taking on a discomforting, clangorous stridency was widely shared.

Visual descriptions of New York indicate how widespread these feelings were. Two of the most common representations of New York after their initial appearance in the 1830s were bird's-eye pictures and scale models. As one student of urban symbolism has pointed out, both of these attempts to encompass the city at a glance were closely related. The prints achieved the sense of New York's wholeness, the sense that it was a comprehensible entity, by moving the observer to a point like the tops of high buildings or nearby hills, far above it. The models achieved the same effect by manipulating the city instead of the position of the observer.[32] Both ways of picturing New York were attempts to reduce and simplify a unit that had grown bewilderingly large. Standing above the city—as the viewer of a bird's-eye drawing or of a miniature replica or, indeed, as was becoming popular in England, as an observer of the city from an air-borne balloon[33]—one could take in the whole city without being confused or overwhelmed by the mass of detail attending a tour by foot.[34] As the newspaper editors recommending one model wrote, "The business and commerce of New York can be better seen by a casual inspection of this Model, than by days spent in actually visiting the business localities of the city."[35] E. P. Belden, the model's creator, advertised that his replica differed from the actual city "only in point of size" (p. 26).

32. Anselm Strauss, *Images of the American City* (New York, 1961), p. 6.

33. Asa Briggs, *Victorian Cities* (London, 1963) p. 53.

34. One suspects that the diarist George Templeton Strong began taking horseback rides around the city for similar reasons. New York in 1844, when Strong speaks of the rides, had grown too large for him to gain any reassuring sense of its limits by simply walking as he usually did. See *The Diary of George Templeton Strong,* ed. Allan Nevins and M. H. Thomas. 4 vols. (New York, 1952), 1: 302, 305. See also Diary of Edward N. Tailer, Jr. (1846-1917), April 12, 1850, New-York Historical Society, Manuscript Division.

35. E. Porter Belden, *New York: Past, Present and Future. . .* (New York, 1849), p. 4.

Scale models like Belden's did more than simply make New York comprehensible to its residents and visitors. They also added a sense of stability and solidity the actual city may have lacked. Here the movement and dynamism that upset men like Hone was stilled. The promotional guidebook that accompanied the appearance of Belden's model suggests this purpose. In the book's lengthy descriptive chapters, Belden made it appear that a proper and thorough picture of New York was achieved by enumerating as many of its institutional structures as possible. It may be significant that the author, in describing the city's government, educational and benevolent societies, and commercial buildings, emphasized their physical properties rather than their functions.

This emphasis on physical stability was also apparent in the lithographs and line engravings widespread at the time.[36] Prints appeared depicting Wall Street and Broadway, two of New York's most busy and crowded streets, as if they were avenues for the promenade of royalty. One 1850 view of Wall Street (frontispiece) pictured it as a wide expansive street, perfectly straight and smoothly paved, instead of as the narrow, winding, cobbled lane it was. It was lined with handsome buildings, some of which—generally the ones made of brick—were unusually tall, narrow, and linear; others were made of clean white marble with prominent columns. All were solid and imposing, literally towering over pedestrians disproportionately. Whatever interfered with this effect had been altered. Two- and three-story buildings had become four- and five; the balconies, trellises, awning posts, abutting ledges, and overhanging signs had been either removed or greatly modified. Retail stores had become staid residences. Male figures were remarkably few and impeccably dressed. Instead of being engaged in business, most were simply out with ladies for a leisurely stroll. The street, scrubbed and swept clean,

36. Excellent collections of these materials can be found in John A. Kouwenhoven, *The Columbia Historical Portrait of New York* (Garden City, N.Y., 1953); Henry Collins Brown, *Old New York: Yesterday and Today* (New York, 1922); I. N. Phelps Stokes, *The Iconography of Manhattan Island.* 5 vols. (New York, 1915-28); and Frank Weitenkampf, *The Eno Collection of New York City Views* (New York, 1925). The views that Weitenkampf has catalogued in this booklet are in the Prints Division, New York Public Library.

was devoid of the vendors, cartmen, traders, newsboys, and animals that normally cluttered it. The effect was one of serenity and stability. No one seemed in a hurry; no one seemed pressured. The frenzy and disorder associated with the area vanished. Even Trinity Church appeared more majestic and dominating than usual.[37]

Another print, of Broadway at City Hall (fig. 2), achieved the same effect through less-obvious but equally effective manipulation

New York City Hall, Park, and Environs, c. 1850. COURTESY ENO COLLECTION, PRINTS DIVISION, THE NEW YORK PUBLIC LIBRARY, ASTOR, LENOX AND TILDEN FOUNDATIONS.

37. The Eno Collection of New York City Views, 5 vols., Prints Division, New York Public Library, 3, no. 251, "Wall Street." Compare with Kouwenhoven, *Columbia Historical Portrait*, pp. 202-3 and photograph in Leonard Louis Levinson, *Wall Street, A Pictorial History* (New York, 1951), p. 118.

of its elements. Broadway, like Wall Street, was widened and straightened and was now able to accommodate its bustling traffic without appearing crowded. City Hall Park, dotted with exotic-looking trees and an outsized version of the Park fountain, became an American copy of the gardens fronting the palaces of European nobility. The perspective of the scene added to the effect. The artist had drawn the view so that only the east side of Broadway was visible; the side with the shops was hidden. Chatham Street, another commercial avenue on the other side of City Hall Park, was obscured by foliage and reduced by the angle of the view so that its activity and gaudiness also left the peace of the scene undisturbed. The effect of stability—unnecessarily underscored, perhaps, by the large stone slabs the artist placed in the foreground—was also emphasized by the background of rolling hills. To an extent the hills confined the scene and set limits to an expansion that appeared to many indefinite and uncontrollable.[38]

Other prints simply denied that any change had taken place at all. Almost in counterpoint to scenes of frenetic and often violent activity were views that pictured the same areas as if they were streets in quiet country towns. In one view of Bowling Green, trees almost completely blocked out all buildings, which stood hazily in the background. Few people were visible and the only vehicle was a coach and liveried driver at rest, apparently waiting for its occupants to return from what might easily be a country stroll. In another print (fig. 3), Broadway was viewed from City Hall Park and the street's usual traffic was literally dropped below street level. Buildings were visible but there were no store fronts or business activities pictured. As in the print of Bowling Green, the viewer was able to see the city only by making his way through the trees and park that dominated the foreground of the scene.[39]

Here, as in the other examples we have examined, New Yorkers dealt with disorienting and discomfiting aspects of the physical

38. Eno Collection, 3, no. 242, "New York City Hall, Park and Environs." Compare with Eno Collection, 2, nos. 138, 150.
39. *Ibid.*, 2, no. 128, "View of the Bowling Green, Broadway;" Eno Collection, 2, no. 257, "St. Paul's Church, Barnum's Museum, and Astor House."

St. Paul's Church, Barnum's Museum, and Astor House, 1850.
COURTESY ENO COLLECTION, PRINTS DIVISION, THE NEW YORK
PUBLIC LIBRARY, ASTOR, LENOX AND TILDEN FOUNDATIONS.

landscape by presenting them as they hoped—in fantasy—they might
appear. Similarly they also transfigured the aspects of the human
landscape that provoked reactions of uneasiness. In the way they pictured groups like the poor and the rich just recently risen from their
ranks, they showed once more that the easiest way to deal with
changes both new and upsetting was to transform them into something more comforting and less threatening.

2

Making Sense of Change

According to men long acquainted with the life of the city, New York was changing with disruptive speed. It was becoming strange where it had been familiar, and mysterious where it had been predictable. To many of New York's most prominent residents, the obvious proof of this was the increasing differences they noticed between residential districts. By the 1840s, New York no longer seemed like the "village" that Philip Hone had talked about a decade earlier. The social consequences of expansion were too obvious to ignore. Like Hone, many New Yorkers in his social position had reluctantly given up the idea that New York was a single harmonious unit.

Social changes, especially the social segregation accompanying the influx of both native young men and European immigrants, made such a view impossible. Inevitably, as differences between neighborhoods became more pronounced, they began to see New York as a different kind of place from the community they had once envisioned. While to some extent a certain social segregation was always apparent in New York (and other cities as well), it was only in this period that such divisions became part of the effort to define the nature of city life. The poor especially, New Yorkers began to emphasize, now lived in a part of the city inaccessible to and divorced from the lives of respectable citizens. Earlier they had felt that benevolent organizations like the Association for Improving the Condition of the Poor would help to maintain New York as a community of close-knit members. But their participation in the work of these groups had the opposite effect; it convinced them that the poor lived distinct and separate lives and were not so easily assimilated to middle-class standards of gentility and rectitude as they had thought. New York, they began to feel, was composed of two separate communities, not one temporarily rent apart.[1] By 1847 Philip Hone noted that New York was a city "overburdened with population . . . where the two extremes of costly luxury in living, expensive establishments, and improvident waste are presented in daily and hourly contrast with squalid misery and hopeless destitution."[2]

This feeling that society was divided into such sharply separated groups had already become widespread in the descriptive literature that began to appear in this period. Yet, this literature did more than simply describe the new demographic and social changes noted in the last chapter. In its sheer quantity and in the way it departed from

1. These changes are particularly noticeable in the annual reports of the New York Association for Improving the Condition of the Poor. Founded in 1842 primarily through the efforts of Robert M. Hartley, a former merchant and temperance crusader, the Association's purpose was to channel contributions from private donors to the "worthy" poor. It encouraged charitably minded members of the community to direct the poor to the Association and never to relieve them individually. This, it was hoped, would discourage begging in the streets and the petitioning of the rich in their homes. It would enable the evils of poverty to be controlled by the careful scrutiny of those who administered relief. The investigation of applicants was accomplished through the efforts of volunteer "visitors," many of whom were merchants, bankers, and lawyers. See Robert M. Hartley Papers, Archives of the Community Service Society, New York; annual reports of the New York Association for Improving the Condition of the Poor; and Dorothy G. Becker, "The Visitor to the New York City Poor, 1843-1920: The Role and Contribution of Volunteer Visitors of the New York Association for Improving the Condition of the Poor, State Charities Aid Association and New York Charity Organization Society" (Ph.D. dissertation, School of Social Work, Columbia University, 1960).

2. *The Diary of Philip Hone 1828-1851,* ed. Allan Nevins (New York, 1936), p. 785.

earlier materials depicting life in New York it represented an effort to reduce these changes to manageable proportions by placing them within familiar categories.

These categories were readily available. By this time Americans possessed a well-developed set of terms to talk about the two groups that came to be most closely identified with upsetting urban change. The growing numbers of poor people (generally immigrants, specifically Irish) and the expansion of an acquisitive bourgeoisie eager to take advantage of new economic opportunities had for the past two decades begun to alarm Americans as they had not done before.[3] Both groups were easily connected with the changes remaking mid-nineteenth century cities and the negative moral judgment imputed to them soon began to color and define the scene of their activities. Americans, upset by the growing visibility and vociferousness of these groups, convinced that a disorganized society could not bear the added disruption of citizens unattached to the social fabric because of their idleness or because of their single-minded aggressiveness, transferred the moral judgments rendered upon the poor and parvenu to the urban world they seemed largely to have overrun. Both inhabitants and the arena they inhabited were seen as corrupt and venal, either prone to, or offering, awful temptations to personal and social morality. If picturing them in this way did not diminish their social or political presence it did seem to diminish their ethical standing. This, at least for a short time, enabled them to be banished to the moral fringes of the society, thereby securing its center for the forces of virtue and stability. These views allowed urbanites some measure of comfort, at least until the political power of the banished groups became too obvious to ignore.

Finding conventions to express such views did not prove to be a task requiring any special originality. It was not necessary to create them after a careful examination of their society. Europeans were experiencing many of the same changes and had already elaborated a view of the city and its denizens that incorporated the moral sentiments that Americans too were voicing. Charles Dickens in particular

3. See David J. Rothman, *The Discovery of the Asylum* (Boston, 1971), pp. 161 and 174 and William R. Taylor, *Cavalier and Yankee* (New York, 1961), p. 119.

was especially well known and had conveniently included a chapter about New York in the volume describing his travels to the United States in 1841. Writers freely borrowed his perceptions, and often his very words, in casting their own accounts of the city.

The profusion of guides for travelers, handbooks for businessmen, and journalistic exposés for the reading public (such as the popular *New York in Slices by an Experienced Carver*) differed in important ways from earlier descriptive accounts of New York. The earlier accounts, like the prolific James Hardie's *The Description of the City of New York*,[4] were full of information certain to be both familiar and useful to a rising middle-class audience. Hardie's readers, for example, were introduced to a New York open to enterprise and investment, well supplied with churches of all denominations, complete with institutions ready to provide for their sons' education, and theaters and parks to enable them to spend their leisure enjoyably and wisely. They would discover street guides that would assist them in getting around efficiently and quickly, and lists of hospitals that would take care of them should they fall ill, of the benevolent organizations that would clear paupers and beggars from the streets they walked, and of the prisons that would harbor those who might rob or assault them. The guides, in other words, assumed that visitors or resident New Yorkers would know how to use the city if they could only find what they were looking for. The city was there to serve its inhabitants; Hardie's purpose was to help them uncover what they needed to get on with the business at hand.

In contrast to these books were the more narrative, discursive journalistic accounts first published in the late 1840s and continuing with little change in form until the end of the century.[5] Here, for the first time, fascinations almost totally absent from the earlier books made their appearance. The literature overflowed with descriptions of a netherworld of vice, sin, and pauperism. These were not the only subjects dealt with. But whether the writers were clergymen and doctors claiming to retell personal experience or newspapermen recount-

4. James Hardie, *The Description of the City of New York* . . . (New York, 1827).
5. I have included fictional accounts employing the same conventions and content in this category.

ing their journeys through New York's principal neighborhoods and institutions, they all seemed devoted to "stripping away . . . the cloud of appearances in which . . . the glories of our magnificent city . . . is [*sic*] veiled" to disclose "but a vast abyss of crime and suffering, with here and there [only] a crystal shooting out over the horrid recess of filth."[6] That "[no] very nice arrangement of subjects" had been observed or "that [one author] has left altogether unnoticed many interesting appendages of New York" was lauded as a virtue contributing to, not detracting from, the pursuit of fact required "if the dark side of the picture [was] not to be altogether concealed." Only by exposing New York's underside could "a picture of the city . . . in all its various phases" be presented. As Dr. Joel H. Ross explained, it required "much more labor to present facts than fiction. And . . . it is not unfrequently [*sic*] more difficult still to make the former so acceptable as the latter.[7] No doubt this was intended as a statement of high resolve rather than as an indication that the writer would have considerable difficulty keeping the two apart. But readers about to be treated, as one title page promised, to "full and graphic accounts of [New York's] splendors and wretchedness; its high and low life; its marble palaces and dark dens; its attractions and dangers; its rings and frauds; its leading men and politicians; its adventurers; its charities; its mysteries, and its crimes"[8] might not be overly concerned with the distinction.

By and large the authors of these books hoped to present a balanced picture of New York, thereby warning "the thousands who visited the city against the dangers and pitfalls into which their curiosity or vice may lead them . . . ."[9] Ostensibly directed to these "country citizens" bent on leaving "their quiet cabins, and kind friends, and shady groves and green fields [to] be crammed and crowded, and packed and stuffed into some gloomy garrett, or

6. [G. G. Foster], *New York in Slices by an Experienced Carver* (New York, 1849), p. 5.

7. Joel H. Ross, *What I Saw in New York; or a Bird's Eye View of City Life* (Auburn, N.Y., 1852), p. 19.

8. James D. McCabe, Jr., *Lights and Shadows of New York Life* (Philadelphia, 1872).

9. Edward Winslow Martin [James D. McCabe, Jr.], *The Secrets of the Great City* (Philadelphia, 1868), p. 16.

mouldy cellar in a city''[10] the books offered the reader a guide through the vagaries of New York life. He would learn, as he had from the older books, something of the history of the city and the workings of the government and its various departments. Once again, he would be oriented to the street system and transit lines (though more generally and briefly), and given a look into prominent business operations, the workings of the stock exchange, school system, religious organizations, and local press.

But another orientation waited for him also. Interspersed among the chapters of predictable guidebook fare were sections describing customs and neighborhoods apparently just as widespread but assumed to be more bewildering to the average reader. Before he finished the reader would make the acquaintance of the Tombs, the Swindlers and Imposters of New York, the Five Points, the Bummers, Black-Mailing, Dance Houses, Concert Saloons, Assignation Houses, Quack Doctors, Clairvoyants, the Abbatoirs, the Patterers, Thimble Rigging, the Dead-Beats, the Patent Safe Game, the Dens of Midnight, the Bohemians, and the Demi-Monde. The authors took for granted that out-of-towners would find bummers, patterers, or the patent safe game and thimble rigging unfamiliar. The sketches portraying these various city attractions and swindles seemed to assume a level of understanding comparable to that of a child learning a foreign language. As it turned out, pages were often devoted to descriptions of people whose only claim to mystery was the name by which they were introduced. Bummers, for instance, were simply men who hated regular employment; patterers were street vendors. Furthermore, the actual activities of these New York denizens were cast in terms so general and commonplace as to lose any specific relevance to the life of New York City. Even activities and terms common to urban life generally seemed in need of interpretation. The books spoke of women ''shopping,'' of ''foot passengers'' walking the streets, of ''concrete,'' a mixture of ''broken stone, sand, gravel and hydraulic cement.''[11]

It was as if living in a city were so strange and unfamiliar to those

10. Ross, *What I Saw in New York,* p. 135.
11. *Ibid.,* p. 62.

not in the midst of it that the very fabric of urban life had to be recreated. Urban life had to be interpreted and decoded by those experienced in its ways, by those who knew its language. The reader of Ned Buntline's *Mysteries and Miseries of New York* (1849) must have been comforted by discovering that "a glossary explaining all of the slang and flash terms used in the work will be found appended."[12]

Yet, their solicitude for the country dwellers' confusion may have been a way of expressing their own. The way writers overplayed the assumption of rural ignorance of urban ways may indicate that they were writing for people very much like themselves, with intimate rather than remote contact with city life. A good example comes from Junius Henri Browne's *The Great Metropolis*. Here we meet the New York Roughs (young Irish delinquents, more or less), the offspring of immigrants "reared from . . . childhood under the worst influences—all his brutal instincts stimulated, and his moral being suffocated for want of wholesome air." The Rough enjoys reading obscene magazines like *The Clipper* and *The Police Gazette*. His "facial and cranial appearance" is that of a beast of prey:

> All the animal is in the shape of his features and head; but the semblance of the thinking, cultivated, self-disciplined man is very nearly lost. The cheek bones are high; the nose is flat; the lips are thick and coarse; the forehead low and receding; the jaws massive and protuberant; the neck thick and thewy; the head mostly behind the huge, prehensile ears.

His physical description done, Browne passes on to the social habits of the young thug. He speaks generally at first ("they are reared in and trained to idleness and dissipation"), but soon turns to specifics:

> They are fed tobacco and gin from childhood. Ribald songs and the roar of swinish carousals, in place of maternal lullabies, echo in their infant ears. Living much in the open air, and fond of rude physical sports, they grow up stout and hardy, in spite of bad habits and pernicious natures.
> In their early teens, they find themselves lewd and lusty,

12. Ned Buntline [E. Z. C. Judson], *The Mysteries and Miseries of New York* (New York, 1849), p. 7.

thoroughly selfish and sensual, principled against work, predetermined to dishonesty and tyranny. . . . To bar-rooms and brothels they tend by a natural law and soon come to regard ruffians, thieves and prizefighters worthy examples of imitation and objects of envy. The more precociously shameful they are, the more they are flattered and coddled. Their first fight and first debauch are like the first honors of a college; and they mount higher and higher by sinking deeper and deeper into the slough of degradation . . . to rob and beat in the morning, the woman whose arms they seek at night is their idea of gallantry and chivalry. . . . Any part of their brutal education that may have been neglected is readily supplied in such places and by such companions.[13]

This passage deserves examination. The standard by which the Rough is judged and with which his description is informed is thoroughly middle class—morally earnest, respectable middle class. The Rough is fed tobacco and gin, food shunned by enterprising young businessmen. Instead of the ideal "angel in the house" singing her child sweetly to sleep, the Rough hears only "ribald songs and swinish carousals." Still, he grows up healthy and strong, although ungentlemanly "rude physical sports" are partly responsible. For higher education, prizefighters instead of clergymen or professors provide the models, while whorehouses and barrooms instead of the university provide classroom space. Finally the Rough's code of manners sanctions the abuse, not the respect of women.

More important, the passage exposes Browne's ignorance of the people he is describing. He practically admits this himself as he watches a crowded ferry cross the East River. Speaking about the sober, hard-working laboring classes packing the boat, he reflects that "they are honest and industrious and ought to be happy no doubt. But," he goes on, "I question if they are. I know I could not be if I were they. They do not give the impression of supreme felicity, but rather of men who have duties to perform for others, and who would be glad when they could lie down and sleep forever."[4]

Here, for a moment, the plainness and drudgery of working-class life was more than Browne could color, in his usual fashion, by

13. Junius Henri Browne, *The Great Metropolis* (Hartford, 1869), pp. 68-70.
14. *Ibid.*, p. 104.

pointing to strange dress or unusual life styles. His language is tentative and vague, his description diffident and barren, in contrast to the confident and certain detail with which he describes the Rough. For once Browne cannot escape the pedestrian reality facing him by resorting to exaggeration and distortion. When he does not embellish his subjects, he has barely conceived them at all.

On the whole, such moments of honesty were rare. It was too easy to represent the poor (except for the small number of deserving "unfortunates") and the areas in which they lived by their most unusual and bizarre examples. The maimed and infirm as well as the exotic, colorful, and occult were continually trotted out for view. Dr. Ross, at the beginning of his book, introduces us in turn to a colored female beggar whom he convinced passersby not to help ("The more I saw her the more I disliked her face, without any regard to color or physical conformation"), a blind beggar whose faith in God assures the author of his worthiness, and a blind sailor whose "dog is nearly as peculiar as his master."[15] But rather than have us "come to the conclusion that our citizens are all beggars," he finally passes to other urban inhabitants. The street sweepers, chimney sweeps ("useful and happy"), rag pickers ("they had plenty of money at interest"), bone-boilers, bone-grinders, dog-killers, horse-skinners, hot-corners, ice-creamers, and bell-ringers all attracted his attention. Other authors were not to be outdone. In all accounts streetwalkers, thieves, and con-men abound; almshouses, madhouses, undergound oyster parlors, and opium dens were their constant setting.

With such fields of endeavor nearby, missionaries, many believed, did not have to look to other continents to exercise their talents. No "darker, deeper field" of activity than New York City existed anywhere. Ned Buntline's New York merchant Mr. Precise had only to go as far as an underground nightclub in the Five Points area of lower Manhattan to find himself in surroundings as exotic as any in Africa:

> And yet wider opened he his eyes, when he stepped within. He saw a sight! Not less than two hundred negroes, of every shade, from the light, mellow-cheeked quadroon, down to the coal-black,

15. Ross, *What I Saw in New York*, p. 52.

were there. Some were dancing to music made by a fiddle, a tambourine, and an exceedingly ancient looking guitar; all of them played with more strength than sweetness; and speaking of this latter the atmosphere was not tinctured with too much of it. Those who were dancing, of course, kept neck and neck with the music; to do so, it was impossible not to sweat some, and the odor raised therefrom was less agreeable than some of the perfumes which Goraud has invented.[16]

The Reverend E. H. Chapin, New York's leading Universalist minister, saw vast evangelical opportunities in such areas. Surely, he felt, one need not go far to "seek the benighted and debased." The "jungles of violence" were much closer.

No one needs to be told that there are savages in New York as well as in the islands of the sea. Savages not in gloomy forests, but under the strength of gaslight . . .; with warhoops [sic] and clubs very much the same, and garments as fantastic, and souls as brutal, as any of their kindred at the antipodes. China, India, Africa, will you not find their features in some circles of the social world right around you?[17]

This vision of the poor led, however, to serious problems. Portraying the poor and their neighborhoods as foreign and obscure, as unknown and dangerous places with fearsome and ferocious inhabitants, did not help New Yorkers to see them as the most manageable or docile members of the community. Who could tell when uncivilized barbarians might go beserk? Such fears mushroomed later in the century. But even now troubled middle-class residents were questioning the ability of urban institutions to insure social stability.[18]

Underlying these worries was the knowledge that the areas of vice and poverty were merely a stone's throw from respectable, "bright" New York. One lady, working for the Five Points Mission House, filled several pages with obsessive repetition of her discovery that

16. Buntline, *Mysteries and Miseries*, p. 89.
17. E. H. Chapin, *Humanity in the City* (New York, 1854), pp. 17-20.
18. See, for example, the unpublished work of Ann Garvey (Department of the History and Philosophy of Education, New York University, School of Education) on the Children's Aid Society, and Rothman, *The Discovery of the Asylum*.

"one minute's walk from that Broadway point of wealth, commerce, and enjoyment will place [the stranger] in another world of vision, thought and feeling,"[19] In *The Newsboy,* Elizabeth Oakes Smith was struck by a similar realization. Certain neighborhoods were separated by boundaries as clearly defined as national lines on a map. "The denizens [*sic*] of Broadway and the Bowery," she said, "are as unlike as the population of France and Germany." The boundary fixed by habit and culture as well as by wealth, was so rigid that "a Bowery dog, even, never encroaches upon Broadway any more than the women and men do so."[20]

Before entering the shadows of these dismal regions east of Broadway, therefore, it was not at all surprising that most sightseers, like travelers to distant unexplored lands, engaged guides to protect and direct them on their expeditions. Accompanied by "two sturdy and obliging police officers," Dr. Ross prepared himself "for such a journey as few are permitted to take." Seeking the most "perfect specimen of wretchedness and destitution that New York could exhibit . . . [he] started on Indian file . . . with club and candle in hand. It reminded me," he said, "of Putnam's going into the wolf's den, with his blazing torch."[21]

The Reverend S. I. Prime, no less than Dr. Ross, had to see the notorious Five Points. As Editor of the New York *Observer,* one of the largest denominational newspapers in the city, and a man by his own avowal interested in the poor, he might have been expected to know a great deal about the area. It seems, however, that his curiosity was aroused only after reading Charles Dickens's narrative of his experiences in the Five Points region—a narrative included in the published account of his 1842 visit to the United States.[22] Unfortunately, according to the Reverend Prime, Dickens was "altogether better at fancy then fact, and when we read his descriptions of things real we are all the while inclined to believe that he is romancing."

19. *The Old Brewery and the New Mission House at the Five Points. By Ladies of the Mission* (New York, 1854), p. 33.
20. Elizabeth Oakes Smith, *The Newsboy* (New York, 1854), p. 83.
21. Ross, *What I Saw in New York,* p. 102.
22. See Charles Dickens, *American Notes* (New York, 1961), pp. 108-10, for this description.

Gathering his journalistic curiosity, the Reverend set out to uncover just how much truth there was in his story. Not that he contemplated visiting the area himself—Prime couldn't be expected "to make a personal investigation of such localities." To relate the story told him by a friend who had just made such a visit—accompanied, of course, "by a friend of his and under the escort of a well-known police officer"—would do well enough. For the sake of continuity Prime told the story, entitling it "A Nocturnal Subterranean Excursion," in the first person.

> We groped our way to a flight of stairs down which we marched, the officer being at the head; till we came to another door guarded by a porter . . . he threw open his infernal ballroom door, and there, as sure as life, was a sight such as the disordered brain of a madman might conjure, but which we had never ventured to believe was one of the many nightly similar scenes in this Christian city.

Standing before him, as it had stood before Dickens or Buntline's Mr. Precise, was the "underground ball," where Negroes, attired in brightly colored dresses and suits, were dancing gaily, or, as Prime put it, "making 'night hideous' with their lascivious orgies."[23]

Prime's language, filled as it is with terms emphasizing his remoteness from the neighborhood and its people (he often speaks of the Five Points residents as "specimens"), is typical of many writers sharing his social sympathies. But more remarkable is his use of identical language to talk about groups whose material accumulations one would think might qualify them for different handling. Commenting on an exclusive men's club recently built in Manhattan, qualifications for membership in which included "plenty of money . . . [and] a fondness for spending it," Prime admitted that he "should be as much out of [his] element in one of these . . . as a fish out of water." Entering the place, he was struck by its sumptuousness. The establishment, he noted, "is splendidly furnished, no elegance of embellishment, no luxury of furniture, no attraction of comfort or display, being spared to render it the . . . envy of all those who have not the means to make a successful push for admis-

23. [Samuel I. Prime], *Life in New York* (New York, 1847), p. 175.

sion into the club." Yet a superficial walk around was not enough to reveal very much of its true nature. "The *penetralia* will not be discovered," said the Reverend, *"until you make a subterranean excursion and explore the winding recesses of the labyrinth of rooms upon which you have entered. Without a thread or a guide it would be difficult to find your way out and the safest way to escape from such places is to keep away from them altogether."*[24] By using the same terms to talk about two very different social groups, Prime keeps himself equally distant from each. Even the use of the word *penetralia* takes on importance in this context. To speak of the innermost parts of a place with a word generally reserved for the mysterious recesses of temples and palaces further reveals where Prime locates himself in relation to social groups like the poor and parvenu. This is particularly clear in a paragraph Prime appends to his discussion of Dickens' "underground ball." Seemingly at home among the "horrid group," a young man from a respectable family was recognized by the Reverend. Quickly he thought of the boy's mother, how her "heart would be wrung with agony at the ruin of her son." But then he realized that she was

> one of the many mothers in the ranks of fashion and pride, perhaps this moment flaunting at a more splendid ball, yielding to the voluptuous blandishments of elegant vice, and listening to the flattering tongue that will lure her to meet her lost boy at the door of a lower hell.[25]

Prime was ready to invoke the image of the pious, devoted mother grieving for her wayward child, an image that might be conjured up to speak of the angelic women of his own class, until she disqualified herself for such treatment by engaging in forbidden moral behavior. The parvenu no less than the poor who also lacked the genteel manners and life style of the established middle and upper class, were considered outside the circle of virtue in which Prime located himself.

The minister was not alone in his feelings. Junius H. Browne, another member of the circumspect middle classes also found himself

24. *Ibid.*, p. 193. (italics mine)
25. *Ibid.*, pp. 176-77.

unable to penetrate the interior of what he called New York's "fashionable" classes—those groups who have "the age, the wealth [and] the caste-feeling . . . that so largely aid in forming what is known as Society"[26]—very deeply. Like Prime, he found their expenditures on social climbing, their ostentation, and their waste just as hard to comprehend as the life of the poor. The "best society" of New York has "more divisions and subdivisions than ours—more ramifications and inter-ramifications, more circles within circles—more segments and parts of segments. They begin in assumption and end in absurdity."[27] And while Browne had little praise to bestow on *any* group engaged in artificial display—the exception perhaps being "the cultivatedly comfortable"[28]—he reserved his most biting ridicule for the nouveau riche. Strangers regarded these people as examples of the finest in New York society, but, Browne noted quickly, "they really represent the worst. While they have the most imposing residences on Fifth Avenue, the most expensive furniture and jewelry they have "the worst manners and the most barbarious English."[29] Browne was also bothered by the conclusions people of a lower rank might draw from their example:

> They prejudice plain people against wealth, inducing them to believe that its accumulation is associated with indelicacy, pretense and tawdriness, and that they who are materially prosperous are so at the price of much of their native judgment and original good sense.[30]

If that was the price one paid for riches, Browne perhaps reasoned, too many "plain people" might decide not only that the price was too high but that the goal itself was worthless.

In view of these feelings it is hardly surprising that writers like

26. *The Great Metropolis*, p. 31.
27. *Ibid.*, p. 32.
28. This group was "independent, broad and sensible"; it had "ideas beyond money". . . . it believed that "refinement and generosity are the best evidence of a developed character"; and was least devoted to "vulgar parade or cumbersome form." *Ibid.*, p. 35.
29. *Ibid.* For a discussion of why a lack of proper etiquette was so deplored, see chapter 8.
30. *Ibid.*, p. 36.

Browne seized opportunities to ridicule the upstart rich with particular relish. Authors smugly recounted anecdotes in which the newly rich, blinded by the chance to rise in the social scale, were duped out of thousands of dollars by underworld swindlers. Possibly men like Browne and Prime had been reminded of the Elizabethan satires of Nashe and Greene, which for many of the same reasons also delighted in portraying a gullible bourgeoisie. Like the poor and their slums, the nouveau riche also signalized a changing city, one whose stability was no longer assured and whose future was no longer predictable. The rise of the parvenu, like the appearance of the slum, confused and disoriented the soberer middle and upper classes.

The preoccupation of guidebook writers with the nouveau riche and the poor was overwhelming. To Browne the life of the entire Metropolis could be polarized between them. New York was a mixture of the worlds of two classes, "those who passed their days trying to make enough money to live and those who, having more than enough, were troubled about how to spend it." The bleakness of one was countered by the brightness of the other:

> Clouds and sunshine, corpse lights and bridal lamps, joy anthems and funeral dirges, contrast and mingle in New York! Every ripple of lighthearted laughter is lost in the faintest echoes in a wail of distress. Every happy smile is reflected from a dark background of despair.[31]

Most authors, in one way or another, found such a conception useful in organizing the material in their own books. The ostentatiously wealthy were contrasted with the vicious and miserable. "Light" was played off against "dark", "sunshine" against "shadow." We catch glimpses of each while the life of the virtuous and pious middle and upper classes remains out of sight.

No matter how vigorously they denounced the newly rich and prosperous, most writers at least had a language for talking about them. But words often failed them completely when it came to describing the horrors of poverty. At a particularly appalling display of filth, Dr. Ross was unable to find words to talk about what he saw, able

31. *Ibid.,* p. 28.

only to "mention a few things [he] did *not* see." For this he had a
vocabulary: he began to enumerate the contents of an antiseptically
clean middle-class home *missing* from the scene before him rather
than grope for words to portray the scene itself.[32]

Luckily, when their own words failed there were other writers to
turn to for assistance. Most frequently it was Dickens. Whether in
part or whole, adapted or verbatim, countless writers of descriptive
literature used the British novelist's picture of the Five Points. Even
where specific experiences differed, the language in which the narra-
tives were cast was drawn from Dickens's 1842 account.

In the talk of using guides, of groping one's way along dark and
rickety stairways (in Dickens's account the author groped his way up;
others, Americans, felt it was change enough to have the traveler
grope his way down), for the amazed reaction as piles of dirty rags
turned into awakening Negro women, for the visit to underground
nightclubs, Dickens supplied the terms and images from which others
freely borrowed. One writer, acknowledging Dickens's fine description, hesitated to retrace the same ground himself. Finally he decided
to go ahead anyway, reasoning that "no description of New York,
no matter how discursive or superficial, could pass over this." The
result was an account drawn, with minor changes, directly from the
master.[33]

Most interesting was the book written by the ladies working at the
Five Points Mission. Of seventeen anecdotal chapters, only two described the neighborhood in which the women worked. Half of the
first of these was taken verbatim from Dickens's book. The rest was
a combination of quotation and paraphrase from a biography of the
Scottish minister, Dr. Robert Chalmers. Chalmers, in the mid-1840s,
had begun in West Port, an Edinburgh slum similar to the Five
Points, missionary work akin to that of the ladies of the New York
area. The similarities were not lost on the New Yorkers. An account
of West Port, they may have felt, was an excellent way to introduce
their own experiment. The other descriptive chapter quoted two accounts—one, Frederika Bremer's *Homes of the New World,* and one

32. Ross, *What I Saw in New York,* p. 103.
33. Foster, *New York in Slices,* p. 24.

taken from a local newspaper. Nowhere was there a detailed description of the Five Points by any of the contributors to the volume.[34]

Dickens proved especially congenial to New Yorkers looking for ways to talk about their own city, although writers did make use of other Europeans like Sue and Reynolds also. Writing as a traveler, Dickens struck a responsive note in New Yorkers who themselves may have felt somewhat alien on their native ground. Dickens, furthermore, had a language—taken from his familiarity with life in London—for discussing what he saw in New York. That he may have transferred his perceptions about England's capital to his picture of New York hardly bothered Americans. Disoriented by the changes around them, they were willing to settle for any description that released them from the responsibility of using their own eyes. It was much easier to make sense of what they saw by imposing the categories of another observer on the scene before them than painfully to recognize and assess what was actually happening to their city.

Even when experience contradicted expectations, stereotypes held fast. In one passage, one of the Mission ladies went up Murderers' Alley in the Five Points looking for two children absent from school. Upon reaching the Old Brewery, the dilapidated and infamous tenement where they lived, she found the building agent waiting for her, apparently blocking her path. Her heart beating rapidly, breathing deeply from walking the "darksome ways," she quickly began to retrace her steps in an effort to get up the back stairs of the building before the agent could stop her. Once again, however, he was waiting for her. This time she "resolved to speak to him." Gathering all her courage she timidly asked where she might locate the parents of the two truants. Instead of refusing the information or swearing at her, as she fully expected, the man "gave directions and then said very kindly, 'You may go all over the house, wherever you please, and so may any of the ladies, and if anybody speaks wrong to you, let me know.' " Greatly relieved, she continued her search for the two youngsters, groping her way along the passages and stairways "so dark that [she] had to pass her hands along the wall until [she]

34. *The Old Brewery*, pp. 15-44.

felt the casement of the door opening on some poor family. . . ."[35] Even if she did actually grope her way along the passageways, she still clung to and lapsed back into a vocabulary of fear and distaste that her experience should at least have partly dispelled.

Dickens may have been congenial to New Yorkers because his picture of their city, like the picture of London he drew in *Oliver Twist* (1839), accorded with their own developing view of New York. As a place composed of separate, almost free-floating, units, lacking the functional ties of the countryside, it was fragmented individually, on a human scale as well as structurally, on a physical scale. Writers of guidebooks and novels, in representing New York, could not see it as an entity or as a connected set of interdependent institutions and activities. Instead, they saw it as congeries of the bizarre and the anomalous, of the unusual and the mysterious, of, for example, the "Bacchanals" of the rich and the "orgies" of the poor. No coherence was portrayed because none was felt.

Seeking to express their feeling that the expanding city was taking on aspects unfamiliar and strange, remote from their experience, many New Yorkers began narrowing, at least metaphorically, the boundaries of their society. Here was one way to deal with the changes engulfing them. What could no longer be contained within their quiet, perhaps more static, world—a world where men knew what their positions in society were—they thrust outside of it. In this way their security was again assured. By picturing both upstart rich and poor as groups actually outside society's regulatory framework, by morally quarantining them and in effect representing them as members of the criminal classes, they could once again reduce their city to manageable dimensions. If bewildering changes were invariably associated with depraved, felonious paupers and grasping, corrupt nouveau riche, there was good reason to avoid trying to make any sense out of them.

Poverty and crime were traditionally associated anyway. "Wherever sin is, there is misery," intoned the Reverend Prime, actually comforted by the knowledge. "One fact . . . is a consolation to a man who tries to do the right thing," he reasoned. "It is, that the

35. *Ibid.*, p. 57.

wilful vices of the inhabitants of these refuges of the poor have reduced them to this condition."[36]

There were exceptions, of course, like Elizabeth Oakes Smith's *Bob the Newsboy* or Dickens's *Oliver Twist*. One might be poor and honest if innocent and young enough. The chances of being both, however, diminished rapidly as one got older. Any truly virtuous pauper, it seemed, would have made his fortune not long after reaching puberty. But even while young, the chances were good that one would be assessed in much the same way that the rich merchant Mr. Dinsmoor judged Bob's cohorts in *The Newsboy*. Before hearing Bob's story, the good merchant had "regarded them as all bad without redemption. A horde of miserable evil-doers, *hunted down by the law, and entirely without the pale of human sympathy.*[37]

The nouveau riche, as portrayed in this literature, were not much better. They were profligate, lazy, irresponsible, dissipated, and hollow. The men were given to speculation and gambling, and were inevitably led by their greed to mental illness and such criminal behavior as extortion, embezzlement, and forgery.[38] The women stole jewelry and clothing and scorned their maternal chores.[39]

The notion that urban society was not a social or moral harmony was uncomfortable. Writers realized that society could not be seen even as it had been in the 1830s. In *The Poor Rich Man and the Rich Poor Man* (1836), Catherine Maria Sedgwick, for example, could picture the working class and the middle class as virtually indistinguishable. Harry Aiken, a poor but virtuous New Englander living in New York, judging by his speech, manners, and the furnishings of his home, was thoroughly middle class—except for his lack of money. Mrs. Sedgwick did hint that Harry's condition was partially due to chronic ill health and his virtue literally did become money in the bank by the novel's end. Yet, the very conception of a working man whose life style was middle class and who serenely extolled the "mutual interdependence of the rich and working classes"

36. Prime, *Life in New York*, p. 99.
37. Smith, *The Newsboy*, p. 373. (italics mine)
38. See the discussion of Joseph A. Scoville's writings in chapter 4 and T. S. Arthur's business novels in chapter 7.
39. See such books as Martin, *Secrets of the Great City*, for examples.

was noteworthy.[40] Later writers, like Mrs. Smith, could not be nearly so sanguine. Her hero Bob was as virtuous, and ultimately became as rich, as Harry. But he and the other newsboys were crude, unlettered, and slovenly. They lived by their own rules, oblivious to social regulations. Even when Mrs. Smith romanticized their lives and had a kindly angel watch over them, they never became middle class. Only by literally making the poor over could this come about. And while one of the Mission ladies thought a "thorough ablution" in a tub of water and a reoutfitting in her children's hand-me-down clothes might accomplish the feat,[41] it generally took an unexpected turn in the plot, like the discovery of high birth, to turn the trick, even for Anglo-Saxon youth.

The appearance of the kind of guidebook literature we have been examining, a literature new to this period of rapid urban growth, reflected an awareness that far-reaching changes were altering the social landscape. In all its various forms, this material pointed to the way increasing numbers of poor and parvenu were forcing themselves into the consciousness of New Yorkers. Writers who pictured the behavior of these newcomers as bizarre and exotic, who connected them with aspects of life far removed from their own experience in the city, indicated how unsettling was the emerging visibility of these groups. The constant expressions of surprise and consternation, of shock and wonder, demonstrated that the understanding and tolerance normally accorded social groups to which these authors did not belong had been withdrawn. In this they revealed a new degree of bewilderment about, and distaste for, the poor and ambitious who, they felt, threatened their own comfort and security.

40. Catherine Maria Sedgwick, *The Poor Rich Man and the Rich Poor Man* (New York, 1836), p. 178.
41. *The Old Brewery*, p. 117.

PART II

Problems

3

The Rise of William E. Dodge

One of the changes most often noted by prominent mid-century merchants was the way the behavior of aspiring clerks and young merchants differed from their own early years in business three or more decades ago. Strongly influenced by the evangelical religion of the day, they viewed the narrowly pecuniary activity of these upstarts as little short of criminal. Young men of the present day seemed to have little regard for the canons of propriety that once governed mercantile life. Few seemed content to work hard, loyally, and patiently for a single employer until the fundamentals of mercantile practice had been learned. They were unwilling to wait until their superiors decided they were ready for promotion. They had little feeling that in joining the mercantile profession they were heirs to hallowed social traditions or that they had a duty to maintain and pass them on to those who would follow. To the young men of that day, entrance into commercial life meant nothing more than becoming part of a group whose principal object was making money. Few saw themselves as belonging simultaneously to a group also motivated by traditions of benevolence, charity, and philanthropy.

Even young men with good intentions, it seemed, could not evade the powerful attractions of this new moneymaking spirit. In one of the popular writer T. S. Arthur's formula novels, *True Riches* (1852), Edward Claire, a young and basically honest clerk, was repeatedly tempted by the fast dealing around him. Even his wife's urging that he abandon his present employer, a young merchant on the make, and pay no attention to the voice of ambition, had no lasting effect. He could not down his restless seeking for gain or his envy of those around him who were quickly advancing. Against his better judgment, he began to steal from his corrupt employer. His actions did not sit well with him; he could not help feeling uneasy and uncomfortable. But he quickly rationalized his deed in a way that would have alarmed the older, more venerable members of the mercantile community:

> It's the way of the world and unless I do as the world does, I must remain where I am—at the bottom of the ladder. But why should I stay below, while all around me are struggling upward? . . . Where each is grasping all that he can lay his hands on, fair or foul, one must scramble with the rest or get nothing. . . . So Edward Claire, if you wish to rise above your present condition, if you wish to get rich, like your enterprising neighbors, you must do as they do.[1]

To writers like Arthur, there seemed to have been a time when men like Claire would never have been tempted. Before the number of young men seeking positions had increased beyond the demand for their services, the competition that encouraged the excesses of ambition had, it seemed, been unknown. Early in the century young men had been willing to work long hours without complaining about the

1. T. S. Arthur, *True Riches* (New York, 1852), pp. 36-37. At the book's end the young clerk was reclaimed, but this required extreme measures. The author had faced the issue of ambition squarely but the only solution he could offer was a strict isolation of the young man from the evil forces surrounding him. Claire's earnest resolve to resist temptation in the future was not enough. Under his wife's promptings, he finally agreed to leave his present place. Even though it meant a cut in salary, he would take a position with an elderly—the breed was on the verge of extinction—but upright merchant who was so "old school" that he was called "a man behind the times."

tasks required of them. They seemed without the eagerness for gain that often pushed today's youth into brash and reckless ventures. Perhaps they recognized that such behavior might not have enabled them to get ahead any more quickly. For at that time the stages of advancement were too closely controlled by the traditional practices governing entry into and promotion within the profession. The mercantile activities of the port they served were not yet expanding so quickly that the avenues of entry into responsible positions could not be carefully supervised.

The career of William E. Dodge, one of the city's most prominent mid-century merchants, contrasts sharply with that of Edward Claire. Claire was constantly plagued by fears that he was not getting on fast enough, that others were outdistancing him and would continue to do so unless he personally and aggressively took control of his future. Dodge, on the other hand, beginning his career thirty years earlier, suffered, especially as the tale of his rise was later told by Dodge and his son, from no such anxieties. He proceeded, it seemed, within an accepted set of conventions and moved easily from one stage of advancement to another.

William E. Dodge was born in Hartford on September 5, 1805. His father, David Low Dodge, a descendant of a long line of Connecticut farmers, had moved to the state capital to take up shopkeeping. His success there brought him to the attention of S. and H. Higginson of Boston, who offered to accept him as a partner if he would establish an importing and jobbing business for them in New York. By 1813 the Higginsons had failed, and David Low Dodge was chosen to be general agent for the Bozrah Manufacturing Company, an early cotton mill located near Norwich, Connecticut. In 1815, with the end of the War of 1812, the elder Dodge, with his family, moved back to New York, hoping once again to set up his own business.[2]

William got his first position in 1818, when he was thirteen years old. E. K. Merritt, a friend of the family, had secured a promise

2. Richard Lowitt, *A Merchant Prince of the Nineteenth Century: William E. Dodge* (New York, 1954), chapter 1.

from William's father that, when Merritt and his brother formed a wholesale dry-goods partnership, William would become a clerk in the new firm's New York store. In 1818 the partnership was struck and Merritt reminded David Dodge of his promise. The father wrote the son, then away at boarding school and living with the Reverend S. H. Cox in Mendham, New Jersey, asking for his decision.[3] William chose to join the firm and ended forever his formal schooling.

Dodge discussed his new job in a lecture he gave in 1880. "It was a very different thing in those days," he said, "to be a boy in a store from what it is now. I fear that many young men, anxious to get started, would hesitate long before facing such duties as had then to be performed."[4] Not that his duties were too strenuous or intellectually demanding; rather, he was probably worried that they would be considered too menial. Dodge was expected to fetch water, sprinkle and sweep the street in front of the store, carry wood, light fires, and trim lamps. ("Junior clerks," he noted by way of further explanation, "did the work now done by the porters.") In addition, to earn his fifty-dollars-a-year salary, he had to carry goods bought at the auction houses in Wall and Pine Streets to the store on Pearl Street and make deliveries, often as far out of town as Greenwich Village.[5]

Dodge's prospects soon improved. In 1819 David Low Dodge, his commission business snuffed out by the Panic, moved back to Bozrahville to take complete charge of the cotton mill. William, who was hardly self-supporting on the wages the Merritts paid him, returned to Connecticut with his family and got a position clerking in the country store connected with the factory his father managed. He worked so hard at the job, neglecting both meals and sleep, that an attack of "nervous prostration" overtook him at one point.[6]

3. D. Stuart Dodge, *Memorials of William E. Dodge* (New York, 1887), p. 21. Just how binding the promise by the elder Dodge was is unclear. D. Stuart Dodge indicates that the choice was left up to William. William E. Dodge, in his own brief account, seems to imply that he had far less freedom in the matter. See William E. Dodge, *Old New York* (New York, 1880), p. 6.

4. William E. Dodge, *Old New York*, p. 6.

5. *Ibid.*, pp. 7-12, 58.

6. D. Stuart Dodge, *Memorials of William E. Dodge*, p. 24.

In 1825 the mill was sold and the family once again returned to New York. For the third time David Low Dodge began mercantile life on Pearl Street. He opened a dry-goods store with William to assist him. Two years later he retired and William began business on his own. He entered into a partnership with the son of a retired merchant with whom he had done business while a clerk. The man wanted to set up his son, a recent Yale graduate, in New York. According to Dodge, "Having heard that I was intending to commence for myself, [he] proposed a co-partnership with his son. He offered to furnish an amount of capital which, with the small sum I had (mostly from savings from my salary) would make for those days, a respectable beginning, and furthermore promised to endorse for us to any reasonable amount."[7] For the next six years William E. Dodge was an active partner in the dry-goods house of Huntington and Dodge.

In 1833 the sudden collapse of father-in-law Anson G. Phelps's warehouse brought a new offer of partnership. William had known Phelps's daughter Melissa for many years. Their families had known one another in Hartford and had renewed acquaintances after both had resettled in New York. Anson Phelps had come to New York in 1815 to enter business; when the Dodges returned to the city in 1825 they again saw the Phelpses frequently—in each other's homes and at the many prayer and benevolent society functions in which both families took part. In William's twenty-first year he proposed to and was accepted by Melissa Phelps.

At the time of the accident, Phelps was one of the city's leading merchants. Upset by the property loss and business interruption, he turned to his son-in-law to help rearrange the firm's affairs. Phelps's old partnership with Elisha Peck was dissolved and Dodge, along with Daniel James (who had married another of Phelps's daughters), was taken on to form Phelps, Dodge and Company, a metals importing house.[8] In this firm Dodge remained and prospered for the rest of his life. In time he assumed great stature in New York's mercantile community, serving as its representatitive in Congress from 1864 to 1866 and as president of the Chamber of Commerce from 1867 to 1875.

7. William E. Dodge, *Old New York,* p. 38.

The steps that Dodge took to obtain prominence and wealth were repeated by many others of his generation who came from backgrounds similar to his own. As Robert Albion points out, and as the five volumes of Joseph Scoville's *Old Merchants of New York* amply confirm, between 1820 and the Civil War, New Englanders in general and Connecticut River valley men in particular dominated the mercantile life of New York.[9] By 1805 their numbers and position were already great enough to encourage the formation of the smug and self-congratulatory New England Society in the City of New York "to commemorate the landing of the Pilgrim Fathers on Plymouth Rock and to promote friendship, charity and mutual association. . . ."[10]

In categorizing the New England arrivals, Albion spends a good deal of time discussing "the self-made man who came ot New York young and worked up from the bottom in the New York business district."[11] The example he gives of such a pilgrimage is Anson G. Phelps. Phelps was born in Simsbury, Connecticut, in 1781. Orphaned before the age of twelve he learned the saddler's trade from his older brother and soon moved to Hartford, where he established his own saddle-making business. In 1815 he moved to New York, where he entered, as we have seen, into the partnership with Elisha Peck that was to bring him his great fortune.[12]

But Phelps's career may be typical of his generation only. Albion, whose case is hardly strengthened, as we will see in the next chapter, by using the often inaccurate testimony of Joseph Scoville to bolster it, talks in a way that would extend generalizations based on the careers of this first generation to the second as well. Before he asserts that a group of merchants are "self-made men" who "worked up from the bottom," he should be sure such terms do not cloud over important historical distinctions. While many of this early gen-

8. Lowitt, *Merchant Prince,* p. 18.
9. Robert Greenhalgh Albion, *The Rise of New York Port, 1815-1860* (New York, 1939), p. 241. Walter Barrett, clerk [Joseph A. Scoville], *The Old Merchants of New York.* 5 vols. (New York, 1885).
10. Albion, *The Rise of New York Port,* p. 250.
11. *Ibid.,* p. 242.
12. *Ibid.,* p. 248; Lowitt, pp. 14-15.

eration of New York merchants, like Phelps, may have risen by their own initiative alone, many of the succeeding generation did not. Their rise, like that of son-in-law Dodge, was softened by a number of social practices aiding advancement. All New Englanders may have "worked up from the bottom" if the term refers only to the social and pecuniary *distance* between the beginning and end of their careers. But in everyday speech the term has also come, as Albion tacitly acknowledges by coupling it with the phrase *self-made man,* to refer to the *process* by which that distance is traversed. Yet, the process through which Dodge and other members of his generation passed appears to be considerably different from that of his father-in-law. When a historian overlooks these distinctions (by using language which does not take account of them), he begins to obscure the very generational relations that determine the descriptive terms with which he has chosen to characterize his subject.

Whatever the case for men like Phelps and David Low Dodge, Albion's description probably cannot be used to characterize the careers of many men of the following generation. Men like William E. Dodge and Arthur Tappan—who came from another Connecticut River valley town, Northampton, Massachusetts—for example, found that the way to prominence was hedged by a highly formalized set of procedures that were as clearly defined as the apprenticeship system that operated for mechanics and artisans. Interestingly, many of Peter Cooper's tasks as an apprentice carriage maker were identical to those William E. Dodge performed for the Merritts. He too "was supposed to clean the office, fetch water from the pump, sprinkle the sidewalk, push the rubbish into the street . . . trim the lamps, carry in wood, and make fires."[13]

One important difference was that among merchants the procedure was more personal, familiar, and informal. Friends and relatives were expected to provide clerkships for one another's sons. There they would get the education necessary to prepare them, after about four years time, to begin business on their own—by themselves or in partnership with other young men who possessed capital. Or, as was

13. Edward C. Mack, *Peter Cooper, Citizen of New York* (New York, 1949), P. 39.

more common, they might be taken in as a partner of the already well-established business of a relative, as a junior member. Scoville frequently spoke of young clerks "graduating" from established mercantile houses to go on to businesses of their own; these houses were no less considered educational institutions than were colleges. In fact, during this period, for one headed into a mercantile career a college education was considered largely superfluous; William E. Dodge never seemed to regret terminating his formal schooling to clerk for the Merritt brothers. A clerk, said Scoville, "took his regular degrees." His first duties included the delivery of goods, the tallying of numbers of packages received, and the copying of letters and invoices. When he could copy letters without error, he was promoted to making the duplicates of letters that went by packet ships and to copying accounts. Next he was given the responsibility of "making" accounts. For Scoville it "was all a perfect system. One clerk instructed and one inspected the work of another. It was impossible to make mistakes."[14]

Young clerks of Dodge's generation did not, as may have been more generally true of their fathers, simply "find a place"; more often that not a good deal of arrangement between a boy's father and employer preceded the youngster's entry into business. Some idea of the negotiations involved are revealed in a letter written in 1818 by the Boston merchant Henry Lee. Responding to an earlier inquiry by Captain William Farris, one of Newburyport's leading citizens and distantly related to Lee, about the feasibility of placing his son in Lee's store, he wrote that he didn't think he had much work for the boy. But, he added, "if you have no other place in view I will receive him into my store." Lee then stipulated the terms:

> It is requisite he should write a very good hand and understand Arithmetic and Book keeping, if deficient in either he will have time to improve this winter—I am willing to allow four Dollar per week for his board, and I recommend your getting him into some family you are acquainted with, who may feel an interest in his welfare. . .as it would be a means of guarding him against many

14. Scoville, *Old Merchants,* I, 110. See also Kenneth Wiggins Porter, *The Jacksons and the Lees* (2 vols.: Cambridge, Mass., 1937), I, "General Introduction." and Albion, pp. 216-61.

temptations which young men are exposed to, more especially when absent from their friends and parents.

Lee also added that he did not consider himself obligated to keep Farris's son if ill health or commercial setbacks forced him to "diminish or abandon" his business or if the boy turned out to be "disinclined to business, or acquire any habits which may unfit him for it." In view of those conditions, Lee thought it might be a good idea if Farris read the above to his son—"it might be a restraint upon his conduct on some future day." Apparently Lee shared the beliefs of his colleagues in New York concerning the difficulties and anxieties life in a large city would pose for a young man.[15]

In spite of the careful scrutiny he would have to endure, Farris must have considered himself a fortunate young man. He would arrive in Boston knowing that he already had a secure position and that someone was at least minimally interested in his welfare. The comfort this knowledge afforded must have been more than enough to offset whatever uneasiness the arrival in a strange city and the undertaking of new duties provoked. And William E. Dodge, coming to another large city to assume a prearranged situation, may have been similarly comforted. His entry into the close-knit mercantile community of New York (at the time he began working for the Merritts, his father, who had his own dry-goods business in New York, lived just around the corner) was not calculated to produce the anxiety or uncertainty that might make a young man susceptible to corrupting influences. Although we do not know to what extent those who came to large cities like New York lacking in contacts or prearranged positions found themselves more anxious, uneasy, restless and more readily distracted from their chosen path whatever the career happened to be, there is fragmentary evidence that suggests that such arrivals were attended by crises of determination and conscientiousness. The experience of Harry Hopkins, who came to New York in 1825 to pursue a career as an artist was, as we shall see, shared by other young men who left family and friends to pursue other careers as well.[16]

15. Porter, 2: 1321-22.
16. See, for example, the career of William Hoffman discussed in chapter 5.

Harry Hopkins, born in 1804 on a farm near Stockbridge, Massachusetts, was the younger brother of Mark Hopkins, the noted educator and president of Williams College (1836-72). Writing his brother about a month after arriving in New York, Harry was plagued by the way he was wasting the money collected to aid him with his training. He seemed most bewildered by his powerlessness over his situation:

> I have been in agonies ever since I have been in the city at seeing my money leak or rather stream away at such a rate without a possibility to stop it. And I have not until late made the discovery that it goes just as fast whether I fret or laugh.

He seemed to have so little ability to control what was happening that he half seriously talked about having "got to be a firm believer in the destinies since I started from home—that is to say I don't believe I shall die til my turn comes, when my money is gone I shall probably live somehow. . . ."[17]

As the month wore on, Harry wrote home that he felt forgotten by his family and lonely in New York. He urged his father to visit in the spring. Archibald Hopkins sympathized with his son—New York, he agreed, was a "solitary place without a friend . . . although it is crowded with people"—but he was afraid spring farmwork would prevent him from making the trip. He was sorry that his son couldn't find any business in "so great a city" and that he had not been able to provide more assistance when Harry left. He enclosed a ten dollar bill to help make amends (pp. 128-29).

On February 19, 1826, Harry wrote his brother again from a third story room in the Bowery. He confided that he was thinking of coming home. Our parents, he said, were getting old and he was more than willing to "sacrifice . . . any anticipated scheme of life or pleasure [of his own] which is necessary for their happiness." Although he said he was still convinced that "with proper advantages" he would be able to support himself painting portraits, his doubts were growing. Even the best, he rationalized, were poor. He could not decide whether the fault lay with the painters or with the profes-

17. *Early Letters of Mark Hopkins* (New York, 1929), p. 124.

sion itself. In any event he was sure he would never regret having spent the winter in New York (pp. 130-31).

Writing again three weeks later, Harry revealed even more of the uncertainty and confusion that had characterized his earlier letters. It was true that he had by then worked out arrangements for boarding with relatives and living with a friend on the Bowery. But somehow the lonesomess for his family kept increasing. "Endeavoring to talk with a Brother who is 150 miles from me," he lamented, "is like feeding upon ashes." And then as he discussed his tenuous financial situation and coming plans, he fully revealed the muddle his thoughts were in. His writing became a mass of contradiction, vacillation, and repetition of fragments of earlier letters. His ability to decide between and choose among his own perceptions and feelings appeared to have broken down.

> I have not yet got any business and have not been particularly anxious about it as my expenses are not very great though there are a thousand little contingencies which wear away upon my little treasure pretty fast. Tell Pa I am greatly obliged to him for the ten dollar note which he sent although I was in no immediate want of it, yet probably it will make considerable difference in my calculations though at present I have no calculation about anything, but the Spring will determine one way or the other what I shall do.

Harry then went on to consider his professional prospects and once again confided his certainty that he "could get before long to support myself by Pourtrait painting." Once again he noted, in language almost identical to that of an earlier letter, that most painters found themselves in only modest circumstances and that he didn't know whether "it was owing to the painters themselves or their Profession." Again he asserted that even if he did return in the spring "I shall never in the least regret having spent the winter here."

He closed with a reference to his father's most recent letter; his longing for home was evident. "When he spoke of the old swamp, my dog and my gun, the Mountains, the old south room and apples and cider I was upon the point of packing up my duds and starting right off" (pp. 132-33).

But Harry remained in New York for some months longer. The

experience must have been increasingly painful. His letters that fall were full of expressions of disorientation resulting from the "noise and excitement which is produced on first coming to the city" (it "causes a person almost to forget every thing he ever knew") and of discouragement about his art ("I have got to be so old and so poor with fingers stiff as pokers") (p. 141). During the winter and spring of 1827, an offer of easy money in a coal mining venture lured him away to Rhode Island. But by the following summer its most tangible results were the memories of the fantasies of affluence the venture had stirred up (p. 164). Encouraged by his brother, he resolved to return to New York and take up painting again.

About a year later (the remaining letters do not allow us to determine exactly when he came back or what he did after his return to New York), his prospects as a painter did not seem any better than they had before. By February 26, 1829—almost four years after he first came to New York—in the only letter we have during this period, he wrote that he had been unsuccessful in trying to establish an apprenticelike relationship with an established artist. "I have been treated with coldness by nearly all the artists in the city," he said. "By coldness I mean that they have showed no disposition to assist me any farther than mere selfishness led them to do." Unfortunately, without their help his chances of developing his ability were slight. "A person cannot learn to paint well in a week or a month nor scarcely at all, let his natural talent be what it may, without the advantage of instruction—this you know is what I came here for, but what I have not yet got." He seemed hopeful that someone would take him on the following May, but when May came Harry had already returned home (p. 189).[18]

Unlike Harry Hopkins, William E. Dodge was able to find someone to take him on. Instead of an experience filled with longing, anxiety, and unsettledness, Dodge's was filled (or at least was *pictured* as being filled) with assurance and security. At every point in his elevation to responsibility and eminence he was surrounded by famil-

---

18. For a different perspective on the problems and anxieties artists faced in choosing to move to a large city, see Neil Harris, *The Artist in American Society* (New York, 1966), pp. 107-22.

iarity and approval. His first position was arranged by his father and a friend; his next, involving greater responsibility, was in the family business; his third, while it involved more uncertainty than the others, was still backed and virtually underwritten by his partner's father; his last, joining an already prosperous firm, was with his father-in-law. Each step took little calculation or planning for advancement. None called for dangerous innovating or risk-taking. At each point Dodge moved within established conventions and practices. Showing himself to be honest and hard-working, he was chosen by others to be their associate. He was never placed at a juncture requiring choices that might have an indeterminate effect on his future. Nor was he ever forced to make decisions the results of which he could not foresee. His habits were steady and regular, and so was his progress in mercantile life.

William E. Dodge prospered in a system that did not often reward daring and imagination,[19] and it is not surprising that Dodge never manifested those qualities. As his most recent biographer notes, "He seldom led the way in any of the business enterprises with which he was associated."[20]

By the time he reached middle age, Dodge sensed that many of the institutions that tied men to their society, which gave them an interest in its orderly well-functioning, were badly faltering. Institutions like the apprenticeship system through which he had risen to mercantile prominence, the family, and the church seemed to be losing their power to regulate the social life of the community. An examination of certain religiously motivated aspects of Dodge's philanthropic work seems to indicate that he realized, though he may not have been able to conceptualize it, that the faltering arrangements either had to be replaced or shored up so that they could perform their essential functions.

19. The anonymous manual *The Young Merchant* (Boston, 1840) specifically ruled the qualities "brilliant imagination" and "bold fancy" out of those required for mercantile success.
20. Lowitt, *Merchant Prince,* p. 188.

Dodge was an evangelical Christian. "Thoroughly convinced that men are lost,"[21] he was prepared to support the various measures evangelical ministers thought might help reclaim them. He was one of those responsible for inviting revivalist Charles Grandison Finney to New York in 1829 and he himself actively took part in revival efforts. He often visited his outlying business holdings to gather his workers for prayer meetings or temperance discussions. Wherever he had mills or held timber lands he built churches and kept them staffed with ministers (p. 212). Dodge also drafted numerous letters to friends urging their repentance. To one business associate during the 1858 Revival, for instance, he wrote, "Oh, my dear friend, that you could but open your eyes and see your true position, and the danger that, with all this world can give, you may go unprepared to the bar of God (p. 213)." In order to help his friends' efforts toward Christ, Dodge presented them with the books, tracts, or hymns that he thought spoke most directly to each man's situation (p. 220).

He worked as a volunteer for the American Tract Society, was among the founders of the New York City Mission and Tract Society, a manager of the local branch of the American Bible Society, a vice-president of the American Sunday-School Union, and one of the earliest patrons of the Young Men's Christian Association (pp. 221-32). He served several times as a commissioner to the General Assembly of the Presbyterian Church and was a member of the Executive Committee of the American Protestant Society and a director of the American and Foreign Christian Union (pp. 235-239). Very early in life he began contributing to a number of educational institutions. In 1836, for example, he was one of the original subscribers to the Union Theological Seminary. He also directly supported from time to time students preparing for the ministry. As his son D. Stuart Dodge points out, he devoted a great deal of time to making these selections, requiring recommendations from the teachers, pastors, and friends of the applicant (p. 250).

In his zeal to reclaim "the lost" and to insure the safety of young men, Dodge apparently felt it necessary to provide the thickest institutional network possible—the more fine-spun the web, the fewer

21. D. Stuart Dodge, *Memorials of William E. Dodge*, p. 208.

were those who could slip through it or escape getting caught in it. Summing up the church involvement of his father, D. Stuart Dodge noted the following among his most significant accomplishments:

> he loved to see churches established in needy districts, and he made it his duty to attach himself to feebler congregations, where the presence and efforts of each member have a distinct value. He deplored the custom or necessity of concentrating in a few strong central churches the wealthiest and most influential supporters of a religious body . . . he was a warm advocate of union efforts wherever the majority of attendants or residents were not of one denomination, or wherever, in sparsely populated neighborhoods or places, there was not sufficient strength to maintain adequately more than one organization. (pp. 198-99)

Interestingly, every one of these activities involved the extension of institutional coverage to groups neglected by community leaders or the strengthening of coverage within groups already organized. Without such a web it seemed to be impossible to keep track of the spiritual state of a community or to encourage its progress. When he felt his support was necessary, Dodge eagerly involved himself to achieve these ends.

One example in particular concerns the community of Wellsboro, Pennsylvania, where Dodge had extensive timber holdings. Here the merchant secured the pastor—the young Reverend J. F. Calkins, just graduated from seminary—and encouraged him to stay on by providing for his support. He also built the parsonage and contributed heavily toward construction of the church. Upon visiting the area, he often accompanied Calkins on trips to neighboring schoolhouses to preach. When a revival developed in 1856, he joined the pastor in house-to-house visits, inviting men to the mercy-seat. At times Dodge seemed to consider himself the spiritual father of the small congregation, directly responsible for its salvation. Writing to his wife from the small town on March 13, 1856, he explained why "he did not dare to leave." "God's power," he said, "has been so wonderful for the last two days and *I have so many on my hands and heart, apparently just on the turning point of their destiny that I cannot go.*" The night before, he noted, four or five of the town's most prominent men who a week earlier were among the anxious "and for whom we had been praying and laboring'' got up during a meeting, recounted how God had helped them, and urged others to come to Christ. If he stayed, he implied that only God knew what new results might occur (p. 213). (italics mine)

Mixed with this evangelical concern were others of a more purely social nature. While the umbrella-work of religious associations helped men to become spiritually rooted, the associations could also root them socially in the life of the community. William E. Dodge may have been aware of this when he began writing to a friend about his drinking habits at the very moment that one of the man's links to society, his family, had dissolved. The friend's wife had recently died and Dodge felt that his friend was now passing through "the critical time of [his] life." He worried that "in the midst of your loneliness and affliction you will be tempted as never before. If you yield you will, I fear, soon find yourself beyond control." Dodge urged total abstinence and called upon his friend to seek the grace of God by uniting with a recognized church (p. 219).

Only when the man's wife died did Dodge think it urgent that he intervene. Perhaps he reasoned that the woman's death removed the check that kept her husband's habit from becoming uncontrollable, perhaps he felt that, although attachment to a church was not interchangeable with the domestic bond, it might provide another link to replace one which had been severed. Dodge's conviction that men were easily lost could have more than a theological sense.

This conviction may have been particularly strong among men who, in their capacity as employers of young, impressionable clerks, were in a special position to watch the often fitful progress of young men trying to establish themselves in an unfamiliar environment. As merchants, they had a unique vantage point to observe one of the chief manifestations of the social changes marking the decades of the 1840s and 1850s—the young man seeking his future in the city. Each day they watched young men who had left lives closely regulated by family, church, and local job responsibilities begin careers. As they viewed these arrivals, the feeling that the agencies binding people to society might need supplementing took on special meaning.

4

A Passing Tradition

The concern with society's institutional fabric that William E. Dodge demonstrated by his philanthropic and religious work was manifested in writing by a retired merchant, Joseph A. Scoville. While Dodge worked to plug the holes opened by the demise of certain social patterns and traditions, Scoville penned memorials to mark their departure. He centered his writing around the differences between the style of life of the older mercantile generation and that of the generation just coming to maturity. In doing so he demonstrated the extent to which many prominent merchants already understood, if only indistinctly, that the way of life they knew, unable to perpetuate itself, was irretrievably passing. The mercantile community in which they had prospered was believed to be characterized by a smooth and unremarkable transition of leadership from one generation to the next. It was a community that was considered closed, by practices of recruitment and training, to all but the members of a social elite who shared, regardless of age, common goals and values.

But by the time Scoville wrote, this harmony, especially that of young and old, seemed to have disappeared. In his books and articles

the old merchant now descried great differences between the life
style and social position of the young men petitioning for entrance
into the mercantile community and its older, more venerable members. Scoville drew contrasting pictures of each group: the old merchants were heir to an aristocratic social tradition marked by dignity,
magnanimity, and self-possession and the young arrivals, often low-
born or of unknown social origins, were grasping, meanly competitive, selfish, and uncontrolled.

Unlike young clerks of past generations, clerks who, as apprentices, were intimately tied to the social and professional sides of the
mercantile community, young men of the present day were frequently
pictured as living outside any moderating institutional arrangements.
They were often depicted as living in segregated boarding-houses
and having strange social habits.[1] On this level their description as
bizarre and distant creatures closely approached that of the poor examined in chapter 2. The reasons for this association are not hard to
find. Both poor immigrants who were seen as exotic savages and native young men of rural or uncertain urban origins who were seen as
unknown outlanders were feared because of the disruptive potential
they added to the community. Like the poor, newly arrived young
men were placed beyond the legitimate boundaries of the society to
deny their claim to the positions or prerogatives held by community
leaders.[2] In viewing young men this way, Scoville revealed how
wide the distance between young and old had become.

Joseph A. Scoville was one of those, like William E. Dodge, who
had prospered in New York mercantile life. He too had come to New
York from Connecticut seeking a clerkship, and he had found one
with Archibald Gracie and Son. There he "had been regularly
educated."[3] Although available evidence is sketchy, and unreliable
besides, coming from Scoville himself, it appears that about 1838, at
the age of twenty-seven, he entered into partnership with John Turner

1. See, for example, Scoville's account of a society to marry rich girls, below.
2. See the discussion in chapter 2.
3. Walter Barrett [Joseph A. Scoville], *The Old Merchants of New York*. 5
vols. (New York, 1885), 1: 128;31.

Welles Sargent and Lloyd L. Britton, who were being set up in business by their uncle, Samuel Welles. How Scoville was chosen as the New York partner (the other two would open offices in Boston and Europe) is unclear. Apparently the firm prospered; "the business that was done by the New York house was immense." Soon their trading activities spread from Europe to the Middle East, and the three partners bought four ships to carry the increasing load of goods. Then a series of sudden misfortunes involving the loss of three of their ships forced the firm to suspend operations. Sargent and Britton were able to start business again; Scoville could not. Instead, he turned to politics and journalism, becoming John C. Calhoun's private secretary until 1850 and owner of a South Carolina paper, the *Daily State Register*. There was a rumor that he died in South Carolina in 1857, but Walter Barrett, the name under which Scoville later wrote his multi-volume recollections of New York merchants, knowingly assured his readers that he had "the very best reasons for believing that it was not true" (1: 131).

It was true, however, that Scoville had dropped from active life and by the early 1860s was again back in New York living quietly and writing short pieces about the city's old merchants for the New York *Leader*. The unexpected popularity of the articles and the demand for back numbers convinced Scoville that they ought to be revised, expanded, and published in book form. As a book the series was even more successful. After a number of editions it was still in demand, and Scoville offered a second volume, then a third, fourth, and, just before his death in 1864, a fifth (1: 7).

Bits and fragments of information about merchants and their families—where and how they lived, how they prospered or failed to prosper, whom their children married, which of them followed their father in business, where the offspring lived, how they prospered and how *their* children prospered, together with anecdotes about business morality and family traditions—were strung together to form chapters that in turn formed volumes of three- to four-hundred pages each. This organization was simple enough. It was complicated, however, by Scoville's habit of adding newly unearthed or remembered material, or corrected mistakes of earlier pages, by simply inserting the new or corrected material after the last sentence he had written.

Rather than holding the material for later editions or going back over his manuscript and inserting the information at its appropriate place, Scoville just kept building his manuscript as if failure to record each newly unearthed detail would result in its loss or neglect. With each volume Scoville reached farther and farther back in time. From the merchants of the 1830s, whose stories dominated the early volumes, he backtracked to those of 1800, then to those of the late 1700s. By the time his last volume appeared, Scoville had collected data on and written about hundreds of merchants spanning as many as four or five generations. An alphabetical index at the beginning of each volume allowed the reader to find the reference to whomever interested him. Today the books are used primarily by scholars as a source of information available nowhere else. This recent attention would have gladdened Scoville. Even though he must have been aware of how well his books were selling, his comfort came in believing his work might be valued in the distant future; he realized that many "regard[ed] it as of no merit now" (5: 21). In recording the history and remembrances of New York's past merchants, Scoville was providing a tangible monument to men whom many New Yorkers, he seemed to feel, were quickly forgetting. He intended to aid "all those who do not wish prominent merchants to be buried in oblivion forever. I am rescuing men and things from such a fate" (1: 174). His volumes, in other words, were not meant to be simply storehouses of accumulated trivia; they were an attempt to salvage a great tradition on the verge of extinction.

Scoville could see a race of men dying without any marker being placed to indicate that it had lived or mattered. Each day he scanned the obituary notices and came across names of men he had planned to write about. Sometimes he recorded the deaths matter-of-factly; at other times he was surprised, hesitant to admit a loss that had caught him unexpectedly. He noted the men who had died before he had been able to write about them and remarked that he was sad that they would not see his article when it appeared. Scoville seemed to consider it his personal responsibility to see that the memory of these men did not perish. The rising generation had little interest in perpetuating or even preserving the tradition of mercantile royalty to which many of them were heir. "The memory of such men as John

B. Coles," said Scoville, using the prominent early-nineteenth-century flour merchant as an example, "ought not to die. But where has aught been written about them, save my *Old Merchants?* These will not perish in this handsome book" (2: 41-45).

At various places in his books Scoville inserted asides that were clearly mean to resurrect this tradition. In the beginning of his discussion of Coles's career, Scoville talked about how ideal were the locations of Coles's business and home (on the tip of Manhattan Island—at No. 1 South Street and No. 1 State Street respectively). "If in the whole city of New York, such a combination of convenience, health, pleasantness and near to business [*sic*] can be found," he began, "I do not know where it can be. At both places he could look upon the ships passing up both the North and East rivers. The slip at Whitehall must have come up within a few feet of his house." But as Scoville continued, it became evident that the site recommended itself for other than pragmatic considerations:

> [Coles] could stand on his handsome door steps, whistle or hold up his finger, and in an instant he would have had three or more of the original Whitehall bargemen rowing up to him. Then he could go out with one and have a row all around the harbor, at that time without being run over by anything more furious than a slow moving houseboat. (2: 42)

Like the princes of Venice or perhaps like the lords and barons whose estates lined the Thames, Coles had a retinue of boatmen jumping at his command, ready to chauffeur him to any point in New York's harbor, so uncluttered that a man might think it his own.

Scoville pictured New York's mercantile community as an aristocracy as closely knit by ties of marriage and common interests as were knights of the Middle Ages. At one point Scoville happily traced the ancestry of the Lawrence family back to Sir Robert Laurens, who had accompanied Richard the Lion-Hearted on the Crusades. Then, realizing that his democratic readers might be more disgusted than pleased with the revelation of "a family claim 670 years old," he hastily tempered his enthusiasm. He could make his point just as well, he decided, by "go[ing] back to the landing in America and giv[ing] credit for [only] 220 to 226 years" (2: 83). In a later volume he seemed to have forgotten this compromise. He could not resist presenting the results of his most recent researches into the Laurens family's genealogical past. For the benefit of his readers he carefully detailed the brushes of Sir Robert's progeny with royalty and patiently decoded the symbolism of its coat of arms (5: 84).

A true aristocracy needed the traditions and accoutrements of nobility, and Scoville tried to provide them. He attempted to unravel the alterations in spelling that the Kiersted name had suffered over the centuries in an effort to make the family aware of its connections with a respected ancestry (2: 87). He readily approved of old Daniel McCormick who, until his death in 1834, wore short breeches, white stockings, and buckles, and kept his hair curled and powdered (2: 52). He delighted in describing the voracious Elizabethan eating habits of the merchant called Old Salles (2: 164). He recalled funerals, especially that of Thomas Buchanan in 1819, with particular relish. Unlike the private arrangements of a later day, this was a "grand affair." In fact, admitted Scoville, it was worth living in those times just to have the pleasure of going to the "stylish, comfortable funeral" of an old merchant like Buchanan. The family mansion became the scene of an enormous public spectacle. "Nothing of the kind," rued Scoville, "can be got up now" (2: 47).

Scoville denied that the aristocracy he had in mind was only one of wealth. Instead, he maintained that the American aristocracy was as distinct as "in any land upon earth." It was an aristocracy based on heredity and peopled by merchants. Just "as hereditary descents give crowns and coronets in Europe," said Scoville, "so in America hereditary merchants have their claim to honor" (2: 84). Honor, important as it was, was hardly the same kind of payment as the crowns and coronets of Europe could collect, but Scoville did not seem to notice the difference. If he did, it probably did not bother him very much. His point was undiminished: a great tradition was passing.

Most significant about the way Scoville defined this tradition was that he did so in social terms. His concern was with family, with a patrimony based not on wealth or traditions of professional excellence, but on social position conferred by one's name. For Scoville, the men entitled by heredity to high standing in the community could have belonged to any vocation; they could have made their living by any honorable means. It was simply a fortuitous combination of circumstances that, in New York, led so large a number to concentrate in mercantile dealings.

Scoville's look at the past seemed to convince him not that it was continuous with the present, but that it was so different and remote that it was forever lost. At the very outset of his first volume, Scoville expressed his amazement at the changes that had occurred in the past thirty years. The whole scale of life in New York had changed. The New York City of 1830 was for Scoville a small, compact community. Even a citizen of "no very extended acquaintance" knew the names of all the prominent merchants and where they lived. By the 1860s all that had changed. In the 1830s "very few merchants of note" (Scoville was always talking about a group familiar with one another by virtue of membership in a common aristocratic club) lived above Chambers Street; "but now," he added, "it is impossible to tell where they do not live" (1: 9).

To point up the changes from 1830 to 1860, Scoville reprinted old advertisements, which spoke in familiar and personal tones to readers, listed buildings no longer standing, and recalled gathering places and neighborhoods once the homes of the wealthy but now abandoned to the poor. But slowly, almost imperceptibly, the city Scoville contrasted with that of 1860 became a New York more than one generation past. By degrees, it became the New York of 1800 and 1780. Realizing perhaps that by 1830 New York was already far from the stable, comfortable place he envisioned, Scoville found himself reaching further back into the city's past for materials that adequately set it off from the place he presently inhabited. In contrasting the New York of 1860 with a city where "a wealthy old merchant could get up at daybreak, look out of his window and see what old cronies were walking upon the Battery," or where travel from Chambers Street to Spring Street involved "cross[ing] the fields, jumping brooks and little streams" he was talking about the New York of 1800 and not, as he said, that of 1830, when the merchant community had largely abandoned the Battery area for residences uptown and when New York was well filled and well paved as far north as Fourteenth Street (2: 40, 42). Although Scoville had begun writing about a city and its residents within memory of a possible audience, he was increasingly forced to talk about a different past, using a longer yardstick, in order to measure how far things had changed by mid-century. New York by 1860 had become unrecognizable to Scoville, partly because he compared it with a past sixty and seventy years old rather than thirty, as he started out ot do.

This was especially true concerning one of the differences most upsetting to Scoville. Although he maintained that "there are mercantile houses who have father to son succeeded each other in business from 1661 to 1861" (2: 84), he was constantly presenting evidence pointing to the opposite conclusion. Often appearing in the midst of chapters tracing typically the distribution of a father's legacy were despairing statements by merchants whose profits had been devoured by uncaring, irresponsible sons. In one instance, Scoville reported a conversation with S. B. Munn, "a Connecticut farm boy," who got rich in the dry-goods trade and land speculation. "When I left business about 1820," the old man told a friend, "I was worth, clear of the world, $800,000. I have not got half of it now. It has been eaten up—drank up—squandered—spent—all used up. . . ." (2: 26).

At other times, accounts of family progress in mercantile life were interrupted by anecdotes about gambling exploits and ruin as theatrical as episodes from the novels of Ned Buntline or T. S. Arthur. Scoville, for example, interrupted an account of Jonathan Goodhue's funeral service by recalling that Stephen Whitney, about whom he had already written, shared many of the same qualities of character as Goodhue. He mentioned some of these—his openness and candor—and then started talking about Whitney's troubles with his sons. By the father's admission, they "were all more or less dissipated when young." One of them did, however, later become a source of pride to him and he set the boy up in his own business, in 1824, at the age of twenty. Whitney's charge to Sam as quoted or, as is more likely, imagined by Scoville was familiar. It included the typical exhortation to exercise discipline over one's character, noted the difference between the relative advantages of the two generations, and made clear that independence was not unrestricted:

Now my son I have given you ample capital. If you are steady, and take care of yourself, you will do well and make a large fortune. I only wish I had such a beginning as you have. Keep out of bad company; avoid gambling. I will indorse all your business notes for tea and other purchases. If you do not do as I wish you will incur my serious displeasure. (5: 57)

All went well for over eight years until the son tried to pass a check forged with his father's name to cover a Faro debt. Whitney, informed by the bank, confronted his son and, as Scoville told it, resolved to "put a stopper on such goings on." He went to a saddler's shop, bought a thick piece of rawhide and administered, as to a schoolboy, "a most terrific cowhiding." He then demanded that his son liquidate his business immediately. This done, Sam lived quietly in New York for the rest of his life. According to Scoville he "was never regarded as of any account by his father, or any one else" (5: 57-58).

By contrast, the father continued to act with the "nobility" and magnanimity that marked his class. When another son, also "wild and extravagant," left two illegitimate children at his death Whitney sought out the mother and gave her $20,000 worth of stock. "Well would it be for this great commercial city," commented Scoville, "if her merchant princes could make wrong right in the same noble manner as was done in this case" (5: 59). Like many of the anecdotes in Scoville's volumes, the truth of the incident may well be questioned. (The penciled "x" next to the accounts in an 1885 edition in the Barnard College Library together with the notation in shaky handwriting at the bottom of the page, "x Sam Whitney lived to be a respectable man and quite a help to his Father and so did Charles. . ." hardly adds to our confidence in the account's authenticity.) But the point Scoville wanted to make rhetorically seems clear: the sons of the "noble" merchants of Whitney's generation had fallen away sharply from the standards of virtue and character maintained by their fathers.

Besides difficulties with young men within their families, merchants also faced problems from young men outside them. Unknown, untrained, and unqualified young men were infiltrating, at alarming rates, the ranks of a profession once highly selective and rigorous in its educational preparations. A profession once staffed by men of substance and intellect was being challenged by men of style and dash. What other lesson did Scoville intend to be drawn from his account of the rise of Homer Ramsdell to the presidency of the Erie Railroad? The circuitous way he approached Homer's story was characteristic. Early in an account of Rogers and Company, Scoville noted two French houses that always worked closely with them. In a single paragraph he then moved from Bouchard, a partner in one of the firms, to his daughters, to their husbands, to the mother of one of the husbands, to her employer in a millinery shop, to the employer's brothers, to one of the brothers who became a large leather dealer, to his forewoman, to her son, and finally to the son's friend—Homer Ramsdell.

Ramsdell had little to recommend him. "A little brainless counter-jumper at a small dry-goods store," said the old merchant, "[he] lacked everything but the impudence of Satan." Scoville ticked off the young man's most noteworthy traits, all of them related to Ramsdell's outer appearance, and none, as was usually the case in describing a worthy youth, related to his inner nature or character. "He was pious in order to prosper; taught at the Sunday-School of the Reverend Dr. Potts in order to have a good shye at girls of fortune; . . . combed his hair beautifully [and] dressed to kill." Before long he married the daughter of Thomas Powell, a powerful merchant who installed his new son-in-law in the presidency of the Erie Railroad. Under Ramsdell's mismanagement, the road quickly failed. Scoville wasn't surprised; he hoped the merchant community would be well warned. "Merchants, listen! . . . Bankers, hearken! . . . Why was it done?", Scoville asked rhetorically, his answer ready. "Because a little chit of a girl fell in love with a . . . half simpleton in intellect [and] experience . . . and then persuaded her father to impose the son-in-law upon the directors of a mighty corporation." But this was not what angered Scoville; such arrangements were common. The source of his outrage was that "nobody knew this Homer Ramsdell but a few fellow dry goods clerks and members of Potts' church, until Powell made him president of the Erie road." This is where the departure from established practice had come; this is where the door to the unqualified had been opened. That a "trifling chap" like Ramsdell could be placed in such a high position with barely anyone in the merchant community knowing who he was signaled a breakdown of a system intended to maintain the purity, social exclusiveness, and high standards of the profession (1: 49-50). It was to prevent such malfunctioning that perhaps encouraged Scoville to invest the system with the trappings of hereditary relations. So strong was his feeling of decline that he was willing to draw out these associations even if it meant offending the feelings of an audience just then fighting a civil war to preserve free labor and democracy.[4]

Fears about the entry of unknown, unqualified, and potentially disruptive (what could be more disruptive to a businessman like Scoville than one man, Ramsdell, causing the ruin of a large corporation?) young men into the merchant profession found expression in a theory of conspiracy not unlike that conjured up by Americans for different purposes a century later. According to Scoville, Ramsdell was not infiltrating alone. He and his friends were organized. Scoville revealed that "there were about ten . . . young counter-jumpers that formed a society to marry rich girls. They swore to protect and aid each other. All succeeded." The system of older practices and traditions was not breaking down because it was outdated but because it was being subverted by a small but determined group of intriguers who planned their scheme in the privacy of their cheap, secluded dwellings. "The society of young clerks," said Scoville, "boarded generally at twenty shilling boarding houses, curled each others [*sic*] hair on Saturday night, went to Sunday School as teachers, and became members of the Presbyterian Church, which had the richest members and the prettiest daughters. Their piety game was the card that won in every instance."[5]

Although Scoville made no attempt to disguise these fears, they were often lost among a more widespread and more heartening picture of mercantile succession. Most often, there was little indication

4. See Eric Foner, *Free Soil, Free Labor, Free Men* (New York, 1970) for an account of the ideology motivating many Northerners.
5. *Old Merchants*, 1: 50-51.

that the practices marking the rise of the earlier generation had ceased also to mark the rise of the next. Generally these practices amounted to the informal apprentice system discussed in chapter 3. But instead of emphasizing that apprentices were secured most often by family negotiation, Scoville maintained a more fanciful view.

At a number of places in his narrative Scoville spoke of the generations of self-sufficient, virtuous country boys and their steady rise to prominence in the merchant community of New York. As Scoville told it, a young lad, typically from a New England farm, had all the schooling he needed by his fourteenth birthday. By that time, if he was smart, he could

> parse pretty well . . . [and] needs no more towards his future success than a trunk, "Sunday-go-to-meeting" clothes, and a Bible. This the family provide, and with a few dollars and a mother's prayer, the young hero goes forth to seek his fortune in the great mart of commerce. He needs but a foothold. He asks no more, and he is as sure to keep it as that light will dispel darkness. He gets a place somewhere in a "store." He is honest, determined and intelligent. From the word "go" he begins to learn . . . and no matter what the commercial business he is engaged in, he will not rest until he knows all about it. (1: 57)[6]

Not only were the elements of this picture almost pure convention, but Scoville's own evidence, in the details of countless individual sketches, contradicted it. While the details of his family histories gave a picture of intermarriage, introductions, family interrelations and arrangements and hereditary dynasties, the above passage pictured an untutored but honest youth marching heroically toward the city lights protected only by his virtue and the Bible. He got a place "somewhere." The details seemed irrelevant—there was apparently no need for us to know how he got his position or in what kind of store. Indeed, Scoville quickly added, lest the concern with particulars obscure the larger picture he wanted to paint, "It is all store to him. He hardly comprehends the difference between the business of the great South Street house . . . and the Bowery dry goods shop." The barest advantage, a "foothold," was all the quarter he asked.

6. See also 2: 101-2.

Nothing could shake him—"Wherever this boy strikes, he fastens" (1: 57). Hard work only strengthened him. Soon he was promoted, earned the confidence of the chief clerk and his employers and before long was taken in as a partner. "It's so in nearly every store, counting room or office," Scoville assures us (1: 195).

But why did Scoville feel he had to picture the young merchant's rise in this manner? Why did he ignore the system of apprenticeship and family assistance his details so often describe? Why, in short, did Scoville use the convention of what has been called "the country-boy myth"[7] to cloud over, whether consciously or unconsciously, a process involving substantially different relationships and social routing? One answer may be that Scoville's perception of declining integrity and virtue in the younger generation encouraged the above romanticizing about the older. Any young man who succeeded with only a suit of clothes and a Bible had to have just the qualities Scoville felt were most lacking in the rising generation. To make it by yourself, amid the temptations of urban life and the pressures of business life in the 1850s, you would have to be as virtuous and as perfect of character as the "country boy." More often, young men of a later generation—the 1850s—succumbed to the pressure. They began to speculate, to make deals, and to bilk unwary customers just as Edward Claire did in *True Riches*.[8] The virtues of honesty and mercantile honor were vanishing. The traits of character upon which a merchant's reputation had rested now counted for little.

To the older generation, however, they counted for everything. And, in order to set this generation off from its offspring, to distinguish the older one decisively from the upstarts. Scoville pictured it as succeeding by the one path guaranteeing that it possessed the character that young men of the present day seemed to lack. To picture its rise by arrangement and family connection may have smacked of the conniving and collusion its present-day counterparts parlayed into promotions and quick profits. A self-made country boy relied only on his inner qualities to bring himself to the attention of his superiors.

7. Anselm Strauss, *Images of the American City* (New York, 1961), p. 179.

8. See chapter 3 above.

This was the road to success, one that Scoville may have felt could hardly be mistaken for the road to success taken by so many at the time he was writing. It mattered little that this picture contradicted his view of the merchant class as a privileged aristocracy. The country boy's virtue and self-sufficiency would seem to be irrelevant to a class in which membership was conferred by hereditary status. But so important apparently was it to emphasize both qualities about the passing generation that Scoville couldn't be bothered if the componenets of his portrait didn't fit into a coherent whole.

Scoville was not without suggestions for closing this gap between the generations, for bringing the young men, where they were of similar social background, back to the high-minded standards of their elders. During a discussion of grocer-wine merchant Peter Embury's family and fortune, for example, Scoville offered what he might have considered an answer. One of Embury's close friends was Philip Hone; in their meetings they often discussed family problems. Both men had numerous sons. Embury's worked; Hone's, according to Scoville, "relied upon the wealth of the father, and were not remarkable for their activity." Hone wanted to know why his sons were only good for spending money while all of Embury's were smart and hard-working. "How have you brought up your sons," asked Hone, "that there should be such a difference?" Embury began his reply somewhat inaccurately by saying that Hone, "a fashionable man" with a "fashionable family," had brought his children up in the "fashionable school." Uncle Peter, on the other hand, had brought his children up to be self-reliant. His formula was simple:

> They are all employed, but all board at home. I make them pay me board just as regularly as if they were entire strangers. If they want money, I lend it to them, and take their notes for the amounts, with an understanding that they pay those notes to me when due, the same as if they had been placed in the bank for collection. They pay those notes. I make them know that they must take care of themselves as I did myself, when I was a boy, and when young.

Hone, listening to this sage advice, gave his approval. "Everybody should hear your experience. This is where I have failed my family."[9]

To those who considered the changes of mid-century painful, the appeal of Embury's advice was easy to see. It involved no coming to grips with the present; it looked rather to the past. It involved no less than making the second generation recapitulate the experience of the first. Embury's sons would in effect proceed exactly as the father had. Peter Embury, as a poor boy in New York apprenticed to a chair maker, probably had to board with strangers and scrimp until he had saved enough to open his own grocery. His sons, therefore, would be forced—even though they lived with their wealthy father——to live as if they too were on their own in a strange environment.

The prescription that Scoville had Embury offer Philip Hone was meant to restore the high character that seemed to be in short supply among a younger generation. To an extent Embury's sons were to repeat the experience of the virtuous country boy whose progress Scoville idealized. But there was an important detail that the author, for all his willingness to tamper with reality, did not alter. Embury's sons would live *as if* they were on their own; in fact, they were to remain at home under their father's watchful eye. Given the danger of being independent in such uncertain times, keeping the sons under the father's roof was a way to maintain careful tabs on their moral progress. In this way Scoville could offer a way to monitor conduct that would replace some of the control that had lately seemed to vanish. If a system of apprenticelike relationships was unavailable to envelop the young protectively, he would turn to whatever unit, no matter how small, isolated, or fragile, it was. Like other writers who surveyed their fragmented community for stabilizing agencies, Scoville found it hard to conceive of any other place besides the family to turn to.

Unless, that is, they abandoned the real world for a world of imagination. Considering the magnitude of their problems, the alternative was welcome. In the way it allowed a man of affairs like

9. *Old Merchants,* 1: 203-6.

Scoville to relieve the tensions and despair that plagued him, the flight into the realm of fiction upon which he briefly embarked becomes understandable.

Near the end of his life Scoville published two novels, both of which dealt with the initiation of young men into mercantile careers. In them Scoville seemed to be working out the tensions and differences between young and old. In *Clarence Bolton* and *Vigor* he could have the harmony and agreement he was not always sure to find when he examined actual cases. In fiction he could have history unfold the way he wanted it to. He could have respected merchants seek out poor but deserving youths with offers of clerkship, and he could have the poor youths happily and obediently accept the positions offered them. He could provide them with a patron-tutor under whose watchful eye (as in the apprentice system) their every action was programmed, executed, and assessed. He could in effect have all the benefits of surveillance and education provided by the system he and William E. Dodge were trained up in without reintroducing that system itself. In doing this, Scoville demonstrated perhaps better than any statistics that a set of practices were disappearing but that the functions they performed were too important to do without. In his novels Scoville kept the process intact but eliminated the institutional arrangements that had previously carried them out. In Scoville's novels a young man, alone and friendless, was recruited by a patron who personally oversaw the youth's entry into and rise within the mercantile community at every step. Once taken in, he was never again left alone. The role played by the comfortable surroundings of family, friends, and business associates for someone like Dodge was appropriated by the self-appointed tutor. By his constant tutelage he provided the security a young man from the provinces or from a different social class (this was practically the same thing if, as we will see shortly, one's "blood" was good) within the city could rarely be assured of finding on his own. Scoville recognized that, in order to fill vacancies in mercantile ranks, it would be necessary to go outside the strict confines of the social group to which its most prominent members belonged. If recruits were of "good blood," if their families, though presently poor, had ties to noble ancestors, they were acceptable for training to enter positions to which—by virtue of heredity—they were heir. Because the group of noble ancestors Scoville had in mind extended to any of West European Protestant stock, his insistence on ties of blood became just another way to uncover those with a possible reserve of good character. This quality was so hard to detect with any certainty that, even locating it in so large a group as that defined by the term "good blood," was considered helpful.

The elements of both Scoville's novels are similar; for our purposes it will be sufficient to examine only *Clarence Bolton,* the one that expresses them most clearly and directly. Clarence Bolton, the seventeen-year-old son of a ship's carpenter who had died in a shipyard accident, was living at home with his mother while attending college. One day, through a series of coincidences, he was introduced to a Colonel Vanderhoost, a man "of the pure Knickerbocker breed." As it turned out, the Colonel was as delighted to meet Clarence as the boy was to meet him. Vanderhoost had lost his fortune ("his history was the history of hundreds in this community") but still retained real estate holdings that enabled him to live comfortably as an "independent but reduced gentleman." He was, we are told, a noble-hearted, generous, and liberal American.

The Colonel wasted no time telling Clarence of his interest in him. Knowing little more about the boy than that he had recently rescued his niece from drowning in the Hudson, Vanderhoost resolved to help him. Indeed, almost on introduction he began computing the years until Clarence should reach his majority. So certain was he, presumably, of the boy's worth (saving young ladies from drowning must have been a particularly revealing sign of worth, judging from its recurrence in the didactic novels of the period), that his mind was already running to the work ahead; he was computing the years of preparation, the time he would have to get Clarence ready to enter a business of his own.[10] As if by some inner sense, the Colonel detected "at a glance" that Clarence deserved assistance and he began sizing up his prospective ward. Clarence, he thought to himself was game; eventually he would succeed. What he needed was a friend,

10. Joseph A. Scoville, *The Adventures of Clarence Bolton: or, Life in New York* (New York, n.d.), p. 30

someone to teach him about the world. The Colonel decided to be that friend; he would take the boy in hand. "I will finish his education for the world," said Vanderhoost. "I will bring him out, polish him, and as he goes along the every day road of life, I will point out to him where to make a hit, and where not to attempt it" (p. 35). The Colonel expected Clarence to be a docile pupil. He intended to "mould" the boy into the shape he pleased, to "carve out for him just such a career as he [Vanderhoost] wished." Clarence would be chaperoned until he was mature enough to uphold the standards of the social group he was being ushered into. The Colonel, much like the benefactors of the heroes in Horatio Alger's stories, decided in effect to "adopt" Clarence and "act towards him as if he was his own son" (p. 35). The benefits of the association would be considerable. Scoville spoke directly to his readers. "We must tell you," he said,

> that the friendship of a man who has traveled for years on the various roads of the world, who is acquainted with them, who knows the distances, the halting places, the turnings in and out, the gates, the bridges, the milestones, and the guideposts; and who has acquired this knowledge at a costly price, and from actual experience, can be of more service to a young and talented lad . . . [than] a dozen fortunes or a score of rich relations and friends. (p. 35)

Scoville's choice of landmarks dictated by the metaphor of travel is noteworthy. All of them—the roads, gates, bridges, milestones, guideposts—refer to travel over a physical landscape and not to any movement across a social or institutional one. It is possible that Scoville, like others of his generation, as we will see in chapters 7 and 8, could not imagine an environment with conrete markers of any other kind.

The plot of the novel, if it can be called that, concerns Colonel Vanderhoost's preparation of Clarence to enter "society." When the right moment should arrive, the Colonel planned to "introduce him favorably" into the right circles. To explain his plans to the boy, Vanderhoost invited Clarence to meet him for dinner at Delmonico's the next evening. Apparently the Colonel assumed that Clarence would agree; as soon as the waiter delivered the first course he began schooling his charge. Clarence was told to start each meal with soup, never to drink milk, and to smoke only before he was married. At the end of the meal Vanderhoost seemed more than satisfied with the boy's progress. There was no need to rush matters. "I must bring you along by degrees," he said, "and induct you gradually" (p. 37). He was confirmed in his earlier judgment of the boy. Scoville, wishing no doubt that such judgments of the young could be made so easily, quickly, and with such certainty, noted that Vanderhoost "had learned from *one act* that he was brave, generous and unselfish" and that he had seen "at their *first* interview that he possessed . . . genius, ambition, commanding talent and a lofty high-toned mind and that there was nothing low or grovelling in his composition" (p. 48). (italics mine)

Vanderhoost made his meaning clear enough when he took time during the meal to instruct Clarence on the significance of blood. For the Colonel, blood and ancestry, not money, were the true mark of class. There was good blood and bad, said Vanderhoost, "and one can tell the class to which a man belongs, as certainly by one look at him, as he can at a horse." A man's financial position did not ultimately determine his fate; only his ancestry did that. Vanderhoost could see immediately that Clarence was properly endowed, even though his financial resources were meager. His mother, Vanderhoost knew, was descended from an old foreign stock—"French, but good." His father from the Pilgrims—"common, but good." Clarence's future was therefore assured. "You will succeed and be somebody," he told the boy. "You have got it in you, and it's in the blood." In contrast, the Colonel noted that men like his brother-in-law, banker Gould (the father of the girl Clarence had rescued at the book's beginning and who, Scoville has earlier told us, came from a "mongrel" class of "no known or established origin" [p. 10]), for all their money, could never be secure (pp. 38-39). Vanderhoost, if we can judge by Gould's fate, spoke for Scoville as well. At the book's end the banker suddenly and inexplicably began to lose his money. We are told that Gould hourly watched his wealth disappear "as if by magic." A man of stronger internal constitution might have survived; one of Gould's background could not. He began to lose his mind (p. 93).[11] Here, after all, was Scoville's point. It was no accident that the Colonel always spoke of initiating Clarence into "society" and the "right circles" and never into a business career. It was no accident that his advice centered on manners and etiquette and not business practice. The Colonel himself, Scoville tells us, was a terrible businessman who lost a fortune on ill-considered schemes and the poor management of his resources. But his blood was good and his connections were strong. Membership in the mercantile profession was simply one, and in a city like New York possibly the most important, avenue by which membership in "society" proceeded.

By the time three-quarters of the book is over, Clarence has still not embarked on his career. He did, however, finally accept the Colonel as his friend and advisor. Fairly pummeled by repetition of the Colonel's original arguments, Clarence agreed literally to give up his habit of thinking and acting for himself (p. 63). The Colonel had even gone to the trouble of disclosing his plan for Clarence's future to the boy's mother. She, too, after long opposing her son's entry into what she considered the fashionable circles of society, was won over and told Clarence to go ahead. "Until now," she said to him, "I have never dared to look forward in your career." But the Colonel had convinced her "that he has taken *everything* into consideration—is aware of our exact circumstances, and that his plan for your benefit *for the next five years* is a good one and will succeed." Clarence listened as his mother related the plan Vanderhoost had worked out, and almost supinely approved. "I like it," he said. "If it meets with your approval let the Colonel act *as he pleases and I will do all that he wishes me to.*" (p. 74). (italics mine)

At this point Scoville found that he had really very little left to tell. In the twenty pages remaining in the book he takes Clarence

11. Gould's fate, according to Scoville, was richly deserved. He belonged to a class (the banker himself was the illegitimate son of "an ignorant, silly, half-witted woman" who worked in a rural tavern) that was "composed of men who have acquired wealth and consequent distinction from blundering stupidity and lucky circumstances, rather than from honest, legitimate business talent, industry and comprehensive, extended mercantile combinations. This class cannot boast of family, or personal qualities or attainments. They have no claim by birth, cleverness, occupation, habits, or manners to the title of gentlemen, which they assume." *Ibid.*, p. 10.

quickly from his first clerkship to commercial independence. But because, for one thing, it resembles so many of the details of William E. Dodge's career, the story, though short, has considerable interest.

Clarence took a position in the countinghouse of a "wealthy merchant." He had been recommended, naturally, by the Colonel and banker Gould, to whom Mr. Cottonship, Clarence's new employer, was in debt. He entered Cottonship and Company "under the most favorable auspices," with an agreement that the firm would "afford him an opportunity of acquiring a complete commercial education." When four years "of outstanding service" had passed, Clarence left Cottonship to accept an offer of partnership from a friend, Harry Lee. The two young men, backed by capital from Lee's father, a retired merchant, prospered. Daily advice from Vanderhoost and the elder Lee, it was suggested, aided their rise. Success had its dangers, however. Scoville hinted that Clarence's ambition, stirred by his good fortune, might lead him to financial destruction. "Very few merchants," the writer lamented, "are content to do a slow, sure and certain business." Unlike the English, Scoville continued, who held that a man's position in society is not at all affected by his employment, Americans regarded "a mere clerk . . . as a nobody in New York." Consequently, many of them became overanxious to get into their own businesses instead of prudently remaining in clerkships until they were thirty or thirty-five (pp. 30-31). Clarence appeared to be no exception. Yet, his restlessness did not prove disastrous; he was being watched too carefully. Clarence had turned to politics and, while he served a term in the state legislature, the business, now being run by the "impudent" Lee (his father's judgment), was overextending itself. The elder Lee rebuked Clarence, whom he held responsible; apparently he did not expect anything better from his own son. When Clarence admitted his neglect, promised to leave politics and to advise the retired merchant of all future plans Lee, offered his thoroughgoing help. He intended to "go to your countingroom, arrange your affairs for you [and] assist you with money to conduct to a successful termination such operations as my son has put afloat (p. 85).

Once more the business prospered, and Scoville reiterated his earlier lesson. "How much," he said, "may be lost even under propitious beginnings, if not assisted by advice of those who have long traveled through the mazy intricacies of mercantile affairs?'' The impetuosity of youth had often led them to rush unthinkingly into a course that they would later regret. Luckily, Clarence and Harry had the elder Lee to turn to. "Old Mr. Lee watched after their interests and where it could be done, gave from time to time such advice as, if profited by, would heal up the mismanagement of the young merchants" (p. 90). Both young men proved to be apt pupils. Experience had made Clarence wise and he resolved "to direct his energies in the only true course to obtain success." Young Lee, for his part, had "undergone a complete change," due in large measure to the constant adivce he received from Clarence. Scoville tells us that the "wild and uncertain management he had formerly pursued was given up" (p. 92). In time Clarence married Harry's sister and later, financially secure, returned to the legislature, this time with Mr. Lee's approval. Ultimately, it appeared, merchants did have to resort to political channels if their interests were to be safeguarded.

All this we learn on the final pages of the story. The book is really about preparation, not fulfillment, and the story of Clarence's rise is almost irrelevant. In *Clarence Bolton,* the working out of Vanderhoost's plan is all told in the last fifth of the book, and then it seems more like an afterthought. At first we are simply told that "the plans formed for him [Clarence] by his friend Colonel Vanderhoost were carried into effect, and during a period of five years Clarence pursued the even tenor of his way, and so did all those whose names have appeared in these chapters. Our next chapter will open as Clarence found himself at the expiration of this interval" (p. 77). Nothing has changed, no one has done anything of importance or even of interest; nothing has happened in effect except that five years have passed. Only then, having gotten Clarence to the point where he is running for office, does Scoville decide to "hastily review" his hero's progress.

Scoville is not much interested in this stage of Clarence's development, however. His concern is primarily with Clarence's preparation, in readying the unscrubbed, unpolished youth to move in society. Once the boy is made over, he is sure to rise. And since his rise has little to do with his own initiative (it is someone else who offered the clerkship and the partnership), the actual steps whereby he progresses need not be detailed with any particular care. The important thing is getting Clarence ready, schooling him in the manners appropriate to the station he is destined to assume, and surrounding him with advisers to pass on and oversee his every move. The one thing we never get in *Clarence Bolton* is the one thing Scoville thinks he has given us. At the end of the novel he writes:

> We have shown what happy results arise from early attention to business, and a combination of energy and perseverence, and the honorable issue resulting as the end from a series of honorable means . . . . We leave the subject hoping it may, from its moral, tend to influence those whose aspirations at the present moment may correspond with those as detailed of Clarence Bolton. (p. 104)

But if Scoville thinks he has presented "a series of honorable means" that others could imitate, he is mistaken. Perhaps it is only the "moral" of the tale that he is recommending for study: that it is the virtuous individual who succeeds—and then not by his own initiative. He succeeds by virtue of his recognition and training by others. Until they appear to assist him there is little he can do to advance himself. Such advice may have allayed Scoville's fears about the disruptive consequences of aggressive young men blindly, without regard to past procedures, pursuing their futures. The fantasies he had spun idealizing intergenerational relationships may have proved comforting. But for young men coming to cities in search of mercantile positions, the reality of the present had about it little of the tidiness, regularity, or patient solicitude that surrounded Clarence Bolton.

5

A Tale of Two Clerks

a. WILLIAM HOFFMAN

By the late 1840s the experience of young men entering mercantile careers in New York had become very different from that of William E. Dodge's generation. Under the impact of increased arrivals from the countryside, the informal procedures marking Dodge's rise had become a less certain guideline for young men who were seeking positions in the world of trade.

In this period the duties of young clerks were often similar to those performed by an earlier generation. But in a situation where their predecessors had felt content and secure, young men beginning careers near mid-century found themselves doubtful and anxious.[1] This was true for the sons of established, prosperous merchants as well as for young newcomers from outlying districts. Both groups

1. Although William E. Dodge is known to have suffered a nervous collapse early in his career, the details are obscure. The circumstances suggest, however—he was working at the country store connected to the mill his father ran in rural Connecticut—that sources different from the anxieties experienced by a later generation coming to cities were responsible. See above, chapter 3.

often found themselves questioning the direction and impatient with the halting progress of their careers. Some, like William Hoffman, managed to accommodate themselves—often at great personal cost——to what was asked, or to what they thought was being asked, of them by their superiors. Others, like Edward N. Tailer, Jr., although starting their business careers as circumspectly as Hoffman, began to find obedience impossible. Almost inadvertently they began to chart a new style of mercantile career, a style marked by more overt aggressiveness and self-promotion unknown a few decades earlier.

On Tuesday, March 30, 1848, nineteen-year-old William Hoffman resolved to leave the family farm near Claverack, New York, to seek a new career. "I was very thoughtful all day," he wrote in the diary he had been keeping for a year. "I was calculating as I rose up . . . that today I must after long contemplation, carry such thoughts to their end." For some time now his mind had, as he put it, "long been abstracted from the desire of making farming my business."[2]

Accordingly, he took the stage to Hudson, New York, remained overnight at his uncle's store, and the next morning took the boat to Poughkeepsie. Once arrived, he made his way up the main street of the town and at the first dry-goods store he came to he asked whether they needed any help. When he was told that they did not, he continued down the street, stopping at each store he passed. "I went on with the same inquiry but received but little encouragement," he noted. At one place he was told about a possible opening, but on checking he learned that the proprietor had already taken a young man—who "had a little experience"—to fill it. He had just about written Poughkeepsie off. "O how unlucky I thought I was. Then I had about given up getting a situation in that place." His plan was to continue his search in New York, but he had to wait for the boat due to arrive at about nine that night. To pass the time he wandered around, occasionally dropping into nearby grocery stores to ask about employment. "Not that I wished to follow [that line]," he pointed out, "but to ascertain what they were in the habit of paying

2. Diary of William Hoffman (1847-1850), p. 90, New-York Historical Society, Manuscript Division. The pagination is Hoffman's. In quoting from the diary I have left all punctuation and grammar as they appeared in the original.

the first year.'' Never having sought a mercantile position before, he was perhaps, by asking about salary, trying to accumulate as directly as possible the kind of knowledge he felt might be helpful in securing a position. He knew that he had a great deal to learn about business affairs and took whatever opportunities available to school himself by increasing his ''experience'' of mercantile customs and practices—whether about salary, as in this case, clerking, or establishing, as we will see below, living arrangements in a new environment. He whiled away some more time with a friend he met in a saloon—he ordered, he says, only pie—and then went down to the wharf, where he boarded for New York (p. 92).

The boat arrived in New York at four A.M. William stayed in his berth until daylight and then ''got up, washed, combed my hair and washed to prepare for starting into the street.'' Beginning with Greenwich Street (the lower portions of which had by this time given themselves completely over to mercantile activities), he made his usual inquiry—''whether they wished any aid in their business''—but, as in Poughkeepsie, he ''met with but little encouragement.'' It started to rain and William bought an umbrella before making his way to A. T. Stewart's great store on Broadway. He had heard there might be openings and applied for a position. But once again he was turned away. ''Undoubtedly,'' he reflected, ''[I[could have received encouragement had I a partial experience in the Business—But such unlucky for me was not the case.'' After doing some further looking, he went into the Astor House for a short rest and then went back into the rain to continue his search. He made his way along the major business streets—to Pearl, Nassau, William Streets—but still had no success. At each place he tried he would ''invariably'' be asked if he had any experience. ''I of course could not answer only Negatively—which seemed to raise a barrier to all further progress.'' But he intended to persevere. ''I would push along,'' he said, ''even though many would try to discourage me'' (p. 94).

He took time out to do an errand for a friend, buying some books, and then, probably to get out of the rain and possibly for some weightier reflection, visited Fowler's Phrenological Cabinet, where he saw ''the Busts and Skulls of many distinguished characters (p.

95).[4] As we will see in chapter 9, the science of phrenology, under the skillful promotion of two brothers, Orson and Lorenzo Fowler, exercised a great attraction for uncertain youths seeking new careers but lacking any firm notion of the kind of work they might actually be fitted for. William may have stopped at the Cabinet to ponder additional involvement—like a full-scale phrenological examination of his cranium—with the Fowlers.

Finally the rain stopped, "the pavements were again dry." William began walking again, trying streets haphazardly in the hope of finding a position. At about four o'clock he went back to Broadway and this time "attempted . . . to proceede to the furthermost extremity of the city." After much looking, he again came to a store where he thought he might have a chance and "put the question." The proprietor, busy with a friend, told William to sit down "and he would see." Cautiously, almost timidly, he waited. Watching the time pass, he quietly swallowed his growing frustration at being ignored, fearing to interrupt and thereby antagonize his prospective employer. Longer and longer he sat, growing more and more impatient—the afternoon was quickly passing—but still said nothing. Finally, "provoked at such inattention" and wishing to end the "suspense" of waiting, William braced himself and asked the man if he needed any assistance. The man asked William if he had any experience in the business. William replied that he hadn't and found the interview at an end. The boy maintained his self-control and "condemned him for keeping me so long *to myself*" (p. 95; italics mine). Lack of experience was either a real handicap or the most frequently used excuse employers had available. It was probably both, and William must once again have been conscious of how unprepared he was to seek employment in the unannounced, unrecommended way he was proceeding. Employers were more willing to talk to their friends than bother with another youth from the provinces.

Although it was late, the business day was far from over and William went back to Greenwich Street to see if anything had changed since morning. All he found, however, was a practical joker who succeeded in adding embarrassment to the round of humiliation he had already endured. In one of the stores William entered, a man pretending to be the firm's proprietor succeeded in "playing the fool" with him. The man was able to "carry it to some extent . . . —it was done so smoothly that a person would hardly suspect anything—" before one of the clerks told him that he was being taken in by an imposter. "I kindly thanked him," he said shortly, "and proceeded immediately out of the store" (p. 95).

At the end of the day he returned to the store in which a friend from home was clerking. After his friend convinced him that it was Saturday and not Friday as he had thought, he agreed to stay in New York at least until Monday. When the new week opened, he resolved to try some Brooklyn stores before giving up completely. On entering one place he met, apparently by accident, Jacob Derwith, who had previously clerked in William's uncle's store in Hudson. Derwith had secretly left a store in New York to work at his present place and told William to try there—the position might still be vacant. Sudden departures like Derwith's probably did little to endear other young men untutored in mercantile proprieties to the employers they hoped would welcome them. Undoubtedly such practices confirmed their suspicions that present-day youth were opportunistic and unworthy of elevation to roles that carried important social as well as commercial advantages.

After finishing with Brooklyn, William tried Derwith's suggestion, but discovered from an old schoolmate of his, Bushnell Lumis of Great Barrington, whom he found working there, that the place was long since filled. Eighteen to twenty applicants had already preceded him that morning (p. 97).

William wandered around until noon, when he caught the ferry to Jersey City. Once again he started looking for a situation. In the second place he entered he met another friend, Daniel Boice, stopped to talk for a moment, and then resumed his search, visiting "every store in the city." As he had begun to expect, he "met with but little encouragement" and returned to New York to wait for a boat up river. He did not intend to return home, however. "I had fixed my plans for going to Albany and if I was not successful there—go to Troy—I meant to persevere." Perhaps those cities upstate would be less flooded with young men like himself seeking jobs. Though the sight of friendly faces may have been heartening, they may also have driven home how many competitors he had. New York seemed to be inundated both with boys he knew and with many others he did not. Against such numbers, and with his lack of experience, he may have decided it was not too soon to try elsewhere.

Arriving in Albany four days after first coming to New York, he again began the rituals associated with his search. He "washed and fixed [him[self as slick as possible" and began pacing Albany's streets. He met with poor luck in several stores but finally found a place—by chance. The proprietor, after a long talk with the boy and without seeing any references—William said he would supply them in a week—agreed to employ him. He would "give me $150.00 for one year and I board myself—or he boards me—washes for me, etc. and at the expiration of the year gives me $50.00" (p. 98). The boy chose the latter arrangement. Perhaps he felt that the well-advertised temptations of urban life were worth taking seriously; or else he may have wanted to demonstrate his prudence to his new employer.

With the matter settled, William made his way home, and on arrival did the farm chores "as usual." He remained at home until the following Monday, April 10, when he started out for Albany. On the boat he met a friend, Henry Coon, who asked where he was heading. With all the self-importance expected of a boy embarking on a new career, William answered, "to Albany and there to enter into Business." Henry warned his friend about the temptations that "would gradually spring up around me and lure me from the path of virtue and morality." William was not worried. "I assured him," he tells us, "that my mind is as it always was—that I always held an aversion of the strongest kind against anything that would tempt to moral depravity and disregarded looseness" (p. 101). William's almost textbook avowal of intention was the firs of numerous indications that he seemed to have absorbed the lessons purveyed in current advicebooks directed to young men.

As soon as the boat landed at 7:00 P.M., the boy went straight to the store. Mr. Mesie, one of the partners, asked him for the promised references and then showed him his duties. He was to start by stacking piles of muslins and folding piles of calicoes. That evening, when the store closed, William followed one of the clerks to the house where he would "board and room." He was shown to a room—it was not particularly large, he noted—that he would share with three other clerks.

After a few days, the exhilaration of beginning a new job passed and the routine nature of the work became clearer. Mr. Mesie, the overseer of store operations, was very strict and kept William busy all day sweeping out the store and putting up goods. Routine became drudgery. On Thursday of his first week at work he recorded:

> Perform the regular work today as usual, sprinkle and sweep out the store which is a great chore. . . . I cannot say as I like the place—the Business as well as I anticipated. Everything here is to perform that is heavy.

Yet he refused to become discouraged and consoled himself with the thought that clerks "the first year . . . have to work harder than at any other time" (p. 103). Unlike William E. Dodge, who seemed to have accepted similar chores without complaint, William Hoffman was anxious to turn to more interesting work after being on the job less than a week. Along with others of his generation, he may have felt that his prosaic duties were a waste of time. There was much to learn about mercantile practice; time spent sprinkling and sweeping may not have appeared to be adding to the knowledge young men felt they had to acquire as quickly as possible in order to advance themselves among aggressive contemporaries.

But his work did not soon improve. For two days he and a fellow clerk were dispatched to the far corners of the city to distribute handbills announcing the sale of an old stock of goods at cost. The bills had their effect; the store became thronged, but William soon learned that the announcement had not been strictly honest: the goods were not being sold at cost as the handbills had promised. Buyers were being deceived (p. 103). William was chagrined by the breach of business ethics he apparently expected his superiors to be guided by. Honest dealing, he may have read in any one of the books, magazine articles, or newspaper pieces meant to catch the eye of young men, was a cardinal rule of the mercantile community.

His own eagerness to begin selling was deflated by Mesie's constant refusal to allow him to wait on customers. Mr. Mesie "told me I was not enough experienced," he wrote. But he continued selling when he could, and by the end of the next week confided "that I like my business and situation rather better than at first." Mesie's continued scoldings failed to dampen his enthusiasm.

Only his weariness at the end of a day's work did that. Often staying at the store until 9:30 P.M., he was convinced that he had "to perform twice the work that another one has who has a knowledge of the Business" (p. 106). Once again he seemed aware that he was not learning fast enough.

At the end of another week with the firm, after the other clerks had gone for the day, Mesie took William aside and asked him how he liked the job. The boy told him he was satisfied and Mesie then began reviewing the time William had spent with the firm. He told the boy to expect "a talking to" once in a while; that he should not be depressed because he was occasionally corrected or talked to "pretty loudly." He never expected William, just starting a new trade, to work with the dexterity of someone who had several years more experience. He was aware that he was sometimes "rather quick in censure," especially when his mind was deeply involved with business, but he urged William to keep at it. "He then told and pointed out to me," the diarist noted, "young men who when in his employ were as strictly kept as I am—and that he installed them in Business for themselves when they had arrived at Years of discression." He concluded the day's entry with Mesie's last words of encouragement. "He said that he had no fault to find—that my deportment thus far evidenced a good bringing up and that I showed every indication of becoming a Businessman" (pp. 107-8).

The reassurance that Mesie offered his clerk was significant. He was telling William that part of the criticism he received was an ordinary and necessary part of learning to be a merchant. He was telling William what to expect, telling him that his treatment was not exceptional or unusual. Like others who had been subjected to criticism or censure, he too would survive. Mesie was acting as the pedagogue he at times had to be. More formal educational institutions for merchants and businessmen were, as we will see in chapter 8, being established, but employers still had more explicit educational duties than would later be the case. Merchants knew that the education and training of their clerks depended in large part on the employers' efforts. By reprimanding, by scolding, by encouraging, by cajoling, clerks were being taught. They were also being tested. How well a clerk responded, how well he absorbed and adapted to the discipline of work, how well he accepted his chores and responsibilities told his employer what today's standardized examinations and university degrees at least help to tell him. It is no wonder that Hoffman's record is punctuated so often by questions from others about his experience. In what other way could a clerk's knowledge of or familiarity with a business be demonstrated? How else could an employer determine the capability of a young applicant? Along with character—the problem of sizing *that* up created other problems that we shall examine later—"experience" was the only gauge of progress or capability. There was only one way a young man could "know the business"—by having worked at it previously. Employers who hired experienced workers recognized the need—thought they were increasingly becoming too hard pressed to do as much about it as they might have wished—to provide their assistants with a thorough knowledge of the trade. For a while at least, young men who did gain a wide-enough familiarity with the operations of business practice to earn their promotion to the higher ranks of a firm would do so within the countinghouse.

After his meeting with Mesie, William's entries, understandably, revealed a greater enthusiasm and optimism. There were fewer expressions of despair at the routine or dismay with the hard work. His primary complaint was the length of time he worked. He wished he had more "time left for meditation" at the end of each day. He wanted, he said, time he could use for mental improvement. "Oh had I two hours every day to spend as I wished," he said, "I should think it a great privilege, and I should not spend it prodigally" (p. 110).

After six months with the firm his share of sales continued to increase, but he still seemed lacking in confidence and sensitive to criticism. One day he hesitated to stop a lady customer who had left the store without paying the correct amount, and he asked Boyd, another partner, what he should have done. Boyd replied that he should have stopped the woman and, "somewhat miffed," remarked "that I was milk and water and did not act promptly." A few days later he was thinking of going to California. If the reports from the gold fields continued to be as favorable as they had been, he saw no reason not to migrate there "and become one of those who are so eagerly seeking this gold metal" (pp. 172, 173). What this entry may reveal is that William was caught between a desire to get on as fast as others he knew and a fear of proceeding more aggressively than his employers deemed proper. Earlier he found himself scolded for impatiently approaching customers before he was considered ready. Now, when he found himself being criticized for not acting "promptly" enough, he may have felt it would be easier to leave for California rather that endure the tension produced by trying to internalize directives both praising him for accepting the tasks assigned him and rebuking him for being "milk and water." It must have been confusing to find that traits he had been led to believe would please his employer sometimes produced the opposite effect.

Trade had grown dull—it was midwinter—and Boyd was "quite cross." William was convinced that he should not stay on. Each day he checked the newspapers at the Albany Young Men's Association for reports from California, and on January 27, 1849, he resigned from S. V. Boyd and Company. Boyd urged him not to go to California and promised to help him find a clerkship in a New York wholesale house. He would gladly furnish the necessary recommendations.

William spent the winter at home and made no entries in his diary until early March, 1849. When he resumed writing, he noted that his mother had deeded the farm to him. He was grateful for the added capital he would gain by its sale—he expected it to bring from $8,000 to $9,000. Until the sale was completed, he engaged a caretaker to maintain the property. His California fever had abated, leaving his intellect, as he put it, "clear and unagitated." He knew his prospects for finding work in a wholesale house were only little better than his first attempt nearly a year ago, but he intended to seek another clerkship in New York (p. 178).

On Monday, March 5, William was prepared to leave, and worried only that he had not yet been able to collect the necessary character references. He had written to his uncle, a friend, and "long since" to Mr. Boyd, but had as yet received no answers. The next day he started without them, arriving in New York that night. On Wednesday he began looking again in a steady rain that had turned the streets to mud. Before noon he had visited all the stores on Broadway. He received a warm welcome from two men who knew his parents—"they showed me a great deal of respect, treated me with true hospitality"—but unfortunately had no openings in their own firm. Taking their advice, William rested from the weather for the remainder of the day. The next day brought some luck. After turning down a few positions that he felt did not pay enough, he was hired by the Wall Street house of Robertson Brothers and Company. After an interview, after an examination of handwriting samples, and after Robertson telegraphed Boyd for references, William was offered a position at $250 a year. Though he had been hoping for $300, he accepted (p. 180). His second trip to New York had been successful. He now had "experience" and could demonstrate it by producing references from past employers. He had a way to set himself off from others, from those like himself a year ago, seeking the same openings. He went home happily to tell his family the good news and collect his belongings. He then returned to New York, in the midst of a severe cholera epidemic, and business.

As usual, William's habits in New York were regular and disciplined. He tried to keep his expenditures down to the "absolutely necessary" and had just moved to an area "pleasantly located aloof from vicious characters who are not always introducing themselves in one's society to tempt in any way." He paid $3.50 for board—fifty cents more than he paid in Greenwich Street, where he had been living—and had a single room where he could come and go as he pleased. He did not stay there long, however. In a week he moved a third time. He decided to take a room at Booth's House, a rooming house for young men. The cost was one dollar a week and he would board himself (pp. 181, 190).

He found work at Robertson's agreeable. It was "most natural for my temperament," he remarked. Yet, by winter time he found himself "losing flesh" and declining in strength. With the consent of his employer he quit his position and returned home for the winter. There, he felt, he would be able to "regain his vitality."

At the end of February, 1850, William was back in New York

looking for a new position—his old one had presumably been filled. He hoped that "by perseverence and unflagging exertions" he might find a situation even though the season for hiring had long passed. But contrary to his expectations he had no difficulty finding openings. His problem was choosing among them. After a day he narrowed his decision to four good houses. Cautiously he considered the advantages and disadvantages of each and finally decided on Gilbert, Prentiss and Tuttle, "settling for $50 less that at another house of a much lower standing." When he reported for work the following day he found that the house was all he had hoped it would be (pp. 214, 215, 216).

In these deliberations William at last seemed close to possessing the confidence and assurance he had earlier lacked. As he described this third "search" for a position in New York, he seemed less desperate, more in control of the situation, more in a position to choose among options he had created. As he considered the possibilities before him he could now assert, "I kept them all in view and carefully managed to have one out of the number to engage in at any time I desired." In asserting that he would wait until he found "a situation in *exactly* [italics mine] the house I desire," he made clear that he no longer had to settle for any position that was offered him (p. 215).

On Friday, June 21, 1850, after a lapse of four months without making any entries, he recorded his continuing satisfaction with the new firm. Although he admitted working hard, he maintained that the firm was a desirable one for any clerk anxious to get on. "Every opportunity is offered," he noted. He was happy and at ease in New York.

As he continued working at Gilbert, Prentiss and Tuttle, he came more and more to identify his interests with those of the company. He noted the firing of an intemperate bookkeeper and approved the "businesslike and gentlemanly" replacement. He worried about the health of his employers, especially Mr. Gilbert, fearing that overwork might make them ill. For his own part, he expected to increase his sales during the coming fall season. With evident satisfaction he reflected on his most recent stay in the city: "I have enjoyed myself very well since my return and know the foundation and basis of all true felicity is contentment: a happy disposition and the indispensable blessings of good health" (pp. 228, 229).

Late that summer, near the start of the fall season, William allowed himself—a rare occasion—to reflect at length on the nature and duties of his career. He asked himself

> what makes [a clerk] most valuable to himself and employers—in fine what duty to be performed on the part of the clerk to promote and exalt himself and command a salary commensurate with his worth and suitable to his age, position, and desires. What will enable those clerks whose enterprise and ambition demand for themselves an advance in this earthly career—to become valuable and gain a competency—for themselves.

His answer was ordinary enough. He counseled hard work, and an obedience and attention to one's duties that would bring him to the attention of his employers. He urged

> unflagging exertion and an industry commendable on their part—A perseverence in the occupation embarked in—at all times endeavoring while employed during the hours of business to work and sedulously too, that nothing devolving upon a clerk to be neglected and left undone that can be done thereby giving satisfaction to employers and gaining their esteem. (pp. 235-36)

The most interesting thing about Hoffman's advice was its conservatism. His words read as if he were his employer's mouthpiece. His emphasis was on duty and obedience—on satisfying the employer—not on personal ambition. The quintessence of his reflections was "Do your job and you will be recognized and rewarded for it." Further on in the entry he spoke of his efforts to build himself up—to improve his sales and thereby "insure a respectable salary." Here he gave one more indication of how limited his personal ambition was. His goals had become those of the perennial employee, always striving to better his position within the organization but never trying to get beyond it. The passages above stressed values that would be most certain to recommend their bearer to his superiors. He talked of his quest for independence but seemed able to conceive of this as operating only within the boundaries of the firm that had hired him.

William had worked for what he had achieved. Long before, he had begun disciplining his desires and regimenting his needs. It is possible that the diary was started both to further his resolve and measure his progress. Although he nowhere said so directly, the journal may have been undertaken at the same time the decision to change his career was made. On its opening page dated March 1, 1847, he had written, "The design of the author is to keep a strict account of the transactions and occurrences of each day—good——Bad—or otherwise. Believing that such a course if rigidly adhered to will be highly beneficial in the end—in short—for future reference." The way he used business language to couch his intentions——the diary was to be an account book of daily "transactions"—may have been the only hint he allowed of his future intentions. His announcement on March 30, 1848, more than a year later, that he would not be a farmer, an announcement made the very day he planned to start his search for a clerkship, was the first concrete expression we have of his intentions.

There were numerous indications that the diary would be in part a way for him to keep track of the preparations—their object was not revealed—he was making. In the year before he left the farm, he made entries rebuking himself for falling asleep early ("It will not do for me; for the future I must betake myself with renewed energy"); noting that he had made resolutions calculated "to remove all corruption from my morals . . . and instill me with purer, nobler and higher feelings than I have ever before possessed"; and recording his intention to subject himself to "governing laws which I am not allowed, or will not allow myself to heedlessly violate" (pp. 74, 76). Since he used the diary to look back on his daily activities, he had a convenient record of his progress. With a diary he could see "clearly how the greater part of my time has been spent" and discover the "many errors committed which might have been shunned." With the aid of a written record he had a way to help his determination to discard habits "that I have nurtured that are not part of a desirable nature" (p. 82). Without any other guides to follow, he created one of his own. In keeping a diary he had a way to record his daily activities and resolves, and to see which ones were helpful and which ones were not. In this way a useful pattern might be discernable from the only experience he could turn to—his own.

It may be significant that Hoffman's diary ended a few pages after the observations he set down during the afternoon of August 31, 1850. Having attained his goal—a secure place, open to steady improvement—the journal, he may have felt, had accomplished its purpose. He would no longer need to consult it for "further reference."

His determination had rewarded him. He had made a comfortable place for himself. In doing so, however, he seemed to have limited himself to the goals and timetable set by his employers. In order to advance in a highly competitive trade, he had done as the hiring agents desired. That Hoffman's progress cannot be traced after this point may confirm what the foregoing has already suggested: that his subsequent career was not particularly successful or noteworthy. It is possible that he had so assimilated the rhetoric of advancement of the employing class as to make his survival in the increasingly competitive New York business world extremely precarious.

What is ironic is that the ethos he internalized may have been only partly intended to produce men as cautious as himself. To the extent that it operated to quiet the aggressiveness of the many who may have been unsure of their own predilections and, in a sense, thereby "self-select" themselves out of the field of competitors for important mercantile opportunities,[3] it was certainly counted a blessing by its purveyors. But even more important, it may have been intended to discipline those like Hoffman's contemporary, Edward N. Tailer, Jr. Tailer, a young man from a prominent mercantile family, might have been expected least of all to need the advice directed at someone like William Hoffman. With his social background and family connections, a promising career was a certainty that should have caused little dissatisfaction and uneasiness. His future was secure. Yet, as we shall see, Tailer was neither satisfied nor at ease.

Paradoxically, his advantages seemed to encourage an attitude toward advancement within his own chosen profession almost wholly different from William Hoffman's. With his advancement virtually

3. See chapters 9 and 10 especially for a consideration of the way merchants faced the problem of selecting workers they needed from the mass of applicants.

assured, we might have expected Tailer to be content with the customary timetable by which he would move into the higher echelons of mercantile practice. Instead, just the opposite appears to occur. Tailer was always sensible that his energies and talents were being shackled, that he was being restrained from acting as boldly as he wanted to. While Hoffman occasionally fretted about this also, he, as we have seen, made his peace with the system. Perhaps his lack of connections or influence made his decision understandable. But Tailer would not wait; his restlessness was translated into movement again and again as he disregarded the advice of employers and relatives and pushed himself ahead. In this sense it was Tailer's career that really marked a departure from the older mercantile style that characterized the rise of William E. Dodge. Hoffman's progress, though it expressed new pressures coming to bear on the old system, was also an expression of the system's continuing, if dwindling, power of coercion. But with Tailer, whose higher social position actually became an aid to rebellion, a new style, which proved to be a far greater threat to the traditions and customs cherished by older merchants like Dodge or Scoville, was being developed. This development was often slow and uncertain; Tailer might not at first have realized how much deviation from its "rules" the system would permit. His progressive boldness may have been due to the results his tentative probings yielded.

b. EDWARD N. TAILER, JR.

Edward N. Tailer, Jr., who was forming plans to seek a business career at almost the exact time as William Hoffman, also left a diary by which we can chart his early progress. On March 23, 1848, Tailer confided that he had left school in New York City "to enter upon the pleasures and misfortunes of a clerk's life."[1] The announcement, made matter-of-factly, was accompanied by no youthful exuberance

1. Diary of Edward N. Tailer, Jr. (1846-1917), March 23, 1848, New-York Historical Society, Manuscript Division. All punctuation and grammar of quoted passages are as they appeared in the original.

or enthusiasm. It seemed to record not a recent or hard-made decision, but the simple observation that the day he was to start looking for a position had come. In fact, he did not seem particularly anxious or eager to begin his career. Considering his background, there probably did not seem to be any hurry.

As he approached his eighteenth birthday Edward was untroubled and complacent, playful and content. His father was a wealthy merchant and a member of the city's highest social circles. His family was well connected, genteel, and properly pious. They attended St. Bartholomew's church, a growing Episcopalian parish where notables like Henry Clay and President Polk often worshiped when in New York. On these occasions Edward dutifully accompanied them, diligently paraphrasing the pastor's sermons in his diary. He was sent to a succession of schools where he did very well, especially, he tells us, in composition.

Surrounded by friends and relatives, he spent his days in any number of pleasurable ways. He took leisurely walks above the city's built-up section, went fishing at Kingsbridge or Greenpoint, traveled to picnic in Hoboken or to tour Brooklyn's newly opened Greenwood Cemetery. He took dancing lessons, was devoted to gymnastic workouts and had a penchant for sleighing or skating in winter. His evenings were no less full; the theater, parties, and other social invitations—even an occasional temperance meeting—all kept him busy.[2]

Edward seemed in no hurry to curtail these activities by beginning regular employment. Presumably, given his family's standing in the mercantile community, he could be sure of finding a position when he wanted one. Not that he had no interest in the matter. He had already turned down two offers—one because his father "put a veto on my operations." Apparently he felt there was no urgency or pressure to find work. Casually and unhurriedly, he was able to sift the advertisements for clerks in the *Journal of Commerce* and to consider offers from friends. A young man in a position to pick and choose, he could wait until the situation he felt appropriate to his talents pre-

2. See entries from November 3, 1847, to March 23, 1848, for a picture of Edward's daily life during this period.

sented itself.[3] He never seemed to question that such a situation would be in the mercantile profession.

Already familiar with a clerk's routine, apparently by helping at his father's office, he seemed to have closed his mind to other options. Whether reluctantly or not, he seemed to be obeying his father's wishes, although not always willingly or gracefully. Throughout the diary, for example, Edward appeared to regret—without ever saying so—that he never attended college, the most certain avenue to other professional careers. On numerous occasions he attended the college commencements of friends, and at the New York University graduation ceremonies of June 1848, he picked out the graduates he knew—some of them had been his grammar school classmates. Quietly he remarked, "If I had remained there, I would in all probability of graduated with them."[4]

There is also evidence that he was interested in medicine—enough to have led a prominent New York physician to make him an offer of partnership—yet, again, he took no action to pursue it. On October 10, 1848, he recorded a long, detailed account of an operation for "phymosis," which Dr. Mott, the performing surgeon, permitted him to observe. On the twenty-second he again noted that he had been observing—this time he did not say what—in Dr. Mott's office. The next day, Sunday, after church he visited the nearby medical school, probably that of N.Y.U. On the twenty-eighth he was stricken with a severe headache, "a thing which I have not been troubled with for more than a year," and the next day Dr. Mott made his offer. "The Doctor," he wrote, "made me quite a favorable proposition, provided I would study medicine with him, which was to study for four years, and he would guarantee me an $800 practice the first year after I graduated, with a prospective of being taken into partnership." Unfortunately, Edward did not add any additional comment to indicate either his inclinations or intentions. He finished the day's entry by talking about the weather—a subject he usually neglected—and two days later, on October 31, 1848, noted that he had answered an advertisement in the *Journal of Commerce*. It

3. See *ibid.*, June 13, 1848; September 18, 1848.
4. *Ibid.*, June 28, 1848.

turned out to be for a place in a lawyer's office. "As my object was to learn the mercantile business I respectfully declined," he wrote laconically. His mind, it seems, had been made up. He would be a merchant like his father. Except for his report of the 1849 N.Y.U. Medical College graduation ceremonies, when he recounted an address dealing with temptations young doctors would face—a social, not a medical subject—he never mentioned medicine again.[5]

Another possibility that Edward may have been considering was writing. He did publish about a year later numerous newspaper articles on the importance of health and keeping fit—extracts from which he copied into the diary—and there is evidence, in the differences in writing style he employed, that he was trying out or trying to find a suitable writing style. (He may have decided to begin a diary for this very reason.)[6]

On December 4, 1848, he decided on a suitable position. Two days earlier he had called upon a Mr. Smythe (presumably a family friend, though he is never identified) "and saw him in relation to *his procuring me* a situation." The next day, Sunday, Smythe sent for him and told him "that he had procured a situation for me with Little, Alden and Co., 29 Broad St., importers of British, French and German Dry-Goods." On Monday morning Edward went to Smythe's store and together they went to see Mr. Alden. Without getting up at daybreak, without walking the streets long hours, without exerting himself much at all, Tailer had a job. His language—a situation was procured *for* him—tells the story very well.

His duties at Little, Alden and Company were the usual for a beginning clerk—he was little more than a messenger and stock boy. The job, if not exciting, was at least secure. At this point Edward apparently felt this was enough. The riches of California so alluring to William Hoffman did not attract *him*. Those who were smitten with gold fever, he said, instead of settling for the security of a New York clerkship, were looking for trouble. Referring to those actually foolish enough to take the chance and go West, he wrote:

---

5. *Ibid.*, October 10, 1848; October 22, 1848; October 29, 1848; March 14, 1849.
6. *Ibid.*, October 14, 1849; December 21, 1849.

They soon find out their sad and irremedible mistake in giving up quiet but sure and productive situations, amidst their friends at home. What must be the feelings of a young man who was comfortably and happily situated amidst endearing friends at home and who foolishly and recklessly gave up all, for the faint hope of gathering unheard of wealth amidst the reputed gold lands of that vaunted country California. When he has at last arrived there he finds that all the boasted stories of the day are proved to be utter fiction and that he has *risked his all like a maniac* upon nothing and a mere bubble.[7]

Like an earlier generation, he still saw risk-taking as foolish and reckless: there were more certain and less anxious ways of reaching prominence.

The first winter at Little, Alden and Comapny was uneventful but not unpleasant. The sleighing was good, gymnastic workouts had added twenty pounds to his frame, and he found that he was having fewer headaches and an improved appetite. He attended lectures (one on Swedenborgianism left him feeling that he would have done better to spend the day in church) and continued his walks, skating, and horseback riding.[8]

By October, 1849, Edward—the volume covering the late spring and summer of 1849 is missing—was still working at Little, Alden and Company. He seemed generally content and filled his diary, for the most part, with a prosaic narrative of daily affairs. One exception was his discussion of his growing interest in physical training. His reasons for it went beyond the merely healthful advantages it bestowed. According to Edward the exercise gave "the persevering gymnast that conscious feeling of superiority which fails not when the hour of danger has arrived, either disguised in the pestilence . . . or when assailed by cowardly assassins." Edward's meaning was left vague—we are never told explicitly what dangers he was expecting, what dangers were disguised by the Plague. His next sentence was, however, revealing.

The wealth of our merchants has eclipsed that of the Florentine or

7. *Ibid.*, December 13, 1848; December 23, 1848.
8. See entries from February 2, 1849, to March 18, 1849.

Venetian Princes of old, but when the hundred or millions of which have been invested in commerce will have exhausted themselves in the pressures and collision of sinking interests and when the rainy day of hard labor, and light earnings, of insufficient food, raiment and lodging shall have arrived then will men be awakened to a sense of the importance of patronizing such institutions as gymnasiums in which the human frame is fortified in a physical sense of the word for the trials of life.

One of two fears may have been in young Tailer's mind. Perhaps he was so worried about the erosion of the merchant's wealth and social position that he was urging him to fortify himself for the struggle against an unnamed enemy. Or, and more likely, he may have been referring to a disaster that would afflict the whole population, not merchants alone. He may have sensed that the economic maneuverings that formed the essence of capitalism threatened to usher in a period of widespread hardship, a period of "light earnings, of insufficient food, raiment, and lodging." Under the conditions of scarcity that would result, only the strong had a chance to survive. Even in this early period of American development it was becoming clear just how ephemeral prosperity could be.[9]

On December 11 we get the first indication that Edward was not so satisfied with his position as he might be. He appeared upset about his salary—a matter apparently left unsettled when he began work—and planned to speak to Mr. Alden about it. When he did so the next day, Alden answered that he had intended to give Edward fifty dollars for the year and one hundred the next. The clerk maintained, however, "by all the arguments which my imagination could summon up," that his services were worth at least one hundred fifty dollars. "It was nearly time," he said, "that I did something toward supporting myself and relieving my father of whatever expense which attended my support." Such a reason certainly seems suspect; it is doubtful that the boy's father, well schooled in the methods of training clerks, either needed, wanted, or expected to be relieved of contributing to the support of his son. The request may have been Edward's first attempt to test the rigidity of the system through

9. See *ibid.*, October, 1849.

which he was supposed to be brought into mercantile life. Alden replied that Boston clerks received only fifty dollars, with a yearly increase of fifty, and that he could get young men willing to work from the time they entered the store until they were twenty-one for nothing. Edward said he would wait for Alden's answer.[10]

As he related the matter in his diary, he insisted that salary was the only issue bothering him. He did not mind the work and certainly did not want to leave the firm. If Haynes (the bookkeeper) thought "from words I have dropped," he wrote, that he was thinking of leaving Little, Alden, he was mistaken. "The salary is the only thing that troubles me, enough I must obtain to support myself."[11] In the next few days he continued to be agitated about the matter, expressing continuing dissatisfaction with a timetable of advancement common for young men in his position. On December 15, 1849, when he still had not heard from Alden, he remarked, "It strikes me most forcibly, as exhibiting a mean trait of character that a man who has made thousands of dollars should refuse the paltry sum to a faithful and hardworking clerk which would make him feel happy and independent." Dunbar, a salesman just elevated to partner, said he would put in a good word for the boy, guaranteeing him $150 at least.[12]

Edward could not get the salary request out of his mind. On January 7, 1850, he noted, "Mr. Alden has not yet made a happy clerk. . . . I am anxiously expecting an answer which [he] promised to give me weeks ago." Once again he spoke to Dunbar; once again the partner promised to talk to Alden. The boy now seemed increasingly irritable and impatient. It began to appear that there was something besides money that was bothering him. On January 17 he remarked

It is time Little, Alden and Co. had a young man to carry out bundles and parcels of pattern cards, as I have now been with them over a year—*and it is not creditable to myself that this kind of awkward and clumsy work should still devolve upon me,* and I

10. *Ibid.,* December 11, 1849.
11. *Ibid.,* December 14, 1849.
12. *Ibid.,* December 15, 1849; December 24, 1849.

hate to offer any objections which might prejudice them against me in any manner, time however will rectify it.[13]

Here for the first time Tailer admitted that considerations of social status and position, about the work and duties proper to a young man of his *social* station, were involved in his uneasiness about getting on. Once, as in William E. Dodge's day, when many of the young men performing such tasks were of similar social rank, feelings like Tailer's probably did not arise. But when young men of different social backgrounds performed them, the pride of rank may have been more difficult for one of Tailer's pedigree to down. The problem was not that the work was wearying, but that it was demeaning. For Tailer, a salary demand may have seemed the only acceptable way to express his dissatisfaction. Yet, he remained cautious and reluctant to question the firm's schedule of promotion openly. Time, he hoped, would "rectify" matters. Until it did, he would contain himself.

On January 28 the issue was finally resolved. Edward was to get the one hundred fifty dollars he wanted—and fifty dollars more if Alden liked his work at the end of the year. Although his enthusiasm was restrained, he seemed well satisfied: "Upon the strength of this interview [with Alden] I have I hope wisely determined to remain where I am as he promised to do well by me."

At home one night, Edward's mother handed him a clipping sent over by his uncle James. The uncle, who cut the article from one of the daily newspapers, thought it might benefit his nephew. It was a piece of advice to a young clerk—possibly his family had heard about the boy's request for a raise and thought the advice relevant. They, no less than Alden, may have considered the request improper. The clipping, or that part of it which Edward copied into his diary, purported to report the advice of a successful merchant who had himself begun as a low-salaried clerk. The mercantile trade, he said, had to be learned. The best way for a young man, especially one without capital, to do this was to begin clerking at a successful house "without regard in the start to the amount of salary." He should devote himself to acquiring a thorough, practical knowledge of all facets of

13. *Ibid.*, January 17, 1850. (italics mine)

the business and, as far as he could, make himself indispensable to his employers. If he remained in one place, "in time it cannot hardly be otherwise than that he will become a principal, some change will most certainly occur to effect it."[14]

The next few months were routine for Edward. If he had doubts about his position, he did not express them. He continued to attend lectures and plays, to keep up with his gymnastic workouts (often twice a day), and to maintain an intensive reading schedule (he was presently involved with Macauley's *History of England*). But on April 16 he again returned to a nagging worry.

"I have been somewhat unhappy," he admitted, "owing to my imagining myself poorly situated and kept down by those who would feign be my superiors, in other things, besides the mere situations which they fill in the house of Little, Alden and Co."[15] The custom that would have him accept a lower status role while at work was becoming a hardship. In a society like mid-nineteenth-century America, status was increasingly associated with wealth, and where wealth in turn was conferred most often by occupation and vocation, the customary long clerkship might become particularly onerous to a young man "of good family." Now, in a rapidly expanding economic situation where so many young men without ties to prominent mercantile families were seeking and finding clerkships, Tailer appeared concerned that customary attitudes toward clerks might be carried from the countinghouse to the street outside. He could accept traditional deference within the doors of the firm, but was troubled that others might feel that the posture was required of him elsewhere. This he could not abide. Unwilling to maintain that he was poorly situated, or that people were actually expecting his continued deference outside the business, he admitted only to "imagining" it all. But he was still unable to squelch his worries. And since the worries persisted, the slowness of his advancement, either real or imagined, became difficult to accept. Even the possibility of an erosion of his social position imposed an impossible strain. There were two things he could do to reduce the tension. He could give up the mercantile

14. *Ibid.*, February 2, 1850.
15. *Ibid.*, April 16, 1850.

profession (as we will see in chapter 7 many sons of prominent merchants did exactly that), or he could try to speed up the timetable of advancement. Without challenging the *process* by which one advanced, he could become aggressive enough to force his passage through its stages more rapidly. The second was the path Tailer took, and it is this choice that explains the kind of doubleness that characterized his rise—its mixture of acquiescence and self-promotion. Tailer accepted the forms governing his rise, but grew restless and impatient within them. It is this doubleness that roots Tailer's career in a particular time and place and thereby gives it its historical significance.

On June 8, 1850, he noted his conviction that he could improve his position. "There is not a day which passes during which I do not imagine," he said, "that I might better my situation as a clerk and receive an ample compensation for services rendered." Yet he was hard put to justify his restiveness. He admitted that he had "all the comforts of life"; that was not the problem. Instead, he wrote, he was upset

> with the want of liberality upon the part of my employers who could without experiencing any inconvenience give a suitable return for services and time rendered. All will justify me in saying that a clerk who bears his full share of the labor of the counting house room, and is compelled to do out of doors work, besides being a young man in his twentieth year, should be better remunerated than with a salary of $150 per year.[16]

Edward himself may have been struck by the feebleness of his reasoning. Unconvinced by an issue of principle—the liberality of his employers—he simply said what he knew was unreasonable: that a clerk (presumably it could be one from any social background) who worked as hard as he did deserved more pay. There was little else he could do without claiming special privilege.

But he took no action. Perhaps he was considering another career, after all. He noted that he had recently been fined twelve-and-one-half cents by the clerk at the Mercantile Library Association for an

16. *Ibid.*, June 8, 1850.

overdue book, George Combe's *Constitution of Man*. Maybe Tailer was turning to phrenology, like so many other young men of his day, to discover what work he was best fitted for.[17] Four days later he recorded that Dunbar had told him his eyesight was too poor for a mercantile career (Edward had been out of work nine days with an eye ailment) and advised him to study for one of the professions. "He also imagined," noted the clerk, "that I lacked energy and wanted that bustling and go ahead spirit which characterizes the active and persevering salesman."

Although discouraged with his mercantile prospects, he took comfort from his gymnastic work and recorded his progress conscientiously. On August 17 he happily wrote, "I equalled Mess. Hall, Montgomery, Leonard and Burke in the performance of what was to be done upon the ladders and bars." Later in the month he noted a new enthusiasm. He had begun lessons in the "art of self-defense." By way of explanation he said only that he feared the opportunity for its use might arise.[18]

By September, 1850, he again announced his desire to leave Little, Alden and Company for a better paying and more responsible position. Besides, he added, "Mr. Dunbar never had any particular fancy or exhibited any lasting signs of friendship for me, and will no doubt keep me down, as long as he can exert any power in the firm of Little, Alden and Co." Rather than expressing a real state of affairs, the entry must simply have been an effort to rationalize his desire to find something better. In five days he was promoted to salesman.[19]

Whatever satisfaction his promotion to salesman may have occasioned did not last long. On some days he complained about working late; on others he nonchalantly left hours early to see the sights of the city.[20] Earlier in the month—it was January, 1851—he complained about not receiving a New Year's bonus. On the thirteenth, saying that he was curious about the results he would get, he placed

17. *Ibid.*, June 11, 1850. See chapter 9 for a discussion of this problem.
18. *Ibid.*, August 22, 1850; August 27, 1850.
19. *Ibid.*, September 14, 1850; September 19, 1850.
20. *Ibid.*, January 15, 1851; January 20, 1851.

an advertisement for a new situation in the *Journal of Commerce*. "A young man," he had the ad read, "conversant with the French language, capable of corresponding, and who has been engaged for the last few years in one of the largest importing houses of this city, is desirous of obtaining a situation as assistant salesman in an Importing or Dry Goods Commission House."

Unfortunately, we have no record of Tailer's progress during 1851. Apparently it had not been great. In his entry for December 26, 1851, we discover that he was still working, with some devotion it now appeared, at Little, Alden. Even so, he continued to express dissatisfaction with his salary and had taken to writing Mr. Little, the partner stationed in Boston, about it. On January 14, 1852, Little, during a visit to New York, told Edward that he had spoken to Mr. Alden about his salary. He warned his salesman, Edward wrote, that "I must not value my services too high as I was yet young and that he would see to my welfare." In a sense Little warned his clerk that he ought not become restless about his position. It was the boy's place to remain modest about his abilities and let others, older and wiser, advance his cause.

The next day Dunbar upbraided Edward for his handling of customers. Earlier he had criticized him for his lack of "bustle" and "go ahead spirit"; the new partner now felt he pursued buyers a bit too aggerssively. Either Edward, much like William Hoffman, had taken the advice too much to heart without realizing that it had limits, or he may have decided finally to take some positive hand in the direction of his career. Instead of continually expressing his demands for advancement in terms of a salary increase, he now began to exercise the responsibility and independence he felt accompanied his promotion. He intended to discover, he may have reasoned, how much of an advance he had actually made. If his promotion was in title only, or even in salary only, the recognition he sought was still being denied. The "blow out" started, said Edward, "by his telling me that I should not put myself out of the way to speak to customers, he laying it down as his opinion that it savored too much of the Chatham Street[21] manner of receiving a customer to see every man

21. Chatham Street was the street just south of the Bowery where the hucksters of the retail trade flourished.

in the establishment running out to salute and shake a buyer by the hand, and that it was only sufficient to speak to them politely, should you accidentally stumble upon them.'' Edward, in characterizing Dunbar's suggestion that selling was best done by being so unconcerned about it that you appeared to stumble upon buyers accidentally, left little doubt about his opinion of the partner's selling technique. To make sure that Dunbar understood his position, he ''insisted upon my right to speak to whoever I pleased.'' As expected, the disclosure ''stirred up [Dunbar's] temper not a little.''[22]

About a week later Edward was again called down for his selling methods and this time told not to wait on any out-of-town buyers. The news, he reported, caused him to feel ''somewhat mortified.'' Although disappointed, he did not sulk. Until time smoothed things over he would be content, he said, to wait on the city trade.[23] The incident must have confirmed Edward's suspicions that the partners considered him accomplished or trustworthy enough to handle only the small local retail trade and not the big wholesale purchases made by the out-of-town buyers, from which most of the firm's profits came.

On February 13 he received the raise he had been seeking. Edward, thinking his recent reprimands would prejudice the outcome, was surprised. ''I . . . am not as bad off as I expected I would be,'' he admitted. His salary for 1852 would be four hundred fifty dollars, an increase of one hundred fifty from 1851.[24] He was apparently not being treated so badly as he sometimes made it appear, even though the recognition that meant more than money to him was still being withheld. It was some comfort to him that his friend Thomas Clark had just agreed to continue with his firm, Ward and Pirson, at the same terms. ''He gets the same salary and *no raise*,'' Edward emphasized.[25]

The salary increase was, however, no indication that differences with his superiors were to lessen. Relations with Dunbar, for one,

22. Tailer Diary, January 15, 1852.
23. *Ibid.*, January 21, 1852.
24. Edward must have received an earlier increase, during 1851, to raise his salary from $150 to $300.
25. Tailer Diary, February 13, 1852.

continued to deteriorate. Edward missed few opportunities to criticize the new partner, feeling confident that he could perform the latter's duties far more effectively. On March 3, after Dunbar returned from a business trip to Philadelphia, Edward remarked that Dunbar had failed to make a single sale. "I am half inclined to think," he noted, "that I might possible have done better myself if they had permitted me to have gone *and called upon the jobbers at their respective warehouses instead of remaining at Ewing's store expecting them to call upon you.*"[26] Some days later, Dunbar did in fact suggest sending Edward. The boy, anxious for the opportunity, wrote Mr. Little, asking him to persuade Dunbar "and get him to send me instead of loosing precious time by procrastination and contenting himself with merely talking about it."

Within two days, at Little's urging, he was sent to Philadelphia. And, according to his diary entries, he appeared to be dealing well. His energy was evident; he visited thirteen jobbers the first morning alone. But by afternoon, since he had sold only one case of goods, the New York office telegraphed him to return home. A bit crestfallen, he came back to New York, disconsolately noting that he had "paved the road for future sales of which we'll be deprived in consequence of my absence."[27]

Edward was somewhat heartened by Little's reaction to his trip. In his periodic Boston letter, Little said he was pleased with the boy's work and sorry he was recalled so soon. Edward quickly responded. "I expressed myself fearlessly," he said, "informing him that Little, Alden and Co. had lost the sale of several cases by my absence."[28] The discovery that Edward had gone over their heads by his letters to Little hardly endeared him to the New York partners, Alden and Dunbar. They "were thrown into a state of excitement," Edward noted, when Little, in the Boston letter, said the youth could be of service in Baltimore and Philadelphia. They reprimanded him, saying that they could best judge the "adaptability" of these markets for taking the firm's goods. In the future, they told him,

26. *Ibid.*, March 3, 1852. (italics mine)
27. *Ibid.*, March 15, 1852.
28. *Ibid.*, March 17, 1852.

I must first submit any letter intended for Mr. Little to Mr. Alden, in order that he may pass his opinion upon them, and erase therefrom anything that may prove to be objectionable. Mr. Dunbar told me that I would only "bitch" to use his expression the Balt-market by going on and prevent Taylor and Gardiner [two other firm salesmen] from selling any more of our goods which I think to be a wrong argument as Mr. Little himself is of the opinion that I might sell ten or twenty packages and all that I petitioned for was a trial which they refused to grant.[29]

Apparently Alden shortly reconsidered. Edward was soon on his way to Philadelphia again. But he did not do well and complained that the bad spring weather had reduced the value of his goods in the eyes of the buyers. From Philadelphia he wrote to Little again——perhaps he would be wiser to try the Baltimore market. But on his return to New York he maintained that he still wanted to try Philadelphia. He was told, however, that Dunbar would go instead. Even his plea that he would sell the goods at a profit or make up the difference from his own pocket did not help.[30] Once more, disregarding Alden's earlier warning, he took his case to Little, who insisted over the New York partner's objection (Alden, said Edward, urged his old excuse, that he lacked experience) on sending the boy to Baltimore. Edward, who noted how impressed even he was with Dunbar's success in Philadelphia, neglected to record the results of his trip. The distance between him and Dunbar continued to widen, Edward no doubt exacerbating matters by asking the older man to address him in "a more gentlemanly and milder manner." Dunbar complied and Edward hoped the change would "prove to be of a durable and lasting character."[31] In requesting the change, Edward may have been trying to secure, by asserting a social claim, the recognition he could not secure by asserting a professional one.

Relations with Alden were little better. A few days after his exchange with Dunbar, Alden called him aside and asked him if he had been discussing the private business of the firm with competitors. Edward, writing of the incident in his diary, recorded only his hope

29. *Ibid.*, March 29, 1852.
30. *Ibid.*, April 3, 1852; April 7, 1852.
31. *Ibid.*, August 6, 1852.

that he had explained everything satisfactorily; but the lack of confidence his employer's question implied surely did not go unnoticed. Charitably, Edward attributed Alden's question to "some mean and insidious character [who] has been poisoning Mr. Alden's ear by telling him that I have been in the habit of disclosing the secrets of the concern to our customers and rivals."[32]

Two months later, in early October, Alden called Edward into his office and circuitously brought up the inevitable. He asked Edward for his views about salary for the forthcoming year. When the young salesman said he wanted $750, Alden replied "that he thought I was much better qualified to sell domestic goods than foreign, and that between now and the first of January I had better procure for myself another situation." They had engaged another salesman at a high salary, he continued, and could not afford to give Edward an advance suitable to his "services and expectations." Tailer may have been a bit disingenuous when he remarked that the communication took him "somewhat by surprise."[33] Possibly this was due to the excuse Alden offered. The reasons for his firing must almost certainly have been personal, not professional. If they had wanted to keep and promote Edward, another salesman would probably not have been hired at "a high salary." And telling the youth that the decision was based on his selling qualifications could hardly have been calculated to spare his feelings. Telling him that he was qualified to sell inferior grades of textiles, or the cheap, durable, but generally unfashionable kinds of ready-made clothing worn by laborers and pioneers that together comprised much of the goods domestically manufactured, and not the finer grades of imported fabrics used by more discerning Easterners, whose clothing was made to order by tailors and dressmakers, constituted an insult.[34]

Tailer was undismayed, however. That afternoon he went to see a Mr. Sullivan, a boxing partner, and told him he was "about to make a change." Sullivan told him that on Monday he would introduce Edward to Reiner and Mecke, the proprietors of a hosiery store, who

32. *Ibid.*, August 12, 1852.
33. *Ibid.*, October 2, 1852.
34. See Robert Greenhalgh Albion, *The Rise of New York Port, 1815-1860* (New York, 1939), pp. 63-64, for information on the clothing trade.

were seeking a salesman. "As he is an intimate friend with one of the partners," noted Edward, "an introduction from him will be of great weight and value."[35] Boxing, it seemed, paid other than purely conditioning dividends. It may also have been a way to make and keep up the personal contacts necessary for business survival. Without the formalized agencies for securing employment that would later develop, such contacts were essential.

Two days after meeting Reiner and Mecke, he was offered a position at the salary he hoped for. One of the partners, Edward related, saw Mr. Alden "in relation to my character," and then engaged him as a salesman at a salary of $1,000 for the first year and $1,200 for the second. He was to begin in November.[36]

The next evening at home, Edward discussed his new position with his uncle James. Like the advice he had sent two-and-one-half years earlier, the uncle pointed out that young men were better off remaining in one situation until they mastered the business. Then, "should the opportunity occur and the capital be forthcoming," they could feel perfectly safe in embarking on their own. "By shifting every year," wrote Edward, who did not seem to tire of collecting such advice, "they might possibly become Jack of all trades but good at none, and liable to fail when they do commence business, owing to their want of experience and proper training."[37] As before, the advice exhibited the careful, unadventurous course a young man was expected to pursue. Opportunities were not created, but could be accepted when they presented themselves. But once again the advice did not deter Edward; he was glad to be making the change. Even the news that he had beaten out another young man—and a friend—who was going to apply for the same position but was taken sick did not dampen his enthusiasm.[38]

On October 19, 1852, when he announced his departure, Mr. Alden gave Edward an assessment of his tenure with the firm. He was told, noted Edward, "*that my greatest failure was too strong an*

35. *Ibid.,* October 2, 1852; October 8, 1852.
36. *Ibid.,* October 9, 1852.
37. *Ibid.,* October 10, 1852.
38. *Ibid.,* October 12, 1852.

anxiety to force myself ahead and a desire to thrust myself in the way of every customer." Displaying a properly humble mien, he took the advice "in a submissive manner reserving the truth it contained for future consideration and meditation."[39]

As he began work with Reiner and Mecke, Edward wondered about the wisdom of his move; he wondered "whether the engagement which I have but now entered upon will rebound to my future welfare and interest." It wasn't long before he saw the answer. He was getting restless again. On February 11, 1853, barely three months after he began working for Reiner and Mecke, he inserted "for the fun of things" an advertisement in the *Journal of Commerce* to see if any importers were in the market for a salesman.[40] And, toward the end of the month, he told Mecke that his eyes were too poor for the hosiery business. He began looking for other employment.

Edward was not alone in his restlessness and eagerness to get on. John Osbrey, another young salesman at Reiner and Mecke and the brother of Fred Osbrey, one of the firm's partners, was also unhappy with the pace at which he seemed to be advancing. As Edward eagerly told it, "Osbrey started a tumult when he insinuated that he could sell goods much cheaper after he had established himself than he could now when he was obliged to abide by company instructions." His brother overheard him and rebuked him for talking like that to customers. This "so irritated John Osbrey," said Edward, "that he refused to remain with them any longer and has left this evening for good."[41]

The episode must have delighted Edward; no doubt it strengthened his resolve to find a new situation for himself. Within a few days he heard from other salesmen that Fanshaw, Millikin and Townsend were looking for a new salesman. Characteristically, though he often

39. *Ibid.*, October 19, 1852. (italics mine)
40. *Ibid.*, February 11, 1853. The advertisement read: "Dry goods, the subscriber who has been for the last four years in the employ of a large Importing House and who has sold goods by sample in the Philadelphia and Baltimore markets, and who is acquainted with the jobbers generally, is desirous of a situation as salesman. A line addressed to "Austin" at this address will receive immediate attention."
41. *Ibid.*, February 25, 1853.

placed advertisements and scanned the advertising pages of the dailies, he always found jobs through personal contacts; friends either told him about openings or recommended him for them.

Two days later, he wrote to Mr. Townsend stating that he "was in the market" for a salesman's berth on or before the first of June. He would be happy to join Fanshaw, Millikin and Townsend providing the latter was satisfied with Edward's references; he named "some of our most prominent jobbers and request[ed] him to call upon them."[42]

The next day Edward, acting with the assurance of an accepted member of the mercantile community, called upon his "most intimate friends" in the jobbing trade and asked them to see if they could find him a place in a dry goods house. One friend, a Mr. Loder, promised that he would call on Townsend personally and see if he could help assure the position for Edward. "I hope that his efforts may be aroused with success," he said, "as I should like to be placed in a position where I could [illegible word] Little, Alden and Co. and sell their customers."[43]

A note from Townsend summoned him to an interview the next day. He was told that he would be notified "as soon as he [Townsend] had satisfied himself as to my popularity with the jobbers." Once again Edward went out to marshall his forces. Feeling that the interview was far from conclusive, he wanted to do whatever else he could to sway Townsend favorably. "I saw Mr. Lambert shortly afterwards," he noted, "and he promised to use all his influence to impress upon Mr. Townsend my qualifications as a salesman, and others of the leading jobbers have assured me that they'd do likewise."[44] In addition to rounding up this supporting claque, Edward himself wrote a second note to Townsend in which he gave his "views upon styles of goods which had done remarkably well with Little, Alden and Co. last fall."[45]

That afternoon Townsend gave in; Edward was provisionally hired. When the merchant stalled about final arrangements Edward, not one

42. *Ibid.*, March 14, 1853.
43. *Ibid.*, March 15, 1853.
44. *Ibid.*, March 16, 1853.
45. *Ibid.*, March 21, 1853.

to place too much trust in prospective employers, applied for a position with another firm, W. and S. Phipps and Company. Perhaps Edward realized that the mercantile community was far from being governed by the honesty and integrity that was said to characterize it. Edward's move was unnecessary. Five days later he was hired by Fanshaw, Millikin and Townsend. He was elated, and vowed he would try hard to show Townsend that his qualifications had not been overrated.[46]

The next morning, possibly to gloat over his good fortune, Edward called on Dunbar at his old firm and later recorded part of his former employer's words. Dunbar told him that his prospects with Little, Alden and Company would have been very good "if I could have *conformed myself* . . . to their ideas of salary, etc. instead of thinking that the concern could not do without me if I left them. He also told me that I was *too self-conceited and not teachable,* and that I must take care and not obtain a position which I could not fill to the satisfaction of my future employers whoever they may be."[47]

On June 1, 1853, he began work at Fanshaw, Millikin and Townsend. He considered both employers "agreeable and energetic," and congratulated himself "upon being associated with men of their business stamp." "It remains for me," he noted, "to give them satisfaction by exerting myself to the utmost."

Apparently Edward failed to do so. Within the year, on April 1, 1854, Townsend informed him that he was going to be fired. Edward's reaction to the news signaled the degree to which his assurance and confidence bordered on unreflective egotism. The only fault that Townsend found with his salesmanship, he said, was a lack of firmness and an "indecision in manning [illegible word] prices, parties not knowing when they had obtained the lowest price." He then continued with a singular lack of introspection. "It must have been some jobber who was a particular friend of his who could have put such a ridiculous idea into his head as I have sold my share of the stock this spring with not half the exertion which attended my movements last fall. . . . I resorted to the gymnasium in the evening

46. *Ibid.,* April 15, 1853; April 29, 1853.
47. *Ibid.,* April 21, 1853. (italics mine)
48. *Ibid.,* April 1, 1854.

for the purpose of forgetting my troubles.''[48] Interestingly, Edward externalized the cause of the criticism. He seemed unwilling to consider the possibility that Townsend's remarks were accurate. At another point, for instance, he attributed his fate to the ''fickle disposition'' of his employer, which led him ''to think that other people employ smarter salesmen, and but seldom experience a dull day.''[49] Edward had been caught off guard. The success of his business trips for the firm—measured by his sales and his familiarity with the Western jobbers—had left him unprepared for such an outcome. But for all the hurt pride, for all the desire to cover any actual failings, he did seem genuinely convinced that the difficulty lay outside himself. The diffident, self-conscious doubtings of the timid beginner did not afflict him.

On May 17, 1854, Edward placed, this time with less levity, a short ad in the *Journal of Commerce*. ''An experienced salesman whose present engagement will shortly expire,'' he wrote, ''is now in the market.'' A week later he again applied to Phipps and Company and was hired at $1,200 per year, to begin in July. Unfortunately, he was not to stay there long either. This time the problem did not lie with him. On October 6, 1854, Phipps told his clerks that the firm would soon dissolve. That he was the only salesman Phipps's son asked to join him in partnership in the commission business was little consolation. Once again he was out of a job.

Yet, he was sanguine enough about his prospects. For a month, while Phipps's other clerks were out looking for positions, Edward held off doing anything. Quietly he passed the word that he was looking for a new place.[50] He seemed confident that, as in every previous instance, he would secure a situation better than the one he had left. His expectation was soon confirmed. On November 23, 1854, through the help of a friend, he was hired by Sturgis, Shaw ans Company as a traveling salesman. The partners agreed to pay him $1,200 the first year and $1,500 the second and third. He was to start January 1, 1855.

The year proved to be his most successful. He was trusted by his

49. *Ibid.*, March 23, 1854.
50. *Ibid.*, November 10, 1854.

new employers and made numerous western trips on their behalf. His social life was just as satisfying. Edward was considering marriage to Miss Agnes Suffern, the daughter of Thomas Suffern, one of the city's most esteemed merchants.

Perhaps the most significant development of the year was the offer he received from John Osbrey. Since meeting at Reiner and Mecke, the two had become good friends and on October 6, 1855, Osbrey told him that he and his partner, Charles Winzer, "would be delighted to have me join them in business provided I could contribute $xx,000 and with my knowledge of the trade we could no doubt sell $150,000 worth of gloves and cotton hosiery the first year and make at least ten per cent profit. . . . They are both honest men and true as steel."[51]

About a month and a half later his marriage plans crystallized. On November 24 he received approval from Agnes's father, and a wedding date, December 27, was set. On December 20 Edward introduced Mr. Suffern to his prospective partners. Suffern was pleased with them and, said Edward, "has given me his consent to go into business with them upon the first of January, 1856." With this approval (it took a more substantial form shortly—Thomas Suffern seems to have paid the capital Osbrey requested of Edward, in addition to assuming many of his notes during the Panic of 1857) and his own business skill, Edward prospered. In 1861 he and Winzer bought out Osbrey, and after the Civil War the remaining link of the partnership was dissolved. Winzer assumed a salaried position representing the new firm of Edward N. Tailer, Jr. and Company in Europe.

By the time he was thirty years old, Edward N. Tailer had established himself firmly—his business, strengthened by the Civil War, was secure. His election to the Union Club and the American Jockey Club some years later confirmed what was already a fact—that he was a substantial member of the mercantile community. Tailer's career, in its disregard of the counsel he seemed eager to collect, signaled how far established practice, no matter what older merchants would have young men believe to be the case, already differed from

51. *Ibid.*, October 6, 1855.

that of a few decades before. That Tailer was not severely penalized for acting as he did shows how little power the system that men like his Uncle and Dunbar thought was operating could in fact exert. Their advice, rather than describing any operational reality, was actually the invocation of a set of customs and social practices that were becoming increasingly rare. It is interesting that Townsend, before hiring Edward, was more concerned about his "popularity with the jobbers" than with his character, and that Edward seemed more impressed with and willing to please this employer than any other. Edward, unlike William Hoffman, who tailored his ambitions and thereby removed himself from the competition for higher business positions, may have recognized that Townsend and his partners knew what business was all about.

PART III

The Search for Solutions

6

Advice to Young Men

Although Edward N. Tailer, Jr., was busy exchanging his elder's counsel for the values of men like Townsend, it was not because the sound of his relative's moral voice was too faint to be heard. At the time Tailer and William Hoffman were pursuing their careers, an enormous volume of literature embodying the message Edward's uncle kept sending him was blanketing mid-nineteenth-century America. This literature, which took the form of books of manners, moral tracts, didactic novels, and magazine articles, is a particularly rich source for examining the tensions and pressures that appeared to dominate the mercantile community in the decades before the Civil War. In its earliest forms, didactic literature consisted of collected sermons concerned with initiating the young into their religious responsibilities. In the early decades of the nineteenth century, it became more specialized: books appeared, for instance, addressed to young women about their domestic duties and to young men about their role as potential leaders of the community.

By the 1830s, the literature directed to young men underwent further changes. More and more it was directed to the youth about to

147

pursue a career in an unfamiliar environment like the city. This new focus may have been an indication that writers felt that the advice they intended to offer was available nowhere else or that the young men who most needed it did not have access to the sources, such as an established apprenticeship system, where it could be found. The appearance of this material also signaled a demographic shift of large proportions, and suggests that the movement of young men to cities was causing a considerable number of problems for those, like merchants, who would be directly affected by it.

To appreciate the differences marking this new advice-literature, it is worthwhile examining Joel Hawes's *Lectures to Young Men,* first published in 1828. The book was a collection of sermons delivered to the young men of his Hartford congregation, and was in many ways a forerunner of the newer literature. Its warning that the slightest deviation from the path of virtue would bring total disintegration of a young man's character, its insistence that life outside the church was a horribly dangerous, temptation-ridden affair, and its acceptance of its audience's desire for worldly success set many of the conventions that later writers of advice-books would use.

Yet Hawes's book, for all its innovation, was still fundamentally a reflection of an earlier way of thinking about the young. There was a closeness of belief, an assumption of shared purposes among pastor and parishioners, that disappeared in later books. Hawes recognized that he was speaking to the sons of established members of the community who would one day inherit what their fathers had accumulated. His audience, he said, would soon be the guardians and defenders of society's institutions and the heirs to all its privileges and hopes. His charge to them was overtly conservative. Their obligation was to preserve intact the legacy bequeathed to them for the next generation. "If you fail to be qualified for the high trust," he warned, "or prove unfaithful in the sacred duties which it involves, how fearful the consequences—how irreparable the loss!"[1]

The duty of the young was to prepare themselves, to qualify themselves, to take over the "invaluable interests" of the community, which would in time be "transferred" to their care. To do this, he

1. Joel Hawes, *Lectures to Young Men on the Formation of Character. . .* (Hartford, 1828), p. 26.

expected them to take up careers in "the various departments of business and trust, the pulpit and the bar, our courts of justice and halls of legislation" (p. 25). They were going to *replace* the community elders, not move up from lower positions in the society to *displace* them. "You are soon to occupy the houses, and own the property, and fill the offices and possess the power . . . that are now in other hands" (p. 8), he told them. It is noteworthy that Hawes's verbs in the above sentence are all static; none connote movement, certainly not upward movement. He did not expect his young listeners to rise to their new positions. They would simply step into positions, already established, that had been vacated for them by their former holders. The idea that the community was expanding and would need new kinds of talent for new kinds of positions was absent. Hawes recognized his audience's aspirations, but never imagined them to have upwardly mobile desires. The cultivation of habits of virtue would lead not to a rise in station, but to esteem (p. 51, 111-12).

Like later writers, Hawes considered the period of youth to be a perilous time. Passions "impatient of restraint" continually endangered moral rectitude. Yet, somehow these propensities were balanced by a degree of self-control, judiciousness, and rationality only infrequently attributed to youth a few years later (pp. 60-61). So certain was Hawes of the agreement of his audience with his own aims, that he unhesitatingly assumed that they, in their turn, would continue the system of promotion that operated to ensconce them in positions of respectability. He took their attainment to prominence for granted and urged them "to perform the angelic office of guardians and advisers to those . . . of fair and promising character . . . younger than yourselves, who look to you for example [and] protection" (pp. 60-61).

Hawes warned his listeners about their susceptibility to corruption, especially while their characters were so malleable. As an example of what might befall them, he pointed to another group, the "great number of youth" from the countryside, naive and unworldly, flocking to the cities in search of work in the business trades, who found it impossible to resist the foulness around them. Speaking with notable detachment, he observed that they "go to swell the monstrous tide of depravity and dissipation which is rolling, as a mighty desolation, over the cities of our land" (p. 41). Unlike later ministers, the problem of accommodating these rural youth concerned Hawes only incidentally. He used their plight to warn his own flock, but it would be some years until he and others like him became sufficiently alarmed to direct words of advice specifically to this group itself. Although it was becoming more difficult to do so, ministers could still echo the sentiments of the eighteenth-century divine John Clarke. "I have taken it for granted," the Boston reverend told a young gathering, "that you have happily escaped the pollutions which are in the world. . . . [If you] have not been long familiar with sin [you] may be easily recovered."[2]

Hawes himself, in a new edition of the *Lectures* published in 1856, acknowledged the changes that had occurred in the twenty-eight years since his first edition had appeared. The text of the original edition was reprinted verbatim. But a new chapter entitled "Causes of Success and Failure in Life" expressed an altered perspective. Here Hawes addressed apprentice workmen, clerks, students, mechanics, laborers, and farmers,[3] and considered their aspirations in terms of upward movement in the social structure. He advised his audience to depend on itself—a new directive for him—and explained why this was especially necessary in the United States:

> Here are no privileged orders, no hereditary honors, no power of caste to depress those who are determined to do well and to rise. The field of honorable enterprise is open to all, and the poorest and most obscure may enter the lists with the richest and most elevated, and compete with them for the rewards of intelligence and virtue, of respectability and influence in society. (p. 124)

His early rhetoric of privilege and inheritance were now put to new uses. What he had once used to assure one audience of an exalted social position, he now denied could hold another audience back. In addition, class differences were explicitly taken into account. The

2. John Clarke, *Discourses to Young Persons* (Boston, 1804), p. 303.
3. Joel Hawes, *Lectures to Young Men on the Formation of Character. Originally addressed to the Young Men of Hartford and New Haven . . . With Two Additional Lectures Not Before Published* (Boston, 1856), pp. 130, 138.

poor and most obscure were enjoined to do battle with the rich and most elevated for the *same* social places. He referred to the rise of Benjamin Franklin from "the printer's stand to the chair of philosophy and the honors of statesmanship," and noted that "there are many young men now before me, apprentices, clerks, laborers . . . who by a right use of time, might be equally distinguished" (p. 128).

The changes that Hawes registered in the 1856 edition of his *Lectures* were apparent in books published only a few years after his first edition. William A. Alcott's *Young Man's Guide* (1833) was one of the most comprehensive. Unlike the Hartford pastor, Alcott saw himself as addressing a group whose aspirations would soon lead them to a world with which they were largely unfamiliar. From farms, from apprenticeships in rural townships, he assumed that there were hundreds seeking places—a high proportion of whom were seeking mercantile places—in the cosmopolitan environment of the city.[4] To help them Alcott filled his book with advice on manners and etiquette—in company it was bad form, for instance, to "take your penknife from your pocket and pair [*sic*] your nails"; on dress—keep it cheap but not shabby; on personal cleanliness—it was shameful "to pass months and even years, without washing the whole body once" (pp. 81, 73, 88). There were also long chapters on business management, amusements, marriage, and sexual behavior.

It appeared that Alcott was trying to provide a schedule of expectations for his readers—a group of young men who were eager to take places among an urban citizenry but who did not yet know the rules of the game they hoped to play. In his chapter on business management, for example, he included a section called "Fear of Poverty." He told his readers not to be ashamed of being thought poor. (The

4. [William A. Alcott], *The Young Man's Guide*. 3d ed. (Boston, 1834), pp. 70-89, 100-108, 158-94. Alcott advised his readers, for instance, to begin keeping a journal and, choosing the haying season as an example, demonstrated how entries should be made. "I selected a common agricultural employment to illustrate my subject," he said, "because I suppose a considerable portion of my readers are farmers . . . ." *Idem*, p. 226. It seemed clear that the habit of method and the improvement of handwriting that would result would be of value in other pursuits that he expected many of his readers soon to turn to.

problem was a uniquely urban one, he noted. Farmers who lived a great distance from their neighbors did not have to worry about keeping up appearances [p. 47].) The effort to disguise the imagined deprivation was sure to produce the real thing. He remarked that the dread of poverty was the most significant cause of suicide in the United States, in effect telling young men to expect to be poor early in their careers and that certainly it was not worth killing themselves about. Like other obstacles to the genteel life, it would pass.

His prohibition of amusements and recreations that he feared would most easily excite the immature passions of the young arrivals may have been partly intended for similar effect. The injunction, prompted no doubt by a concern for the moral development of his readers, also had the effect of removing from their path virtually every activity that made a large city unique and possibly forbidding. Whether intentionally or not, he made the city less threatening and terrifying by barring what was new and strange and urging what was already familiar. Theatergoing was condemned significantly, for health reasons as well as for its moral dangers. "Respiration contaminates the air; and where large assemblies are collected in close rooms the air is corrupted." In a gathering of 1,500, calculated Alcott—he was a physician of sorts—ten were sure to die from carbonic acid poisoning (p. 176). It did not take exceptional mental energy to conclude that attendance at any large indoor gathering might be a risky venture. Outdoor amusement, on the other hand, Alcott enthusiastically recommended. It ought to be "active recreation . . . in the open air," he said. Ball-playing and skating were excellent.[5] The result, for those heeding the advice, was an experi-

5. *Ibid.*, p. 192. James W. Alexander in *The Merchant's Clerk. Cheered and Counselled* (New York, 1856), pp. 51-52, even proscribed young men's associations, which he felt might be too "frivolous and fruitless." He wanted young men surrounded only by "the guidance and protection of superior minds . . . and the corrective pressure of paternal interest." No doubt he excluded the Young Men's Christian Association, which he had early supported. Perhaps he felt that the YMCA was being overseen closely enough by "society at large, especially that governing part of it which comprises our mercantile weight and wealth, [which] should consult its own interests enough to cast an eye upon the nocturnal dangers of persons in their employ, and to devise means for mental pleasures which are as true and as necessary a part of general education as the school or the college." See chapter 9.

ence of city life which, if dull and colorless, was at least predictable and secure.

Whatever its reception among young men, the advice must have been welcome to city elders. For, to the extent that the young newcomers followed it, their range of behavior would be restricted to those activities least likely to provoke excesses, such as stealing from employers to repay gambling debts, whose disruptive consequences alarmed community leaders. To secure such behavior, in the absence of other regulating mechanisms, proper etiquette was urged. Young men acting according to commonly accepted rules of conduct would be less likely to surprise by unexpected actions members of the community they were being ushered into. Adherence to such rules would also serve as a petition of entry signifying one's intention to become a member in good standing of a superior social class. Viewing their audience as they did, members of these classes counted anything that had a tranquilizing effect on young men as a blessing. Young men were seen not only as innocents entering a vile and corrupting world, but also as a dangerous force that required controlling. One writer compared their excitable natures to "keg[s] of powder uncovered amid the sparks of a blazing furnace." The explosive possibilities of "heart[s] easily fired by temptation as powder by a spark" was not easily forgotten.[6]

Many writers were not at all comfortable in addressing their chosen audience, and their clumsy attempts to disguise the gulf were often transparent. The Reverend J. B. Waterbury, for example, admitted that young men of cities and colleges formed a special class, often unwilling to listen to advice from others.[7] He felt justified in addressing them, however, since he had "been placed, by the providence of God, in circumstances favorable to acquiring a knowledge of [their] feelings, principles, and habits" (p. v). Relying probably on his own youth—he was only thirty-two years old—he hoped that he might be able to "convince his young readers, that his intentions

6. William Howard Van Doren, *Mercantile Morals: or, Thoughts for Young Men Entering Mercantile Life* (New York, 1852), p. 167.

7. Jared Bell Waterbury, *Considerations for Young Men* (New York, 1832), p. v.

at least are benevolent." He wished to achieve a "greater familiarity and directness," a relation young and old did not apparently experience together often, and would use, he said, an epistolary form of address. Its use was also intended to overcome "a prejudice" he thought widespread "against essays, lectures or sermons" (p. vi).

But despite this assertion his book was exactly what he said it would not be. Instead of familiar letters, the book was a collection of staid discourses, where he as often spoke about youth in the third person as he addressed it directly. At one point, in trying to justify the distance of other writers from their young audiences, he began pleading for his own exoneration from the same offense. "Some writers, in addressing the young," Waterbury noted in introducing a discussion of the dangers and temptations of youth, "may appear to have approached them in an austere, if not a harsh and repulsive manner." But these writers had no intention of stripping young men of every enjoyment, to have them assume "the coldness and gravity of age." "You must not," he said, "call *us* harsh when we are only ardent . . . if the mode of our address be occasionally pungent, you must refer the point and the earnestness to the interest which we feel in your happiness." He then completed the personalization of his remarks by protesting in the first person that he himself certainly had no desire to censure youth, to smother their youthful feelings or to drive them to premature sobriety. Trying, it seems, to convince himself, he continued at a length that indicated a real defensiveness and need to believe in a harmony between him and his audience. If others did not understand the young, he at least was not one of them:

> You cannot impute to me feelings which have become cold and which would therefore reduce your enthusiasm to my own indifference and apathy. No, I come to you in these letters as one of your own number. I can appreciate your feelings, and participate with as keen a relish as ever, in many of your joys. Some experience I may have had beyond yourselves. That experience has taught me to regard you with an interest arising from identity of hopes, prospects and enjoyments. (pp. 75-77)

It was not long, however, before Waterbury was again speaking to his audience in a detached, almost clinical manner. Within a page he was referring to "the period of youth" as an abstract unit with special urges and needs. It was as if he was delivering a lecture on the psychology of adolescents to a group of parents not as if he was talking familiarly to young men. Part of this posture may have been the result of a genuine confusion on the author's part about who his proper audience actually was. He felt he had written "a manual . . . which the pious parent might commit to a beloved son" (p. vii), and he perhaps saw himself standing between the two groups, trying on the one hand to advise young men as their Christian parents wished, and on the other to "explain" the young man to their bewildered elders. That he tended more often than not to spend his time "explaining" was an indication perhaps of how new and strange this generation of young people appeared to its elders. Waterbury may have suspected that, as much as the young wanted to know what to expect from the new situations they were going to experience, their parents wanted to know what to expect from their offspring.

The young man that Waterbury and other writers were talking about was anywhere from fourteen to twenty-five years old[8] and apparently just barely able to control himself. Alcott attributed to him all the characteristics of an undisciplined, untrained child. He was silly, boisterous, boorish, and at the same time sheepish and timid.[9]

8. Alcott, in a sequel to his 1833 volume admitted the difficulty of fixing "the mind's eye on any particular age. There is a period—and it arrives sooner in the lives of some, and later in those of others—when they may be said to begin to act for themselves; and in the common but not inappropriate language of the day, to form their own character." Like other writers, Alcott assumed that young manhood was a discrete period of life, sharply divided from childhood and full maturity. It was a curious state of unpreparedness. The young man had gone "beyond parental control" to embark on a period of self-education and individual responsibility. Yet, to a large degree, his emotional development had not kept pace with this physical freedom. He was on his own, but dangerously unequipped for his new freedom. William A. Alcott, *Familiar Letters to Young Men on Various Subjects* (Buffalo, 1849), pp. 13-14. See also Daniel Wise, *The Young Man's Counsellor: or, Sketches and Illustrations of the Duties and Dangers of Young Men* (New York, 1854), p. 17 and Van Doren, *Mercantile Morals*, p. 152. Also see F. W. Thomas's novel, *Clinton Bradshaw* (Philadelphia, 1835), for an example of the instantaneousness by which the change from young manhood to maturity was represented.

9. Alcott, *Young Man's Guide*. p. 231; also Wise, *The Young Man's Counsellor*, p. 189.

He seemed civilized only when compared to the young man of interior Africa who, "as soon as he puts off the dress of a child, beats his mother to show his manhood."[10] With his moral nature incomplete, passion was stronger than reason, ready to overpower it and take control at the slightest provocation or temptation.[11] In cities especially, people "whose pleasures consist in ruining the youth by corrupting principles and habits" were everywhere coaxing and taunting young men to take the first step that would lead to their destruction.[12]

To many writers the problems posed by young men were more serious than they could ever remember. The appearance in 1849 of Alcott's *Familiar Letters to Young Men*, designed as a sequel to his earlier volume, was dictated, he said, by a more critical reading of the social situation. Boys were reaching the period of young manhood even earlier, with less experience, and were being forced to assume weightier responsibilities than ever before. Whereas young men of an earlier period were once kept "at too great a distance, when in truth not a few were treated more like servants and menials than like sons," the other extreme was now being approached. "It may be worth while to inquire," he added, "whether there is not danger of going too far."[13] Because young men were more exposed to temptation than ever before, there was an even greater necessity for them to shore up their character, to make it impregnable against the attacks of vice and temptation. In our "hurrying age," said the New York minister J. W. Alexander, boys become men by a sudden spurt. It was therefore essential for young men to make their moral natures strong enough to withstand any assault by evil before the chance was lost. "There is no going back to correct the errors of youth," he said. Once manhood was reached, only the most traumatic shock would alter a wayward nature.[14]

10. Alcott, *Young Man's Guide*, p. 232.
11. See Wise, *The Young Man's Counsellor*, pp. 21-22; Van Doren, *Mercantile Morals*, pp. 152, 210, 221.
12. Van Doren, *Mercantile Morals*, p. 167.
13. Alcott, *Familiar Letters*, pp. 14, 17.
14. Alexander, *The Merchant's Clerk*, p. 5.

Most of the advice found in these books was therefore geared to the moral improvement expected to encourage the development of character. Chapter headings like "Self Knowledge," "Industry," "Economy," "Faithfulness," and "Integrity," could be found in hundreds of advice-books that appeared between 1830 and 1860. Whether the books were specifically directed to aspiring merchants or to young men who had not yet settled on a career (the assumption was strong that in an expanding economy they too would choose business[15]), all concerned themselves with general categories of moral behavior.

Daniel Wise, for example, in *The Young Man's Counsellor* (1856), devoted almost the whole book to a discussion of "the construction of character." Character had to be as solidly rooted as the foundations of a building, said Wise, or "the first rushing flood of tempting circumstances may wash [it] away."[16] One to a chapter, the virtues necessary for success were discussed, with examples illustrating each one. Significantly, the examples never related to particular situations young men might have to face. The temporal and geographical settings were utterly random. To illustrate integrity, examples such as Kossuth's reply to a Turkish Sultan who had offered him wealth and military command if he would renounce the Christian religion and Ulrich Zwingli's refusal to accept a Papal bribe to suppress his reformist beliefs were offered. To illustrate the allurements of vice, the examples of Mark Antony's submission to Cleopatra and Robert Burns's dissipation at the fountain of drink were noted. And, to illustrate the consequences of vice, Wise used the example of a young German apprentice who, having lived an irreproachably moral life, became dissolute on reaching his eighteenth year. Suddenly he became "wanton, riotous, disorderly and lazy; fond of dress and exces-

---

15. See William R. Taylor, *Cavalier and Yankee* (New York, 1961), p. 118. Noting the assertion of one prominent writer of the period that "the engrossing pursuit of Americans is wealth," Taylor then asks, "What American better symbolized this pursuit than the 'merchant'? To those already wealthy the term denoted a kind of status; to the shopkeeper it was a flattering symbol of aspiration; even to the farmer it was a pious hope to be realized, perhaps, in the next generation."

16. Wise, *The Young Men's Counsellor*, p. 27.

sively vain.'' On a whim, the youth stole a watch from the local shoemaker, in the process killing the man, his wife, and their little son.[17]

The result of this battery of examples was to reinforce the idea that abstract character was alone important—it was this that determined whether a young man would survive. Any flaw no matter how minute, any transgression no matter how inadvertent, was sufficient to doom a young man's future. The first visit to the theater, the first chew of tobacco, often even the first perusal of a novel (not to mention, of course, the first sip of whisky) were all it took to start the irreversible process leading to total dissipation.[18] Stories like that of the upright nineteen-year-old who, visiting the city in search of business, fell into dissolute company and then into debt; whose theft to pay off the debt landed him in prison (his cell-mate turned out to be another young man); whose shame caused death from a fevered and tortured mind were common.[19] Because the city was most corrupt and tempting, those entering its domains were more susceptible to the exposure of personal failings more easily concealed in other environments. ''Your escape from destruction,'' said Wise, ''depended on your being strong in resolve to resist the first advances of illicit pleasure.''[20] Only youths so inured to temptation were likely to survive. W. H. Van Doren, in a book written especially for aspiring young merchants, admitted that the clerk ''amid this dark world of doubt and perplexity, of deceit and ignorance'' needed a guide to steer clear of evils and temptatious that may beset him.[21] But he too gave no examples relevant to the specific situations young men faced. Beyond a warning about youth's passional imbalance or an injunction to beware of character defects like pride, inward conceit, or a deceitful heart, he never mentioned what the evils or temptations

17. *Ibid.*, pp. 45-46, 171, 173, 189. See also Van Doren, *Mercantile Morals*, pp. 244, 294.
18. Wise, *The Young Man's Counsellor*, p. 213; Van Doren, *Mercantile Morals*, pp. 370, 374.
19. For this example see Wise, *The Young Man's Counsellor*, p. 199.
20. *Ibid.*, p. 178.
21. Van Doren, *Mercantile Morals*, p. 181.

consisted of or how they were uniquely related to urban life.[22] Even a book called *The Young Merchant* (1840), with such promising chapter headings as "Conduct during Apprenticeship," "On Setting Up," and "Suitable Education for a Merchant," was no more enlightening. Each chapter once again enumerated values and principles the young merchant ought to live by; in virtually none was there any hint as to how the principles were to be put into effect.[23] If writers were trying to speak to specific situations that young men would face, it seemed that they had not yet developed the language for doing so. They had titled their books and even chapters appropriately, but were still unable to fill them out with anything but the moral platitudes they had inherited from an earlier form of advice-literature. To focus their advice occupationally on the central concern of their audience was a significant step forward; such information was never required by the young people to whom previous didactic efforts were directed. As the headings from *The Young Merchant* above indicate, writers had seen that the advice they provided should correspond with life as it was actually encountered by the young clerk. But as one historian holds,[24] it would be some time before writers would fill those chapters with the content their titles promised.

Although his mentors were less insistent about it, the acquisition of experience was the other piece of social baggage a young man needed. Because it often involved contradicting the value of such virtues as perseverance and patience associated with sticking to a given task, the assertion that knowledge of different trades might be useful considering one did not know where he might end up was never advocated forcefully. Experience was subordinated to character development. If the latter was assured, the former was readily acquired. Writers like Freeman Hunt often settled the matter simply. In his *Worth and Wealth,* a collection of advice pieces that originally appeared in *The Merchant's Magazine,* which he edited, he eschewed

22. See, especially, chapter 5, "Dangers Incident to Young Men in Large Cities."
23. *The Young Merchant* (Boston, 1840).
24. Irvin G. Wyllie, *The Self-Made Man in America: The Myth of Rags to Riches* (New York, 1966), p. 200.

principles, announced that readers would find "no formal code of mercantile rules,"[25] and provided all kinds of advice, no matter how contradictory. One never could be sure what might prove helpful. Without the channeling mechanisms of apprenticeship, men had to be ready to seize any opportunity that might present itself. If they had some knowledge about the work they were going into, they were just that much ahead of someone who did not, and therefore just that much more likely to succeed.

Wise went on to emphasize the value of experience. He explained that entering the stage of young manhood was like sailing through the winding channels of a river and the rocky straits of the river's mouth into the great sea of active life. For the first time young men were in command of the vessel. The safety of their passage depended on their inner strength and the chart of experience laid down by previous navigators.[26] They had to be taught by others who knew the route, who had been through the passage before. Great emphasis was placed on securing a tutor who, if he was not to serve as the agent conducting one through each stage of his development like Colonel Vanderhoost, would at least transmit the knowledge, permitting one to proceed on his own. Otherwise, despite one's good character and intentions, one might find himself paralyzed by indecision and ignorance.[27]

Realizing, perhaps, that there might not be enough live tutors to supply the great demand, substitutes were avidly sought. The reading of biography was probably for this reason the most widely recommended form of literary recreation. Biography, in a vicarious and indirect way, was an invaluable source of experience. Freeman Hunt considered biography "a chart on the ocean of mind to assist the aspirant after knowledge." Just as the maps consulted by the student of geography kept him from "forever wandering among dark shadows," biography was a map of human life "teaching all who

25. Freeman Hunt, *Worth and Wealth: A Collection of Maxims, Morals and Miscellanies for Merchants and Men of Business* (New York, 1856), p. v.
26. Wise, *The Young Man's Counsellor,* pp. 18-19.
27. See Hunt, *Worth and Wealth,* pp. 437-42.

consult it its landmarks and beacon lights.''[28]

The signposts and pointers that could be culled from reading a biography of a man's life were, it seemed, hard to come by in any other way. The metaphor most commonly used to express the relation of a young man to his society—the one that Wise invoked above, that of the youth as the sole navigator of a ship heading out to sea—points to this conclusion. Wise used the metaphor to emphasize the experience young men needed; other writers used it to emphasize the plight of the young man undertaking his "voyage of life" without the tutorial advantages that channeling institutions like apprenticeship once performed. "Too often," said a speaker to the Boston Young Men's Christian Union, "the young man is compelled to steer . . . without a guide or a chart"[29] and the strength of his own character was his only resource. These writers used the components of the metaphor to liken the building of character to the building of a ship for a long ocean voyage. Character had to be flawless to prevent weakening in a storm, just as the ship had to be made fast against even the smallest puncture, which would doom the vessel to sinking in the open sea. By implication, character also had to be flawless because help in the event of trouble would be unavailable. On the open sea there would be no way for a ship to tie up during a storm, no sheltering coves for it to pull into, no dry dock for it to steer to to make repairs. The ocean was wide and empty and the ship was alone, cut loose from ties that might help guide it to its destination if it foundered.[30] Writers who saw the society that young men hoped to move in as an ocean knew that its guideless vastness directed voyagers to no safe channels whereby advancement was assured. The centrality of character in discussions of the equipment necessary for success reinforces the feeling then widely shared that many of the disappearing practices that had once helped direct young men to careers and social positions had not yet been replaced by more reliable and efficient ones. The way in which the development

28. Freeman Hunt, *Lives of American Merchants.* 2 vols. (New York, 1858), 1: 494-95.
29. Emery Washburn, *Anniversary Address* (Boston, 1856), p. 6.
30. *Ibid.,* pp. 6-7 and Charles Loring Brace, *Short Sermons to News Boys* (New York, 1865), pp. 169-73.

of character was likened to the construction of a building or a ship may be an indication of the kind of service one's inner resources had to perform.

The changes in the usage of the words "character" and "reputation" are another indication of how devoid the landscape seemed to be of guiding institutions. Writers in this period had great difficulty in keeping the two words apart; the differences in the usages of each often became indistinguishable.[31] Reputation like character was always placed in opposition to the "outward," or easily falsified, signs of virtue; it was thought of as the external badge of true character. The two were so closely associated that one, reputation, began to be used interchangeably with the other. Benjamin Franklin knew the difference between the two very well; for him character was a quality quite distinct from the deceptions and deceits that, he boastingly tells us, established his reputation. When Charles Butler in *The American Gentleman* (1836) said that there would always be men "inclined to flatter their own pride by detracting from the reputation of others [and] that, even if we were able to maintain an immaculate conduct, it would be difficult to preserve an immaculate character"[32] he was using "character," an internal quality, to stand for the external one—the one affected by community whim, that is, "reputation." Once such substitutions were common, any attack on a man's reputation was also an attack on his character—the one thing he depended upon, as we will see more clearly below, to advance him socially. Butler could only offer the feeble hope that men who dealt in defiling reputations would find no audience. Happiness, he said, depended "chiefly on the approbation of our own consciences, and on the advancement of our interest in a world where liars shall not be believed and where slanderers shall receive countenance from none."[33]

It was no wonder, then, that men guarded their reputations so closely and were so quick to react to insult. If reputation could be shaken by rumor or slander, the one, admittedly imperfect, indicator

31. See *Hunt's Merchants' Magazine* 27 (1852): 277, for the problems one writer encountered.
32. Charles Butler, *The American Gentleman* (Philadelphia, 1836), p. 22.
33. *Ibid.*, p. 23.

men had of one another's character would become useless. Without the long association of a formalized relationship like apprenticeship to reveal a man's character, reputation came more and more to be treated as its equivalent. The seeming instantaneousness with which offense and affront to honor were taken, the sensitivity with which such stimuli were perceived, and the ease with which they led to violent outbursts of temper, which even by the late 1840s could reach resolution by duel, suggests that one's good name was defended as if it were the only qualification or credential a man possessed. The most unthinking oversight by one man could easily be interpreted as a gross insult demanding satisfaction. A remote hint that one had been slighted brought brooding, anger, and possibly the exchange of blows.[34] T. S. Arthur, in his *Advice to Young Men* (1848), went to great lengths to lay ground rules for "conduct among men." He hoped the rules would help young men mediate differences between themselves without violence. Young men, he said, should always try to accept "the office of mediator" in arguments among friends; under no circumstances was a resort to deadly weapons justifiable. Arthur gave detailed instructions, both for young men asked to serve as seconds and those directly involved, for the avoidance of bloodshed.[35] Rules of conduct were important not only in maintaining order, but also in presenting oneself, by acting according to commonly recognized rules, in a way that insured that no offensive interpretation could be placed on one's actions.

This touchiness about reputation emphasizes the absence in mid-nineteenth-century society of a formal network through which young men were conducted into their careers.

Unlike many of today's youth, whose careers are determined by a series of institutional associations, whose abilities can be tested and rated, who can be awarded external badges of achievement like university degrees, young men of the 1840s and 1850s had few objective credentials that could distinguish them from others seeking the same place or recommend them for advancement once places had been secured. With the growing numbers of young men looking for

34. T. S. Arthur, *Advice to Young Men on their Duties and Conduct in Life* (Boston, 1848), pp. 121-22.
35. *Ibid.*, p. 126.

work in the cities and with the pressure these numbers placed on an apprentice system that had evolved from less-demanding circumstances, ordered, institutional channels to opportunity were more reduced than they had been before or would be later.

Freeman Hunt's *Merchants' Magazine* is an excellent source by which to chart this change in the personnel and nature of mercantile clerkships. The magazine—a compilation of informed articles about trade; of statistics about commerce, agriculture, population, and transportation; of legal summaries; of anecdotes about prominent merchants and their virtues; and of notices of new mercantile and benevolent organizations—in providing a unique arena for the discussion of the problems and preoccupations stirring the mercantile community registers the changes in attitudes and practices toward clerks that took place during the 1840s and 1850s. Freeman Hunt (1804-1858) had spent his life in journalism. At the age of twelve he left his home in Quincy, Massachusetts, for Boston. Here he became an office boy for the Boston *Evening Gazette* and began to learn the printer's trade. Soon he started working on the Boston *Daily Traveller*. Advancing rapidly, he decided in 1826 to go into the publishing business with John Putnam. Together, among other ventures, they published the *Juvenile Miscellany*, edited by Lydia Maria Child and the *Ladies' Magazine* (1828). After the partnership with Putnam dissolved, Hunt was associated with various publishing undertakings, most of them short-lived. Dissatisfied with his career, he decided to start a magazine in a field he believed was still untouched: he discovered that there was not a single magazine that represented the claims of commerce. With the financial aid of friends, he established in 1839 the *Merchants' Magazine and Commercial Review*. His work on this journal occupied him constantly until his death in 1858.[36] That his concern with the changes in the practices initiating young men into mercantile careers was not peripheral to the copy that dominated the magazine is suggested by the two collections of articles from the magazine that Hunt published separately. Both *Worth and Wealth* and *Lives of American Merchants* were intended to pro-

36. A. Everett Peterson in *Dictionary of American Biography* (New York, 1932), 9: 334.

vide guidance for those entering commercial professions. Hunt must have been well aware of how closely the pieces of advice and reports of new suggestions for bettering employer-employee relations, for example, were studied by aspiring young men and their bosses. It is possible that Hunt, who carefully observed the New York mercantile scene and studied the daily and trade press of the larger Eastern cities, saw his magazine as a way to give national distribution to ideas or developments originating in areas like New York, Boston, and Philadelphia. Hunt may have seen that news of these developments would be valuable to a wider audience, whose experience and problems were beginning to parallel those of the largest urban and commercial centers.

One of the subjects Hunt constantly gave magazine space to was the disloyalty of clerks—now primarily pictured as originating from rural areas—to their employers. No longer, it appeared, did these clerks identify their interests with those of the firms they worked for. One article taken from the Boston *Evening Gazette* discussed several recent cases where young men charged with "defrauding" their employers turned out in almost every instance to be from the country. "Left to themselves in a large city," the author said, "[they] have been dazzled by the gayety and ruined by the profligacy of others."[37]

Hunt did what he could to discourage them from coming. Few issues passed without at least a small filler urging young men from rural districts to stay at home. Generally they were told how few avoided ruin in New York and how the farms they were thinking of leaving were both more profitable and more secure. Writers did not hesitate to indict the mercantile profession. Young men, they said. would be exchanging their independence for a kind of commercial vassalage, bartering a natural for an artificial pursuit and hence debasing themselves morally and physically in the process. In addition, there were simply too few jobs to go around; the city was already overflowing with people seeking commercial positions.[38] One anecdote, from the *Brooklyn Eagle,* made its moral obvious. It told of a

37. *Merchants' Magazine* 20 (1849): 686.
38. *Ibid.,* p. 570; 37 (1857): 784; 11 (1844): 193.

"pale, sickly looking young man" about twenty years old sitting at his desk in a New York countinghouse dreaming of being home on the family farm upstate. While he was asleep the store was robbed and the youth was arrested and imprisoned for the crime. Somehow acquitted at his trial, he immediately fled the city for home where, in a single month, he recuperated from the physical deterioration caused by city life and regained his health. "He never entered into mercantile business again," the author said, "but commenced farming and is now a wealthy and much respected farmer" (29 [1853]: 647).

Merchants seemed to feel that instances of clerk loyalty were extremely rare if they could be found at all. In one fictional episode in the *Magazine* an older merchant whose business was failing was told by his poor young clerk that he was willing to sacrifice years of savings to help him. So unexpected was the gesture that the employer was almost uncomprehending." 'Hawkins, you distress me,' he exclaimed: '. .. will you make this sacrifice, will. . .you incur this hazard for me?' " (6[1842]: 172).

The worry that merchants felt over the distance that had grown between themselves and their employees and about the unfamiliarity with which qualified young men often faced the prospect of finding situations can be seen in the proposals they offered to deal with these problems. Nelson Merrill, writing in the April 1845 issue of Hunt's, denounced the common practice of employers' requiring their clerks to put up security to guarantee the honest discharge of their duties. For one thing, argued Merrill, under the present system a young man well fitted for a position often could not put up the required amount and did not know anyone who could. As a result "he must stand aside for some other one, possessing perhaps less honesty, though more money." The second problem was that individual fortune fluctuated so greatly in the United States that a man considered responsible one day was often insolvent the next. "Hence," said the author, "how seldom is it that defalcations are made good by sureties." To remedy these evils Merrill proposed that a guarantee society—an insurance company, in effect—be established, encouraging clerks to take out policies to provide a reserve to replace funds misused or stolen by delinquent or dishonest members. Before being accepted for membership the "fitness and character" of applicants would be carefully scrutinized by an examining committee. If the committee was not satisfied, the application would be declined, "and the employer would be required to exercise all the usual care and watchfulness over the conduct of the employed" (12 [1845]: 330-33).

By the 1850s, merchants were certain they could see how far the methods of securing help and overseeing its proper functioning differed from an earlier period they remembered. Formerly clerks entered stores in their youth, said the *Journal of Commerce,* and preference was given "to those who had received a proper moral training, and who could bring testimonials of correct habits and an unspotted character." Today, unfortunately, the writer continued, thinking perhaps of Edward Tailer's employer Townsend, moral fitness and experience had given way to the ability to control the patronage of out-of-town buyers. Outward performance, in other words, had now replaced inner qualities as criteria for advancement. But selection of only those who had this qualification, the writer noted, was unlikely to secure the highest mental or moral excellence. The results were plain. Robberies were becoming frequent and merchants were realizing that they once again had to pay attention to the character of their employees. Clerks "who have nothing save their character and capacity to forward them in their career" deserved to have these qualities more highly valued and to be promoted because of them. "If there is no reaction in favor of the old system," the article concluded, "the time will come when clerks will have to be weighed in and out of their respective warehouses, as the slaves are in the silver mines to prevent their depredations upon the property of their employers" (36 [1857]: 135).

Another writer, in the Boston *Herald,* felt that the problem of clerk robberies was simply a matter of economics and could be easily settled. Hunt heartily endorsed the solution. The *Herald* writer related the story of a clerk who had stolen hundreds of dollars of goods from his firm. When his employer was informed of the crime by the officer who had discovered the loss, "he seemed troubled, said the boy had for some time been with him, and to all appearances was a faithful clerk . . . and further stated that he paid him for his services $3.50 per week." The officer asked the merchant if the young man did not need practically all of his salary to pay for his room and board alone. The merchant acknowledged that "he probably did." The boy, called in and confronted with the crime, readily and contritely confessed. But instead of dismissing him, his employer decided to keep him at his post and raise his pay to six dollars a week. He was never troubled again, and later admitted that there was "not a better servant in the store." Hunt hoped New York merchants would follow the Bostonian's example. Their action, he said, would place them among the moral and social reformers of the day. "Pay your clerks an adequate compensation for their services," he urged, "and 'lead them not into temptation' by withholding the means of supplying their every reasonable want" (24 [1851]: 134).

What makes articles like the last three discussed important is the way they reflect a change in the very nature of clerkship, in the nature of the relation between employers and their clerks, as well as in a more narrow concern with the recruitment and character of personnel. The concern with stemming losses from theft reveals a changed awareness that clerks were coming from different backgrounds and had different life styles and aspirations from those they were formerly considered to have. What begins to emerge is a perception of clerks as a distinct group that requires a new kind of attention. When Merrill talks about the need for employers "to exercise all the usual care and watchfulness over the conduct of the employed," he means something very different from the "care and watchfulness" that somebody like Joseph Scoville had in mind when he wrote about the "perfect system" of inspection and supervision that operated in the old countinghouses.[39]

Paralleling the classification of youth as a separate group, as a generational class apart with distinct qualities and urges, is the classification of clerks as a separate group, as an occupational class apart with distinct qualities and urges. That the creation of a separate "natural slot" occupied by youth appears at the same time as a separate "employee slot" occupied by clerks is less a coincidence than a reflection of broad social and economic changes. Large numbers of young people were being brought into the work force, not just as laborers but as members of an expanding group of white-collar em-

39. See above for Merrill quotation and chapter 4 for Scoville.

ployees. As clerks, competing for new openings at various levels in commerce and industry, they were not treated in a paternalistic way meant to ready them for hereditary responsibilities, but were treated in the more impersonal manner that befitted the station so many had come to occupy. Books and magazines of advice reflected not only the threat posed by visibly growing numbers of unattached young men in the nation's cities, but the new vocational status that had been fashioned for them. The *Herald* writer's suggestion that the employer had been ignorant of his clerk's actions, thoughtless about his cost of living and, when the culprit was revealed, without self-righteousness or moral indignation (an attitude eagerly approved by Hunt) indicated a new way of thinking about young employees.

A letter to the editors of the weekly *Dry-Goods Register,* which Hunt reprinted in January 1848, made the change clearer still. The letter indicated that some men saw that an even greater distance between employees and employers had developed. The writer, a New York merchant, sought to promote the interests of the city's clerks. He proposed the formation of an association of dry-goods clerks—an association that "should embody all the points of the present system of odd-fellowship" plus one more. Clerks thrown out of work, for any cause except misconduct, would be entitled to draw a certain sum weekly, for six weeks. The only qualifications for membership, as in Merrill's scheme, would be honesty and morality. Concerned about the great amount of money lost annually by the dishonesty of clerks, he felt that his proposal would benefit the honest, diligent clerks in the city.

> Is it not [he argued] for the interest of the honest young man . . . that the rogues of the business should be ferreted out, and driven from the trade? Would not the profession rise, in point of respectability, in consequence? Is it not the case, that a stigma is cast upon all engaged in the business by the conduct of these evil-doers? And, if so, let us, by adopting some method of self-defense draw a distinct line between them and us.

The benefits would be innumerable. No clerk, said the writer would be subject to "imposition" from an employer; he would be taken care of when sick; "a good understanding" would be maintained between the clerks and the stores employing them; and knowledgeable merchants could be engaged to deliver series of lectures connected with the dry-goods business. Finally, he presented what he considered his most convincing point: "the rogues, being driven from the business, as they invariably would be, the demand for clerks would be greater, and the pay proportionately increased."

The advantages to employers, as might be expected, would be commensurate, for they would be certain of having honest clerks. Although the writer felt that recommendations about a man's capability were of little value, under his plan a young man applying for a position would simply be asked if he was a member in good standing of the dry-goods association. "If the answer is yes, and he produces his certificate, the merchant is perfectly posted up as to his honesty." As an added safeguard, an obligation should be entered into by each member to expose any malpractices of any other member. The accused clerk would be suspended pending the outcome of a trial by his peers. In addition, the writer felt, all employers should also be allowed to join the organization "upon payment of such sum as may be agreed upon," even though they would not be voting members of the association (18 [1848]: 119-20).

Besides the admission that employers were no longer able to distinguish between the honest and dishonest clerk and that they feared the number of dishonest infiltrators was far too high,[40] the author implied for the first time that an earlier harmony had completely vanished. Clerks and employers seemed no longer engaged in a common enterprise to which both groups were devoted. Rather, they were distinct groups with separate interests. Employers wanted honest clerks,

40. One example the writer used was of a European clerk forced to leave the Continent to escape capture for theft. It will become evident in chapter 10 that the concern extended to native young men as well. The worry was less the venality of their former crimes than the impossibility of detecting the men. The writer, following the foreigner to the United States, wrote: "His gentlemanly appearance, his perfect acquaintance with the details of trade, as drawn probably from his experience in first-class houses in Europe, are strong recommendations. His letter of introduction gives him a reference and he easily obtains a situation. And thus this man, who was an ingrain [sic] villain before he left his native land, becomes one of the dry-goods fraternity, and his superior accomplishments enable him to successfully carry out his nefarious practices" (18 [1848]: 119-20).

clerks wanted higher pay and protection against unjust employers. Although the writer tried to engage the clerks' professional pride by calling for the shared guardianship of mercantile respectability and to evoke a fellowship of all good men opposed to roguery, his argument ultimately rested on grounds that looked forward to the later demands of unionized white .collar workers. The plan may have failed, not because it was irrelevant to real problems merchants faced, but because merchants felt that other organizations already performed or could be made to perform the same service for them.[41]

One writer so took this change for granted that he appealed to the divergence of clerk-employer interests to justify his suggestion that wholesale dealers close their stores in late afternoon instead of working a sixteen-hour day. "It is no wonder," he wrote "that clerks who cannot have the same interest in the business which is felt by the master, get fatigued at this eternal confinement at a desk and oftentimes too when their books are posted up and there is nothing for them to do, save to be in company with their employers." Attendance at the countinghouses and close association with the employer were no longer an occasion to welcome for the chance to learn the trade under the master's personal eyes but a burdensome chore to be endured until the work day ended (37 [1857]: 131).

These last two writers show an even greater consciousness than did Nelson Merrill, for example, of the changes that had taken place. Merrill pictured employers and employees as holding essentially the same interests and aims. The only group he wished to place outside that harmonious union were men who, because of their dishonesty or delinquency, had no claim to membership. His standard for dividing the community was moral; all *virtuous* men, whether they were clerks or established merchants, shared common interests. In the cases directly above, both writers assume that the clerks cannot possibly have the same interests as the employers by virtue of their economic position. The moral appeal made by the correspondent to the *Dry-Goods Register* is secondary; it is plain that he does not feel that the argument has the power it once had. He is certainly not willing to rest his case on that ground alone.

41. See chapter 10.

There were other indications that relations between clerks and their employers were felt to be markedly different from an earlier period. Hunt printed other suggestions "for increasing the comforts of those under [the] protection of mercantile houses." In the July 1848 issue, a letter from a London merchant appeared recommending to Americans the arrangements made by a large English drapery house for the benefit of its clerks. After the business closed at 7:00 P.M., the young men so inclined could retire to a large and well-lit reading room well supplied with a fine library and the best periodicals. For others, teachers of French, German, Latin, music, and drawing were hired by the firm. Three times a week distinguished authorities were engaged to lecture on subjects like chemistry, anatomy, geology, botany, and electricity. In addition, every individual was allowed a certain time each day for outdoor exercise. "In short," wrote the Englishman, "the employer's house is made a home to them and few so situated, I hear, feel inclined to idle away valuable time" (19 [1848]: 120).

The scheme was hardly original (some American mercantile houses had similarly tried to regulate all the time of their clerks, in and out of the countinghouse[42]), but it was noteworthy nevertheless for the

42. If Scoville can be believed, Arthur Tappan, whose abolitionist sentiments he detested, established the following set of rules for the conduct of his clerks: "1. Every young man was to be a strict temperance man, drink no ardent spirits or wine of any kind. 2. A clerk was not permitted to visit houses of ill-repute, indulge in fast habits, or stay out late . . . . 3. No clerk was permitted to visit any theater, and no forgiveness was accorded if he added to the crime by becoming acquainted with members of the theatrical profession. 4. Each clerk was obliged to attend Divine Service twice on the Sabbath day. 5. Every Monday morning to report to the proper authorities what church they had attended, the name of the clergyman, and the texts. 6. To attend prayer meetings twice a week. 7. Never to be out of the boarding-house or residence of any clerk after 10 o'clock, P.M." Walter Barrett, clerk [Joseph A. Scoville], *The Old Merchants of New York*. 5 vols. (New York, 1885), 1: 230. Whether or not what Scoville reported was true (the eighth rule was that every clerk had to belong to the "Abolition Society"), there were other aspects of Tappan's life attesting to a continuing concern with the conduct of young men. He was the principal contributor to the building fund for Clinton Hall, the home of the New York Mercantile Library Association; the driving force behind a reorganized Magdalen Society, an examination of whose first annual report reveals that its concern with prostitution was prompted in large part by a fear that the moral foundations of the city's young men were being subverted (see *First Annual Report of*

way it tried to reconstruct an imagined past. It was actually only a blow-up of the apprentice system it was presumably meant to replace, for once again the life of the employee was to be completely enveloped by the employer's home; his trade, education, and recreation (now, it is suggested by the reference to the time allotted for outdoor activity, even more stringently regulated) were all provided for by a single institutional structure. Such efforts generally proved unsuccessful in the United States. Instead, the component parts of apprenticeship were scattered among discrete institutional units. Men like Arthur Tappan notwithstanding, countinghouses became devoted solely to business; organizations like the YMCA became devoted to recreation; and, increasingly, small collegiate institutes became devoted solely to the education of clerks.

If we can judge by the growing number of notices for business schools that appeared in Hunt's *Magazine,* merchants were beginning to realize that new institutions were needed to provide young men of trade with the education they required. In an article in the October 1858 issue, one writer, noting that "the dangerous proclivity exhibited by American youth to rush too rashly, and without due preparation into the varied and hazardous walks of commerce is one of the crying evils of the day," advocated the creation of commercial colleges as a solution. He noted the present-day tendency "to congregate in cities, and to throng the avenues of wealth and honor, which are already overcrowded." The result was widespread personal distress and disappointment; gross ignorance and inexperience were every day producing terribly bitter and expensive lessons. Most of the business failures—fully ninety percent of those who started out—were directly attributable, he said, to shameful mismanagement and ignorance of business. It was all "a sad but very significant

the Executive Committee of the New York Magdalen Society [New York, 1831], pp. 12, 24); and, with his brother Lewis, was a founder of the Credit-Rating Agency (later to become Dun and Bradstreet). The Agency provided confidential data about the financial stability of the city's mercantile houses. (The New York Trade Agency—an organizations similar to the Tappan's—significantly concentrated its reports on business firms around the character of the proprietors. See New York Trade Agency, Confidential Reports on Business Concerns, 1851, New-York Historical Society, Manuscript Division.)

commentary on the deficient commercial education of the times.''

The greatest need of the period, believed the author, was a more efficient and careful system by which young men interested in business careers could be more suitably prepared to enter the ''crowded arena'' of commerce where so many hazards confronted them and where ''they must encounter sharp competition, shrewd rivals and experienced opposition.'' The author, making a point few of his contemporaries neglected, remarked that in business ''the race is not always to the swift, nor the battle to the strong.'' In order to succeed, knowledge, prudence, experience, and regularity were all necessary.

Commercial colleges could remedy the deficiency. The author felt that these ''peculiar institutions,'' as he called them, were growing daily in public regard as a result of the ''widely felt want'' they filled. Although they were still in their infancy, he was certain they would become an important part of popular education. With so many young men choosing mercantile occupations, the schools would be able to render great benefits to society. The author argued that

> the young man who acquires a careful education through the medium of a good commercial college, will find himself in possession of a science which he can apply under all possible circumstances, and which will make him as much the superior of him who is obliged, as an apprentice to pick up his knowledge through a series of years and by costly and varied experience, as the educated engineer is to the ordinary mechanic.

Not only would the colleges provide a more thorough knowledge of the merchant's trade—no small advantage to young men who grasped at any piece of advice in the hope that it might apply to some future situation—but it would also do it more quickly than traditional channels. With the increased competition young men now faced and with the possibility that young men lacking proper guidance might make a false start or two, the advantage gained could be invaluable.

The new institutes were legally chartered and provided ten- to fifteen-week courses in subjects ranging from bookkeeping, penmanship, bank-note engraving, detection of counterfeit money, and forms of letter writing to accounting, mercantile law, political economy, and mathematics. The author, writing specifically about Iron City

College in Pittsburgh, was especially proud of the school's efficiency in securing positions for its qualified students. "The great demand which exists for its graduates," he wrote, "and the high salaries which they command, are the best possible guaranties [*sic*] of the practical and business value of those whom it recommends" (1 [1839]: 77-78).

Most of the prominent mercantile colleges were in western cities like Pittsburgh, Buffalo, Cleveland, Cincinnati, St. Louis, and Chicago, but Hunt, in printing the article, must have sensed their applicability to problems facing merchants in eastern cities as well. The exclusiveness of entry to the older seaboard firms may have been more tightly controlled than in the West, but even there the awareness was growing that former hiring methods were outliving their usefulness.

As early as the 1840s, the New York Mercantile Library Association had debated the possibility of becoming "a collegiate institution." Why it eventually did not become one is hard to determine from the vague accounts found in its annual reports. In the eighteenth report of 1839, the board of directors offered "with great spirit and zeal" a plan for establishing a Merchants' College. "What literary or scientific institution," they asked, "opens to the merchant an opportunity of acquiring an education strictly and thoroughly mercantile?" (2 [1840]: 170). Yet, the 1840 report announced that the plan had been shelved. The board admitted that utlimately it might be practicable and expedient; for the present, however, the board would be content to see the Association's current system of classes expanded to incorporate "branches of knowledge [which] are likely to prove most beneficial to our members as citizens and as merchants." Unlike the proposed offerings of a year ago, the suggested course additions were not of a specifically commercial nature. The directors suggested that classes be formed in "the Classics, in Spanish, in French, in German, in Rhetoric and Oratory, in Moral and Natural Philosophy, in Chemistry, in short, in whatever may be thought necessary."[43]

43. New York Mercantile Library Association, *Nineteenth Annual Report.* . . (New York, 1840), p. 14.

The reason the directors gave for their decision was that the organization, with its present clientele of working clerks, could not make the transition without interfering with the duties of its members. As members were "necessarily engaged during the day, in the busy pursuit of their profession . . . any employment . . . be it ever so worthy in other respects, that shall so engross their minds as to prevent proper regard to their main vocation" was of "doubtful utility."[44] The young directors of the MLA may have balked at becoming a "colegiate institute" similar to Iron City College, because they realized their function went beyond the simple training of clerks. Unlike the business schools that would appear at the end of the nineteenth century, those advertising in Hunt's were probably designed for young men who would never be very upwardly mobile. They were designed for young men who would assume modest positions in commercial houses and, unless they started off on their own, be unlikely to aspire much higher. The MLA's suggestion of offerings in philosophy and language was a way of underlining their differences with such schools. While institutions like Iron City College trained clerks, the MLA was interested in educating future merchants for the wide range of responsibilities they would be called upon, as men of the world, to discharge.

The apparent shift of mercantile education to institutions other than the countinghouse was also indicated by the numerous suggestions in Hunt's *Magazine* and other advice-books that young men, instead of hurrying into business, ought to prolong their formal studies. A story in the February 1844 *Merchants' Magazine,* for example, had a moral far different from those of Joseph Scoville. In *Clarence Bolton,* especially, all the boy's essential education had come from an informal source, the Colonel. Clarence's college education was virtually forgotten. The author of the story in Hunt's, J. N. Bellows, told of a boy whose father, intending him to be a merchant, saw no reason for his son to learn anything beyond the fundamentals of reading, arithmetic, and writing. Just at the time that the boy was beginning to feel some interest in his studies, they were cut short and he was "turned into the countinghouse, to sigh for the green playground, his merry schoolfellows, and perhaps for daily tasks, which,

44. *Ibid.*

when completed, made his mind spring with elastic joy." His whole nature was soon changed. At the age of fourteen, the author said, he was forced to suppress his youthful exuberance and assume a grave, austere, and polished manner. Many years of dull, profitless toil were all he had to look forward to.

Bellows had no doubt the boy would survive. His objections concerned something else. Many young men, he noticed, with similarly incomplete and shallow preparations were forced to seek out the city writing master after they had begun clerking, to supplement the poor training they had received at school. "Not a few," he said, "get their knowledge of accounts and bookkeeping by sad experience of errors, which cost their employers much more than tuition fees." Bellows's assumptions are significant. He took for granted that these lessons were not being taught by employers. He assumed that the educational functions of clerkship, the painstaking initiation into each mercantile task and operation, which someone like Joseph Scoville considered normal, was to be acquired *outside* the countinghouse.

There were other problems that denoted how far removed the countinghouse was from the educational institution it used to be. Bellows was concerned that in teaching the boy only that "which will enable him to perform the duties of his place," his parents had apparently forgotten that he would have many leisure hours—hours when, it was assumed, if he was not doing something good, he would "find something evil to occupy him." Possessed of only the narrow education he had received, the boy was sure

> to fall prey to dissipation and vice, because [he has] not taste for quiet and studious pursuits. [His] business being over for the day [he] seeks that relaxation, in forbidden pleasures, which the fireside, the library, the literary circle should furnish.

Like other writers of the period, Bellows was certain that any foray of young men beyond the library or the fireside of their rooms could only lead to disaster. He never doubted that young men without more complete education would get along very well in business and social intercourse. But their moral nature would suffer irretrievably.[45] What

45. *Merchant's Magazine* 10 (1844): 143-46. See also Alcott, *Familiar Letters*, p. 200.

this assumed was that the development of moral character no longer occurred under an established merchant's tutelage. The coupling of mercantile education and character development was no longer so automatic as it had once been considered. Clerking was coming to be seen as a job occupying a certain portion of a young man's time and no more. It was no longer necessarily the center of his life, and certainly not the source of his moral development.

Bellows, in speaking of the preparation of a young clerk, brought together the two related changes we have noted. He combined the new notion of youth's susceptibility to temptation and moral decline with specific assumptions—expressed in his recognition that counting-houses no longer provided the personalized instruction of older days—about the relation of clerks to their employers. Because of the growth of business operations, more young men were needed to occupy lower-level positions. The presence of these young men changed the atmosphere of the countinghouse and the status of clerking. These alterations, given the newness and uncertainty that attended them, were accompanied by a changed way of looking at young men generally. Merchants, rightfully concerned about the consequences of supervising so many young men of unknown and untested capacities and unsure of the ability of traditional business arrangements to remain stable amid the influx, began to see the young as a dangerous and irrational force that threatened a familiar continuity. Books of advice eased this worry. They legitimized the view of young men as excitable and therefore requiring control, a view the merchants' position as an employing class was forcing on them. And the advice-books provided the code of conduct that might make young men seeking the trappings of gentility behave in a better-mannered and hence more predictable way. By doing so, these books offered to restore some of the stability recent social changes seemed bent on obliterating.

7

The Need for Institutions

Although writers like Bellows pictured the inculcation of moral precepts as slipping out of the merchants' hands, writers knew it could not be neglected altogether—its social value was far too important. But if clerks were no longer sure to receive instruction in such matters in the countinghouse, where would they receive it? The pressure of numbers and the quickening pace of business operations did not permit merchants the time to oversee their clerks' education as they once could. Merchants seemed to realize that it was now even more critical that standards of behavior that emphasized the impropriety of aggressive self-serving and demanded that the young and inexperienced defer to the old be instilled in new arrivals. Increasing numbers of young men were sure to threaten an already fragile social balance unless they behaved in the manner their elders sanctioned.

For merchants, the absorption of these standards by the young might confer numerous benefits. It might mitigate the conflict and disorder that they felt the competition for a limited number of places could lead to and it might enable them to exercise the control over access to positions in the business community that seemed to be slipping away from them. But the standards of behavior that men of trade cherished were an ideal of the mercantile profession that seemed to have lost its holding power. Over and over, business and community leaders pointed uneasily to the erosion of the social position and high prestige that this ideal invoked. Their fear was less that any real social or economic standing they held had declined[1] than that the idealized picture of the merchant as a man with special talents and training, with special virtues and style of life, no longer commanded the wide assent of an earlier time. It seemed increasingly difficult to maintain that the "Merchant Prince" was anything more than a successful businessman. As such, he hardly seemed the embodiment of the high morality and genteel manners that community leaders hoped aspiring newcomers would emulate. The acceptance of the "Merchant Prince" as a model of conduct had important advantages. But if the ideal had about it no distinctive marks of culture or virtue, how would a young clerk know what to do to signify his desire to join the select company it represented? More important, how—unless the young used the ideal as a guide—would his employers or competitors know what he might do?

It was the understanding of the valuable role this ideal played in stabilizing a society lacking a well-developed network for the control of mobility that led business leaders to voice expression of declining mercantile prestige. In lectures, magazine articles, and novels, men of prominence urged merchants to withhold recognition from lower-class intruders, tutored them in the need to maintain or assume distinctive traits of culture and virtue, and implored sons and other colleagues not to leave the honorable profession that had made them wealthy and independent. If those who by their education and breeding invested the ideal with reality should abandon the mercantile scene, both the ideal their presence fed and the stability their supposedly high-toned participation produced would be endangered.

Unlike in an earlier period, merchants were no longer able, with

1. Recent scholarship indicates that wealth and position were probably as secure as, or more secure than at any other period in the nation's history. See Edward Pessen, "The Egalitarian Myth and the American Social Reality: Wealth, Mobility, and Equality in the 'Era of the Common Man,' " in *American Historical Review* 76, no. 4 (October 1971): 989-1034.

any great assurance, to assert their equality with other professional vocations like law, religion, and medicine. The tradition of the "Merchant Prince," with its associations of statesmanship, philanthropy, and charity, seemed challenged by a more recent breed of businessman. One place these doubts began to crop us was in the addresses delivered to mercantile organizations on subjects such as commercial integrity and honor. Instead of the ease and glibness with which these speeches had generally been delivered, a new sense of uncertainty, of wrestling with a troubling problem, now seemed to pervade them.

Hunt reprinted many of these addresses. One, for instance, began by defining the kind of learning merchants needed. If they expected their profession to be invested with a dignity greater than that to which its mere functions entitled it, they had to require the proper intellectual baggage. "What does the merchant do, as such," asked the Reverend George Putnam in a speech to a group in Boston, "but fetch and carry, buy and sell, something to eat and wear, and to keep accounts?" Putnam did not deny that business was as honorable and useful a pursuit as any other. But, he added, "it can enjoy no *peculiar* elevation except such as may accrue to it from enlarged collateral culture of mind and character." A mere merchant, with a mind devoted solely to money-making, would almost certainly become "narrow in [his] comprehensions, low and earthy in [his] plans and conceptions." If he expected himself and the dignity of his profession to rise above this, he had to avail himself of present-day educational facilities and studiously cultivate some branch of learning like the exact or natural sciences, the arts, history, or political economy. Only when clothed with the learning "which [is] proper to be cultivated by him in common with all men as favorably situated as he" did he elevate himself above the "belittling" effects of selfish pecuniary striving. Anticipating the objections of an audience uncertain of the relevance of his remarks, Putnam closed by declaring, "I shall not easily be convinced of the inappropriateness of what I have been saying to the future merchants of Boston."[2] Putnam's insistence that merchants acquire a modicum of culture may have re-

2. *Hunt's Merchants' Magazine* 8 (1843): 302-4. (italics mine)

flected his desire to affirm that the profession was still the province of a well-bred social class that was above openly and single-mindedly pursuing material gain. Like rules of etiquette, a patina of learning was valuable in distinguishing oneself from others who, though they performed tasks that appeared similar in the marketplace, were considered to be of a lower social station. That Putnam had to make the point may have indicated how far from actual cases he was. His remarks and his audience's failure to see their relevance were evidence to him that Boston's mercantile ranks had already been considerably infiltrated by men whose concern was with making money, not with demonstrating their membership in a particular social class.

Another speaker, Joseph Hopkinson, a federal circuit court judge, in an address delivered to both the Philadelphia and New York Mercantile Library Associations, used a similar subject, "Commercial Integrity," to discuss the decline of trust and confidence in the mercantile community caused by the complacency with which the many cases of business irregularity and misconduct were tolerated by its members. To a great extent the problem was that too many merchants were content to think of themselves as "petty traffickers for petty gains" rather than as "*merchants* in the largest and most honorable sense of the term." Too many men never imagined that the work required any special preparation or instruction. Unlike the legal or medical professions, where the candidate put himself through a regular course of study and worked for years to acquire the learning and skill of the occupation, many men aspiring to mercantile professions thought themselves qualified as if by intuition. It was only a rigorous preparation, however, that would allow them "to expect the patronage or countenance of the community for [their] undertaking." The author specifically singled out the mechanic for censure. He had labored hard, accumulated a few thousand dollars, and then turned his back on the honest trade in which he made his money in order to be a merchant. Why he could "not be content to be useful and respected in the business he understood, and in which he was truly respectable, and reject the indulgence of a false and foolish pride, to be something that he is not, [and] which cannot but expose him to ridicule" was something Hopkinson could not fathom.

As soon as the mechanic left his proper sphere of employment, he lost his high standing in the community. Did anyone believe, Hopkinson demanded, that commerce was a pursuit so low in the scale of human affairs, that its qualifications were so common, that it required no suitable education or experience? If a young man sought the honors and profits of trade, if he expected to be distinguished by his ability and success, he had to undergo a process of instruction before a "knowledge of his art" could be acquired. Training, the author suggested, ought to begin in a countinghouse, where all facets of business operations could be observed, where one could learn to accurately distinguish the qualities of various grades of merchandise, and where one could learn the methods of accounting and bookkeeping. Unfortunately, this kind of training no longer seemed widespread. Now, said Hopkinson, a man just says he wants to be a merchant and he is one.

Whatever may have been his previous education or occupation—or if wanting in both—if he can open a counting house, and get an indorser, he is a merchant, and, as such, repairs to the exchange, and is at once admitted to the fraternity. He puts on a bold face and a brave spirit, dashes at anything that offers in the way of doing business, however desperate, and finds everybody eager to trust him. He relies on chances which are a hundred to one against him and his very hardihood obtains for him consideration and credit.

The author was obviously indicting not only his subject but the rest of the mercantile community as well. It was they who were eager to offer trust and to extend credit. It was they who accepted and thereby legitimized this brash behavior. And it was they who, if the man succeeded in a few reckless schemes, extended deference and reputation to him. Like so many of the changes that an older generation of merchants had difficulty understanding, the switch by which the unqualified now assumed mercantile positions was represented by an image of catastrophic swiftness. "The creation of light," Hopkinson said at one point, "was scarcely more instantaneous" (1 [1839]: 380-82). The frustration at being incapable of preventing the transformation and decline of mercantile character (presumably by admixture) that the image revealed only intensified the sharpness of his response.

Hopkinson's feelings about the decline of mercantile integrity, about the decline in the standards the profession professed to uphold, went deep. He was appalled at the assault by men of lower standing on the professions supposedly the preserve of a social elite. But with the erosion of the "process of instruction," the bastions of mercantile exclusiveness were apparently breaking down. It is interesting that the system of education Hopkinson seemed to be urging was an apprenticelike one. He did not refer to business schools or other agencies where the skills of commercial practice could be learned, perhaps believing that among the lot of them only the old apprenticelike relationship schooled its charges to assume a social manner as well as an occupation. Unlike the professions of medicine and law, to which Hopkinson compared business, long years of specialized training were not in fact *essential* to commercial success. Besides informal devices, like those of protracted clerkships when the business community was relatively stable, there was no other mechanism intrinsic to business practice itself that—in contrast to the learned professions—could be used to restrict entry. It might be precarious, but the businessman setting up on a shoestring *could* make it.

Freeman Hunt was himself worried about the supposed infiltration that imperiled a dearly held conception of mercantile prestige. In the introduction to the first volume of his *Lives of American Merchants* (1858), he was led to attack the widespread counsel to obtain as much advanced learning as possible. To Hunt, the widespread extension of collegiate education seemed certain to obliterate the distinctions he wanted to retain by wrongly encouraging those who were better off where they were. Too many people, said Hunt, felt that college training prepared them only for a learned profession; any trade that required manual labor came to be viewed with "unqualified repugnance." Such thinking only maintained "the absurdity that the farmer's son should not return to the plow, that the young mechanic must not again wield the hammer." But unlike Hopkinson, Hunt saw the problem of declining merchant prestige as due less to the intrusion of unqualified men and men of lower social position than to a turning away of the talented and socially qualified. As much as he wanted to discourage men of lesser position from feeling that they had to gain membership in learned professions because they had college degrees, he wanted to attract college-educated young men of high social standing to the mercantile profession—a profession that they seemed to feel was beneath them. The four years spent in college were not lost, Hunt said, if the graduate found himself over the merchant's letter-book instead of Blackstone's *Commentaries.* Appealing to the graduate's vanity and ambition, he asked, "We may inquire whether a scholar would not occasionally consult his own welfare by adopting an active pursuit, in which he might become distinguished, instead of clinging to mediocrity in a high profession simply because he has received a degree from a university and *fears that he might fall from Brahmin to Pariah and lose caste in the descent."* It was one thing to enter the professions of law, medicine, or church out of a devotion to the work involved. But, he added, "it is another thing to adopt a [learned] profession, merely because it is considered respectable."[3]

Instead, Hunt hoped these educated young men could be persuaded to consider mercantile careers. It appears that he assumed these careers to be of lesser status than those in the learned professions and that educated young men, no doubt of good family, would choose the latter unless convinced that they should do otherwise. It was the talent from this group that Hunt felt was most important to lure into business. Although it is difficult to be certain that Hunt was interested in recruiting young men from one social stratum only, the nature of the biographical sketches comprising the book seems to support this view. The portraits consistently emphasize the subjects' high birth and connections, noting how these advantages helped them to succeed. In the case of Peter Chardon Brooks, who did start out poor, the writer—though the sketches are unsigned they were almost certainly written by various men, not by Hunt himself—was quick to quash the impression that Brooks had struggled from the bottom

3. Freeman Hunt, *Lives of American Merchants.* 2 vols. (New York, 1855), 1: xli-xlii. (italics mine)

up by his own resources alone. "Although commencing business without capital, or any *direct* family influence which could advance his fortune, Mr. Brooks no doubt owed something in early life to family associations, *which ought not to be forgotten here.* The name was well known and highly respected in the vicinity of Boston, not merely on his father's account, but also through the late Governor Brooks. . .; to be of his name and kindred was a letter of recommendation for a young man just coming into life in this region."[4] Another exception, Stephen Girard, was clearly labeled as such. His character had been scarred by some early personal experiences and it was suggested that his unbridled ambition—which contrasted sharply with the almost quiescent nature of the other subjects—was therefore excusable. The book was admittedly "a stimulant to the young merchant to imitate the example of purity of life, of integrity of motive," rather than a blueprint for action.[5]

What may have been most disturbing to merchants was the lack of interest shown by their own sons in following their careers. Whether or not it is true that sons whose affluent, successful parents could afford to educate or indulge them no longer cared to experience the worries, uncertainties, or hard work of their fathers' profession, there is little doubt about the extent to which the older generation believed this to be the case. Whether sons abandoned mercantile life for the learned professions or wasted themselves in dissipated irresponsibility as their fathers imagined, the source of talent merchants most counted on to provide continuity, regularity, and hence stability in business life seemed to be evaporating. A tired, aging generation of businessmen had looked to its sons to succeed it and found them sin-

---

4. *Ibid.,* p. 141. (italics mine)
5. *Ibid.,* p. 129. This becomes even clearer when the book is compared with a later treatment of successful businessmen. James D. McCabe, Jr.'s *Great Fortunes, and How They Were Made: or, the Struggles and Triumphs of our Self-Made Men* (New York, 1871), pp. 138-41, included a sketch of the piano-maker Jonas Chickering, which in large part was plagiarized from the account in Hunt's *Lives.* What is interesting were the changes McCabe made. McCabe slighted Hunt's description of Chickering's own apprenticeship and his dutiful overseeing of his children's upbringing. Instead, he stressed Chickering's single-minded drive for success and the struggle of starting business alone.

gularly reluctant. If this were so, one other prop, to the degree that a son could still be depended on for reliable, loyal service, supporting an already interrupted order would be gone. Too many young men of the present day, wrote Hunt, instead of starting out in the world to earn a livelihood and build a reputation through their own exertions as their fathers had done, spent their time in idleness and dissipation. They "depended upon their fathers even for the daily bread necessary to prolong their worthless existence." His remarks prefaced a piece in his *Magazine* that urged such idlers to "wake up . . . help the old man—give him now and then a generous lift in business——learn how to take the lead, and not depend forever on being led."[6]

Another short piece, included in the *Magazine* as a filler, honored the sons who did follow their fathers in family businesses. Too seldom was the son who dutifully performed the functions of a clerk given the honor that was due him, the article began. "Wealth descends best when it falls into the hands of the merchant's son who has been also his clerk, for thus received riches are made the instruments of enterprise and public good, instead of dissipation, evil example, and ruin" (33 [1855]: 394).

Hunt happily printed as news examples illustrating the spirit merchants hoped to see in their sons. One, titled by Hunt "A Worthy Son of a Boston Merchant," told of a merchant's son who sent the headmaster of the school from which he had recently graduated fifty dollars. The money was to be spent on a poor Irish classmate with whom he had competed—"the son of the merchant was the successful one"—for the school's highest rank. The writer was impressed by the interest the boy continued to show in his "less favored rival," especially since they were "placed in different social positions and not likely to meet after leaving the school." As significant as the consciousness of class barriers that the writer exhibited were the terms he used to describe the boy's act. It was, he said, an act distinguished by its kindness, delicacy, modesty, and thoughtful solicitude—all values, it seemed, too infrequently encountered in most youth of the period (17 [1847]: 540).

In light of the infrequency of such examples and the doubtfulness

6. *Merchants' Magazine* 40 (1859): 523.

that young men could be counted upon to manifest such character traits or to exhibit a sincere devotion to their fathers' businesses, the problem of securing trusted replacements often seemed insoluble. To one writer, the popular novelist T. S. Arthur, it was easier to look for a solution in an imagined past rather than in the frustrating, intractable present. If it seemed unwise to move aside and relinquish one's place to young men whose future performance was at best considered unpredictable, it might be safer to prolong the practices of the past, to hold onto methods that men—remembering their own experience when young—had confidence in. T. S. Arthur's novel *Retiring from Business* (1848), in advancing such a solution, pointed up the fears besetting conscientious merchants and also revealed the extent of their uneasiness about the direction in which the business system as a whole was moving.

Arthur's own life (1809-85) seemed to mirror the social mobility and instability he wrote about time and again. The grandson of an officer in the Revolutionary War, he was born on a farm in Orange County, New York. While he was an infant, his parents, presumably lacking the means to make a success out of farming, moved first to Fort Montgomery, New York, and then, in 1817, to Baltimore. Arthur was placed in the public schools, but was soon removed and apprenticed to a watchmaker. Instead of following this trade, however, he entered, through the help of a friend, a Baltimore countinghouse as a clerk. In 1833 he went West, representing a Baltimore bank. When the bank failed, he returned and about this time decided to make writing (in his leisure time he had already started composing verse and sketches) a full-time career. Before long he was editing a number of short-lived literary ventures and by 1841 moved to Philadelphia, where his writing began in earnest. Soon he was contributing regularly to *Godey's Lady Book*, *Graham's Magazine*, the *Saturday Courier*, and the newspapers. Throughout his life he began magazines of his own, but none were particularly noteworthy. His success came from his writing, from the constant stream of moralizing novels, stories, and tracts that he produced. By 1875 he had written about seventy books, some of them, says his biographer, "astonishingly popular."[7]

In *Retiring from Business,* Arthur used the story of the retirement of a prosperous businessman to talk about the chaotic consequences that would result if the older generation passed from the mercantile scene. Howard Franklin at fifty was comfortably prosperous, and with the property he had acquired was wealthy enough to live contentedly the rest of his life. Why should he continue to make a slave of himself, he argued, just to hoard up money for the sake of mere accumulation? He was in the prime of health and wanted to retire while he could still enjoy it. One of his friends questioned his decision. Society, he maintained, still had a strong claim on him because of his ability—we are told only that Franklin was the manufacturer of "some useful article"—to do valuable service as a business man. His wife, "a woman of clear perceptions," was also against Franklin's decision. She feared that his mind, after so many years of devotion to business, would become uneasy and discontented if it remained idle for long. "You will be unhappy with nothing to do," she warned.[8]

It was not long before the effects his wife had foreseen began to appear. Franklin soon became restless and, with no business to turn to, said Arthur, looked to other areas to occupy himself. One by one he undermined every possible aspect of what his generation considered the foundations of a happy and prosperous life. First he interfered with his daughter's education, sending her to a school where her character received, just as it "was in a state of formation . . . and beginning to harden, impressions that no after culture could entirely efface" (p. 37). Next Arthur described how Franklin's idleness disturbed his home life. With the hours hanging heavily on his hands—it is as if the man could not possibly have, or develop, any other interests—he became so tired from doing nothing all day that he was often ill-humored, irritable, and harsh (p. 38). He began to meddle in domestic affairs, "seriously hindering the orderly progres-

7. Allan Nevins in *Dictionary of American Biography* (New York, 1928), I: 377-78.
8. T. S. Arthur, *Retiring from Business* (New York, 1848), p. 21.

sion of his wife's duties." His son Edwin's future also suffered. At nineteen Edwin had just completed his college term and wanted to go into business instead of law as he and his father had previously decided. Franklin was aware, however, that the boy had not received a business education and only reluctantly began to look for a place for his son in a commercial house. While doing so, the thought that he should never have quit business kept crossing his mind. If he had still been engaged in his manufacturing operations, he thought, he could have taken Edwin into his countingroom, "and, retaining him under his own care, have made him extremely useful." At the same time he could have taught him the business. Hopefully, in a few years Edwin could have joined the firm as a full partner while Franklin, "in retiring then, would have left his son in a fair way of amassing an independence for himself" (p. 37). The actual outcome was far different. Franklin was able to place his son in a large firm employing about twenty-five clerks. Many of them had wealthy parents who provided them with liberal spending allowances and "thus . . . the means of dissipation, which a few of them did not fail to use. With no love for intellectual pursuits, and naturally inclined to sensual indulgence, the position of Edwin was anything but a safe one" (p. 58).

Franklin then compounded his previous errors and jeopardized his savings by buying a handsome country house. With his mind still unsettled, he thought he would "amuse himself" as an amateur farmer. His wife again objected, fearing that the move would further decrease their control over their children, who had both taken to staying late in the city with "improper associates." Franklin countered with the hope that his son might become interested in farming; its benefits, in comparison to the fluctuations and temptations of the mercantile life, were obvious. He hoped that together he and his son could learn a new vocation. But away from a business with whose operation he was well acquainted, Franklin was reckless with his money, relying on the advice of a hired overseer who was busy swindling him. And Edwin, instead of taking an interest in the managerial work he was to share with his father, preferred to spend his time fishing, hunting, and reading such books as "The Mysteries of Eugene Sue, Dumas or some other French novelist of like attractions." Edwin spent more of his evenings in town in the company of the young men from his former clerkship, became profligate with his money, and was soon in debt. During an appeal to his father for funds, an argument developed and Edwin, turned out of the house, ran off to the city.

On the fourth day of the boy's absence, Franklin went to New York to find him. In a few hours his search brought him to the home of another merchant, Mr. P————, whose son, a friend of Edward's, was also missing. Mr. P———— noted that his son's habits were also "very irregular and that his conduct caused the family great uneasiness." On hearing that his son might be involved in the illegal sale of the horse Edwin had ridden off on, Mr. P———— exclaimed

> Oh dear! This boy will kill me! I have spent thousands of dollars upon his education, and here is the result. I believe, after all, that we cannot lay a heavier curse upon our children than to give them money. The poor lad, who works as hard as you and I did, twelve hours a day for his plain food and coarse clothing, is really happier and better, and gives more promise of a useful and prosperous life, than the sons of the wealthy. Our children, Mr. Franklin, are the drones of society! (pp. 104-5)

Mr. P———— was sorry that he could not help locate the boys. Referring to his son, he said, "I know but little of his incomings and outgoings. That a father should say this! But it is even so! For more than a year, he has acted toward me with a kind of insolent independence, which has stung me like the fangs of a serpent" (pp. 104-5). Sadly, Franklin could only agree. A visit to Mr. Welford, another merchant whose son was friendly with Edwin, proved no more helpful. Welford's son had also disappeared. The nightmare that seemed to haunt the merchant—that his son was completely out of control, that it was impossible to keep track of his whereabouts—had become epidemic reality. But just as Mrs. Franklin was convinced that her son was lost forever, Franklin found him and brought him home. Edwin did not remain long. Pressed by his debts, he resorted to forging notes on his father's account. Discovered, he ran off again. To make matters even worse, the daughter, Florence, had also run off with an unscrupulous dandy interested only in her father's money. Arthur summed up Franklin's recent past:

> What a change had two years wrought in everything that concerned the retired gentleman! Property had passed from his hands so suddenly and in so unexpected a way, that no time for prudent anticipation of the result was given. His children had gone astray—one of them he feared hopelessly. The health of his wife, under the painful affliction she had suffered was sadly broken. . . . And the home—how sadly was that changed! Once every evening was a pleasant reunion. Now, the members sat silent when they met; or with an oppressive sense of disquietude passed hours in the solitude of their own apartments. (p. 138)

Things were to get still worse. Franklin had sold the farm (taking a $7,000 loss), moved back to New York, and entered into a brokerage business with LeGrand, his daughter's seducer. LeGrand had gained favor with Franklin by returning Edwin, whom he had found in Mobile, Alabama. But Arthur suggested that the association was even more attributable to Franklin's disturbed mind.

Edwin was taken into the business also, and appeared to be substantially changed since his return home. Invoking a widespread theory of learning, Arthur said only that "the remembrance of all he had suffered remained *too vivid* in his mind to leave much desire to court old acquaintances or to indulge in old follies." His new interest in the business also kept his mind from wandering. But the most significant factor in his reformation seemed to be that "Mr. Franklin was at the office almost every day, and thus had Edwin under his own eye for a large portion of the time" (p. 145). While Edwin's interest in business was growing and while his character was developing under his father's constant scrutiny, the resources of the enterprise were being drained by LeGrand. In two years he had diverted all of the business's funds and had run off to Europe before the loss was detected. Franklin was now completely ruined and "forced to retire. . .into obscurity." So reduced were his circumstances that, Arthur tells us, he could not even provide his family with the "absolute necessaries of life."

The disaster did have one positive effect. It brought out a strength of character in Edwin that no one knew existed. Through his efforts a release for his father from his creditors was secured, and for eight months he carried the burden of supporting the whole family. It was only then that "the prostrate mind of Mr. Franklin began to rally." And the same time he realized that no man can be happy in idleness, a combination of circumstances enabled him to reacquire his old business.

The return to business had a remarkable effect. Almost immediately Franklin and his family resumed the closeness and happiness that his retirement had extinguished. By the end of three years his business had grown so that he needed a clerk to help him. Conveniently, there was a young son, James, now eighteen, whom he was able to take into the establishment. Edwin, remaining with the firm he had joined almost four years before, after his father's ruin, had satisfied his employers so well that at this same time he was offered an interest in the firm. Time restored Mrs. Franklin's health and even brought the abandoned Florence peace of mind. Franklin himself "is once more a useful and happy man; and while his strength of mind and body are given, will never think of retiring" (p. 166).

Arthur's story had a tidiness about it that was characteristic. As we will see shortly, a large part of this neatness, this tying up of all loose ends, this accounting for all the pieces that were disordered as the story unfolded, was connected to a belief that society was better off unchanged. Except for Edwin, the family, at the novel's close, had progressed no farther than they were at the novel's beginning. Arthur was careful to tell us that the factory Franklin resumed control of was in great disorder from the mismanagement of the interim operators. The result was that by hard work he was able to regain his former position but not exceed it. It was no accident that he acquired the same factory (in a reduced state) that he had earlier relinquished, rather than a different one. As we will see repeated later on, there was a penalty to be paid for moral lapses or neglect of obligation, but the penalty was not so harsh as excommunication from the class one belonged to.

The changes that do occur in the course of the novel actually look backward to an earlier period. Edwin's development is a good example. Other young men of his position and background were felt to be turning away from their parents' businesses to more learned occupations. Edward's movement was the reverse. At the book's beginning, the father was urging the son to study law and the boy refused; at the book's end he was taken into a mercantile concern. In addition, the pattern of his encounters with business organizations was also chronologically reversed. Instead of ending up in a large, complex, impersonal firm where employees were too numerous to be known by employers and were thrown back completely on what their elders feared were inadequate personal resources, this was where Edwin began. When he returned to business after an interlude of dissipation, he entered a historically more primitive establishment with his father. He returned, in other words, to an older, literally paternal, relationship with his employer, until personal crisis provided the shock energy that in a sense pushed him from one stage of life—from adolescence—to the maturity of manhood. The place at his father's side was not, however, left vacant. As Edwin went off to join a different firm, his younger brother—who had played no part at all in the story so far, who had been presumably manufactured for just this purpose—was taken in as a clerk to maintain the line of succession. Perhaps now, with succession fixed, with James being watched too closely to go astray until he reaches maturity, Franklin will finally be able to rest.

Besides expressing the dimensions of the worry men like Arthur entertained about the competence and willingness of their sons to succeed them, a worry related to their expressions of social decline and instability, the novel *Retiring from Business* reveals a far more wide-ranging preoccupation with the need to root one's life institutionally. Although Arthur is nowhere consciously aware of it, the novel's plot appears to indicate an implicit recognition of this need. It provides a hint to the kind of solution merchants would increasingly turn to in an effort to replace the set of practices that they felt had once supplied continuity in business and social leadership. In most didactic novels of this period—Arthur's own, as we shall soon see, are no exception—the state of one's character determines the course of one's life, especially one's success in business. But in *Retiring from Business,* the process is reversed. Franklin's success in business determines the state of his character. When diligently involved with his manufacturing plant, his life runs smoothly—his business prospers, his character is stable, and his family life is ideal. It is, in fact, this diligence, rather than the success automatically assumed to follow from it, that is most important to Arthur. In this light, his vagueness about the nature of Franklin's business seems less accidental. It is not so much what one does (so long, naturally, as it is honest labor) as it is the persistence and steadiness of the activity that is essential. In a society whose institutional foundations seemed to be crumbling, work itself, especially if connected to a continuing, sustained enterprise like a profitable factory, became perhaps the only certain way to insure order and regularity in the lives of men.[9] It is therefore not surprising that as soon as Franklin leaves the institutions of business everything goes awry. Arthur's summation, quoted above, of the disasters that befall Franklin could hardly have been more complete. His property disappears, his children succumb to temptation, his wife's health breaks, his family become strangers to one another, and his own mental powers decline. His return to business, however, almost miraculously restores his former tranquility. Once he returns to practicing his profession according to the standardized and tradition-laden ways of a passing era, the stability that characterized all aspects of his life reappears. Its utter chaos and complete lack of control evaporates.

In a society much of whose institutional life was disintegrating, Arthur felt it was essential to spell out the disasters that could befall a man if the very cornerstone of a settled existence—regular business practice—was abandoned. As Arthur noted at the end of *Retiring from Business,* "A remembrance of the unhappy period in which [Franklin] sought rest from labor will ever remain too vivid in his recollection to leave him in danger of again committing that folly" (p. 166). The dire consequences of retirement were brought on not because Franklin abandoned business, but because he did so voluntarily. He *chose* to turn his back on his former livelihood. Arthur felt

9. It is interesting that Michael Walzer, in his study of the English Puritans, sees their view of work as serving a similar function in a society also pictured, though for different reasons, as disorganized and "unsettled." See Michael Walzer, *The Revolution of the Saints* (London, 1966), pp. 210-15.

that a stable social order could be salvaged only if business was conducted "on the permanent, healthy, honest, and only true basis of
demand and supply." But lately too many men, aware of the opportunities for making money around them, had become unscrupulous,
vicious, and blind to the disruptive effects of their actions.[10] They
were willfully disregarding the sound business practice that could
alone insure order.

To counteract the activity of these growing numbers it was necessary to keep men with Franklin's credentials actively involved. If
these men suddenly packed up and moved to the country (as Franklin
had done), if they removed themselves from the social structure
whose very fabric depended on the strength their combined force of
character imparted to it, then the tide of disorder would surely over-
whelm the nation. As Franklin's friend told him early in the novel,
"Let all men seek their ease; let all men refuse to work; in other
words, perform services for others, and how quickly would disaster
and wide-spread distress prevail throughout the country" (pp. 13-14).
A man of character, integrity, and industry was a pillar of his community in a very literal sense.

Especially in a society devoid of institutions around which customary patterns of behavior and hence durable social relationships could
develop, men who abided by the rules of social conduct were highly
valued. Arthur emphasized this point by the attention he gave in his
books to the conventions of social intercourse. Possibly, by following
these informal rules closely, the institutional slack created by the disruption of other stabilizing forces like the church, family, and apprentice system could be taken up. Unfortunately, the rules of behavior he looked to were not in themselves strong enough to support
the weight he hoped they could bear. With society growing so
quickly and changing so rapidly, with so many people altering their
life styles and expectations, such rules were no longer so easily applied as they once were.

In his *Advice to Young Men* (1848), Arthur touched on all the
themes commonly discussed by other writers of morality tracts. His

10. See Arthur's novel *Riches Have Wings* (New York, 1847), p. 7.

emphasis, to a greater degree than the others', however, was on etiquette and good manners in polite society. Unlike many of his contemporaries, Arthur felt that "dancing, games, concerts, the opera, scenic representations, etc., are all good in themselves."[11] Their value in allaying selfishness and ambition, he felt, far outweighed the danger of provoking the passional excitement often feared by others. For Arthur they provided an essential antidote to the ugly competition of the business world—competition that, by its new ruthlessness, threatened to wipe out even lip service to distinctions necessary to the preservation of social stability. In the business world, men grew more selfish each day; there was no consideration given to the interests of others. In social intercourse, on the other hand, if there was no longer the "generous deference" he prized, there was still "the *form* of self-sacrifice for the good of others." And, Arthur noted, "we would fain believe no little of its essence" (p. 75; original italics). It appeared that maintaining the form of self-sacrifice was better than neglecting the virtue altogether.

The conventions and forms of proper conduct in general were uppermost in Arthur's mind. Deference by young men to age and station was urged again and again. A youth of real worth was modest and "always ready to defer to others" as a matter of habit (p. 115). Adherence to such customs, Arthur assured his readers, need not involve the violation of one's self respect or the slavery to "mere conventional forms". He realized that his counsel had its dangers; while good men deferred evil men pushed themselves ahead aggressively. "Shallow conceit," he wrote, "is ever thrusting itself rudely forward, and occupying the place of wiser and better men" (p. 115). But so overriding was his belief in the primacy of the values of deference that he quickly overlooked his own objections.[12]

The selfish, self-seeking young man, the man who lacked what Arthur called self-government, and who willfully infringed on the rights and comforts of others was sure to harbor within himself "disorderly

11. T. S. Arthur, *Advice to Young Men on Their Duties and Conduct in Life* (Boston, 1848), p. 74.
12. Arthur even urged that deference and respect be accorded to those occupying elevated stations in society whether or not the men holding those positions were themselves good. *Ibid.*, p. 116.

tendencies.'' Unless they were brought under "proper control," old age would find him "with a host of ungovernable impulses struggling in his bosom and overmastering him in every feeble effort he makes to subdue them" (p. 81). Arthur explained that insanity (which was simply a state of disorder "more or less excessive") was a certain fate. "Is it any wonder," he asked, "that after a man has pursued only selfish ends all his life that in old age there should be something of insanity or mental imbecility as a natural result."[13]

To change the "form of government" or to engage in legislative reform was no answer to the "perverted state of mind" then dominant. Only when each individual was guided in all his dealings with others "by justice and judgment," said Arthur, will an end to business disorder prevail.[14] When all young men entering careers began acting from principles like the above, great changes would be noticeable in just a few years:

> Trade would be in a far more healthy condition, and every man in business would feel himself *more firmly established*. And the reason is obvious. There would be no overreaching; *no disturbance of the regular course of trade* by eager, selfish speculators; no interference as is now often the case, by which it not unfrequently [sic] happens that his prospects for life are ruined.[15]

Predictability and certainty once again could be restored to an area whose practices suffused the whole of social relations. All business had to do was "to use diligence, wisdom, and prudence, and these will carry him through, even amid the wrongs and disorders of society as it now exists" (p. 163).

Yet, despite this professed optimism, Arthur knew that things had changed beyond the point where this assurance was comforting. He realized that he had to counter specifically the charge "that deception and false representation are absolutely necessary to success; that it is impossible for a strictly-honest man to succeed in business." The

13. *Ibid.*, pp. 79-80. See also David J. Rothman, *The Discovery of the Asylum* (Boston, 1971), p. 116 on the connection between insanity and aggressive pursuit of business and social success.

14. *Riches Have Wings*, p. 11.

15. *Advice to Young Men*, p. 163. (italics mine)

feebleness of his reply, however, revealed just how helpless he was
to suggest or envision alternatives that tampered with the system as it
currently operated. His answer—"But this is not true"—was no
sooner stated than denied:

> We believe, however, that in a business community where nearly
> all take undue advantages in trade, an honest man will find it dif-
> ficult to sustain himself, unless he be wary, active and energetic;
> for he will lose by the dishonesty of others, without being able to
> repair the loss by dishonest practices in turn. But what right-
> thinking man would not rather suffer the loss of worldly goods
> than the loss of honor? Who would not be content with a smaller
> portion of wealth, accompanied by a consciousness of having
> done what was just and right between man and man, than be the
> possessor of millions obtained by overreaching and a system of
> successful fraud not recognizable by the laws. (p. 160)

This was all the solace Arthur could offer. Again and again in
countless novels about mercantile affairs, he simply presented this
advice without attention to its obvious distortion of reality. In fact, it
was just this distortion, with its unvarying collection of characters,
virtues, and picture of social mobility that accounted for Arthur's
popularity. An older generation was attracted by the tractability and
docility it might induce. Young men were attracted, as Donald M.
Scott has imaginatively pointed out, by the sense of order that this
advice—by drawing on the most customary moral precepts—imposed
on what seemed to be a bewildering and chaotic world. Many young
men may have sensed that constant attention to these precepts
brought success no closer, but it did serve to give them some confidence that the world they were entering still honored the ethical currency of the world they had left. In doing so it provided at least
some benchmarks by which they could orient themselves and retain
the hope that the world was still amenable to their own efforts.[16] Horatio Alger, when he began writing some twenty years later, would
not have to look much beyond Arthur to find the elements of the

16. See Donald M. Scott, "Making It in Ante-Bellum America: Young
Men and Their Careers, 1820-1860," paper delivered to the Organization of
American Historians, New Orleans, Louisiana, April 17, 1971.

formula that he, generally in a far less interesting way, would employ in his own novels.

Book after book repeated the same plan. Arthur followed two young men—one good, one bad—as they pursued mercantile careers. Invariably the self-seeking, unscrupulous merchant, tempted into error by avarice and impatience for gain, was reduced to poverty (often only temporarily as we will see), while the upright merchant with unblemished character, though forced to live humbly at first, eventually reached success.

In Making Haste to be Rich, first published in 1848 and reprinted later as one of the popular series "Tales for the Rich and Poor," Arthur introduced two young men, Franklin Riddell and Morris Jordan, engaged in a discussion about the methods of setting up in business. Riddell, admittedly of "ardent temperament," acknowledged that he could never rise up by the "slow and sure" way that his friend recommended. And he said, "In ten years from now, you will see me over the heads of dozens of the sleepy tribe who now grope along in the paths of trade." He belittled his friend's caution and urged Morris to change his course or be left behind in the race. "I do not want as I rise," he said, "to look back upon you grovelling in the plain below with the great, unambitious horde." He would never be a merchant of the old school.[17]

After this introduction, the novel proceeded to focus on Riddell's career only. In careful detail Arthur recorded the machinations and scheming attending Riddell's rise until, as expected, he was consumed by his greed. Tempted into greater and greater indiscretions by his insane (it is hinted) desire for money, he was finally incarcerated for forgery. Only at this point, with pages remaining in the tale, do we hear anything of Morris Jordan's progress. After his release from prison, Riddell wandered into his old neighborhood. The elegant mansion he had erected in his days of affluenc was now occupied by a stranger. Next to it he noticed another large and imposing dwelling; "as he passed by, he read the name of Morris Jordan." The story of the rise and fall of the dishonest merchant took Arthur

17. T. S. Arthur, *Making Haste to be Rich: or, the Temptation and Fall* (New York, 1855), p. 14.

165 pages to tell. The story of the rise of Morris Jordan, the honest, retiring merchant was not told at all. Though we are never told how, we discover that he had succeeded. Did Arthur think his readers were not interested? Why then did he detail the career of the failure and neglect the career of the success? The answer possibly stemmed from his view of the process of social mobility and from his difficulty in conceptualizing its stages. The point will become clearer if we first examine one of his longer and most popular works, *Sparing to Spend*.[18]

In *Sparing to Spend*, Arthur again introduced two young clerks, each with temperament and outlook comparable to Riddell's and Jordan's. This time he followed the careers of both men; we are told how the impatient Pinkerton fails and how the prudent, self-denying Lofton attains "peace, prosperity and happiness." Pinkerton, even more than Riddell, is pictured as the "progressive man," the man whose devotion to the passing fashion dooms him to extravagant living far beyond his means. Lofton prudently saves his money—his salary is $200 less than his friend's—and spends his evenings reading moral tracts while Pinkerton, for instance, is out at the theater. In time Lofton falls in love with a poor, gentle seamstress, Ellen Birch. His employer, Mr. Arden, a kindly, fatherly man, hearing of the engagement, assures Lofton that he has made a wise choice—he knows the girl well. And when Ellen becomes sick, the older man, the model of mercantile benevolence, tells Lofton that some of his family will see her immediately to attend to her comfort. A few days later the clerk is given a raise. His old salary is changed simply because Arden feels he is worth more than what he has been receiving. The raise has nothing to do with his engagement or with a change in duties; we are never told what the clerk's responsibilities are or if they change.

With the extra money assured, Lofton and Ellen, after fully computing their present and expected expenditures (this is a sign of maturity; the two are not impulsive or flighty), decide to marry. Pinkerton, hearing the news, tells his friend that *he* could never marry on

18. T. S. Arthur, *Sparing to Spend; or, the Loftons and Pinkertons* (Philadelphia, 1853).

a salary that forced him to "hide [his wife] away in a salt box" as if he were ashamed of her. Lofton replies that he and his wife will find higher satisfaction in acting wisely and prudently than his friend will find in flaunting himself before the world. "Those who seek to maintain appearances beyond their ability," he notes, "usually do it at a heavy sacrifice. It not only costs money, but character" (p. 115).

Character is, of course, Lofton's stock in trade. Nothing will be permitted to sully it, certainly not a challenge from Pinkerton that he should take his wife to a respectable boarding house "where she could be brought into the company of people who have a position in society" instead of keeping her in the humble, obscure residence where they live. Coolly Lofton tells Pinkerton, "We can wait."

Yet, the young clerk is having his doubts. "I believe that I possess equal business capacity with Mark Pinkerton; and a great deal more prudence," he says to his wife one evening. "And yet capital seeks him out, while I am passed by, and left to plod along through life, a simple clerk" (p. 177). His wife, the true moral authority of the household, comforts him. Providence is not to be questioned. "Don't let that bane of all happiness, discontent with the present lot, come in to cloud the sunshine of our happy life," she says. If good fortune is in store for them, she tells him a few days later, it will come in its own time. As if in response to her words, that very day an invitation to attend a party given by Mr. Arden is received. Lofton is gratified. He feels the introduction into society that the invitation affords is a public endorsement of his character, an endorsement of incalculable value to a young man like himself who has nothing but ability and good character on which to build "his worldly prosperity" (p. 183). The affair is the turning point in Lofton's career. Ellen comes to the attention of a prominent merchant, Mr. Ackland, who is just then seeking a new partner. Earlier in the evening she had decided to forgo wearing jewelry offered to her by a friend. She feared it might injure her husband's prospects if she was thought extravagant. Everyone could tell, apparently, that her husband's income was too small to allow such purchases. Ackland asks Arden about the woman and then about her husband. Arden assures him that the clerk is worthy of his wife—his principles were manly and honorable, he shunned extravagance, and belonged to the "slow and sure" school of business (p. 196). Early the next week Ackland called at Arden's store and after little more than an introduction to the clerk, offered him the partnership.

The two went on to prosper in Ackland's business. And, after a few months, the older man suggested that his partner move out of his humble quarters, in keeping with the firm's image. "Our position in trade requires that you, as one of the partners, should assume a more imposing style of housekeeping," he explained. "This looks as if we were not doing a profitable business; and I don't care to have such an impression abroad." Ackland, a bachelor, offered to move into part of the house he had in mind—the one Pinkerton, now married, had just vacated for more sumptuous quarters—and pay for his room and board. The Loftons gladly agreed. Apparently ostentation was permissible if the resources underlying it were honestly acquired.

During the next six years, which Arthur passes over rapidly, the house of Ackland and Lofton steadily but safely extended its operations. Arthur tells us that the Loftons "remained in the comfortable dwelling where we last saw them, and were not in the least troubled with ambitious thoughts." They are not to stay there much longer, however. Once again urged by his partner, and now by Mr. Arden as well, they are going to move into an elegant house just built by Pinkerton. Lofton's old friend had finally come to ruin. Having overextended himself, having gone into debt to pay in part for the expensive tastes of his profligate wife, his business became insolvent. The heavily mortgaged mansion he had just built was to be sold at public auction. Lofton's decision to buy it was not shaken by his wife's misgivings.

Near the book's end, the Lofton's were comfortably settled in their new house when they received their first news of Pinkerton since his failure. Through her Irish maid, Bridget, Ellen Lofton learned that the Pinkertons had not left the city as she had thought. They were living quietly in the house where Ellen had first met Lofton and where the two had spent their early married years. Apparently the neighborhood had changed considerably—it now seemed to be an Irish slum—as had the haughtiness of the Pinkertons. When Bridget had met Mrs. Pinkerton in the street, she had humbled herself to ask if Bridget could get her some work from the clothing stores. The

Loftons, on visiting the couple (who formerly had not deigned to visit them in the same house), found both changed. "We abused our position and our privileges," admitted Mrs. Pinkerton. "I say it in sorrow and humility." Lofton, convinced of their sincerity, offered his old friend a clerkship in one of his insurance companies. Pinkerton gratefully accepted and told Lofton

> I have been a very foolish, reckless man . . . as you know but too well. How often have I thought of your steady, safe upward movement—slow, cautious but sure. I used to call it dull plodding, and I deemed you lacking in enterprise and true business capacity. Ah! if I had but taken a few lessons from your example. (p. 355).

At his new job Pinkerton had changed so much that people hardly knew him. "Some scarcely recognizing the subdued, low spoken, humbled man, as he quietly discharged the duties of his office," said Arthur approvingly. Ten years later, while the Lofton's condition had changed little, Pinkerton had again achieved some degree of success—though on a far more modest scale. Arthur assures us at the book's close that he was in no danger of falling into former errors. As with Howard Franklin in *Retiring from Business*, "the lessons of the past are graven too deeply on his memory" (p. 358).

In *Sparing to Spend*, Arthur's thinking about the process of social mobility is most clearly revealed. Most significant is the pattern of Lofton's rise. It is not just that he is rewarded for his cautiousness and nonaggressiveness. He is also rewarded primarily for qualities unrelated to any specific professional competence. For his first advance it is enough that he is considered "worthy" by his employer; we are never told in what this worth consists. We never know what it is that actually recommends him, except that it can be summed up in a vague phrase like the notion of character. His second promotion, to a partnership with Ackland, was even farther removed from any connection with his business abilities. Except for the confirming interview at Arden's, where little was disclosed but the fact that, as Ackland already knew, he is not extravagant, Ackland's mind was already made up the night before when he heard the story of Ellen Lofton's refusal to wear her friend's jewelry. Lofton's elevation, when it did come about, was both swift—Ackland, like Scoville's Colonel Vanderhoost, could read the signs of good character as if they were stamped on their possessor for any observer to see—and fortuitous. Ackland, struck by Ellen's unfamiliarity, happened to ask who she was. Only then was he told the story about the jewelry.

The message for the attentive young man seemed to be that advancement, proceeding as it did through selection by an established member of the community, was so incalculable a process that any trifle of behavior or appearance might prove decisive. One never knew what particular item might bring him to the attention of those in a position to select him for his overall qualities. Therefore, every detail that drew attention to his inward nature had to be carefully attended to. It was not enough that one was virtuous; it was necessary that knowledge of that virtue be accessible to others. Strength of character and the inward virtue to which these details pointed would ultimately be responsible for a young man's selection by keeping him *available* for selection. After years of clerking he would still be present on the mercantile scene, unlike others who, succumbing to temptation, literally disappeared. In this negative sense a young man could influence his own career. He could be sure *not* to take any action that might remove him from the arena where selection took place. One did not seize opportunity; one was seized by it. Arthur, in advocating "safe upward movement," denied the risk and adventurousness that were the essence of the entrepreneurial spirit of the period. By his haste to reach quick wealth, Pinkerton made an unfortunate business alliance that doomed him both to obscurity—the Loftons lost all track of him—and to the certainty that when available openings appeared, they would be missed. Had Lofton not "discovered" him, he and his wife would have been fated—it was already happening—to a life of illness, poverty, and humiliation. For all the apparent concern about the special education necessary to make a "thorough merchant," advancement seemed to depend only on the unshakable possession of virtue and character. An employer had to satisfy himself about this alone; with it as a foundation he could be sure that the operational skills his employee needed would be easily learned. This explains why Arthur, in *Making Haste to Be Rich,* need not tell us anything about the rise of Morris Jordan. There is no point in telling us. Besides developing character, there is nothing a young man does to advance himself, and therefore no lesson is to be learned by knowing the details of Jordan's rise. Only the development of character can be copied, not the stages of advancement. Advancement itself is fortuitous and beyond one's own doing. Providing such details, whether in novels or advice-books, was simply irrelevant; the circumstances of each man's rise were completely individual and nonrepeatable.

There were other restrictions on mobility as well. Arthur, in arguing that property was "placed within reach of nearly all who have the ability, as well as the desire to struggle for its attainment"[19] was being either disingenuous or blind to the implications of the plots of his novels. Like the writings of the political economists of his day, Arthur's books seemed to express a kind of wages-fund theory of advancement. There was not unlimited room at the top. Just as the increase of one person's wages beyond a certain point meant that someone else would lose part of what he had earned, so after a point, the advancement of young men to higher and higher positions in society meant a corresponding decline for others. Every change in Lofton's fortunes, for example, was tied to and interlocked with Pinkerton's. Lofton's first move was to a house just vacated by Pinkerton; his next was to a house that Pinkerton would have occupied had he not failed. But he did fail, not just for ethical reasons, but to make room for the upwardly rising Lofton. The place vacated by the Loftons was then assumed by the Pinkertons. They moved into the house where the Loftons first lived and Mrs. Pinkerton was about to assume Ellen's old job as a seamstress. More than moral irony was intended; the economy of social replacement suggests a conception of what society was like or of what Arthur wished it was like. It suggests that Arthur entertained a model of society more static than he wanted to admit. Unless a reprobate held each position to which the virtuous aspired, success might not be open to all who were theoretically deserving. Rather than count on this unlikely occurrence, it was better to work hard, be satisfied with a competence, and wait. There

19. T. S. Arthur, *Riches Have Wings; or, A Tale for the Rich and Poor* (New York, 1847), pp. 5-6.

was no point in demanding, even as Lofton demanded, a reward for one's honest labor that the system could not deliver.[20]

This view of society is reinforced by another characteristic of Arthur's novels. In none of them is anyone of good social standing, even if of poor virtue, truly declassed. The actual range of social movement, interestingly, is much the same as in Jane Austen's novels. No one really moves up or down, either into or out of the class to which he is born.[21] Pinkerton is rescued from the humility of living in an Irish slum by Lofton himself. He must live in reduced circumstances thereafter, but we can assume that his life style will be genteel—he is not doomed to join the lower classes. It is significant that the maid, Bridget, on disclosing Mrs. Pinkerton's intention to take in sewing, remarks to Mrs. Lofton, "I felt choked right up, at that. It did seem so hard. Poor, dear Lady! She wasn't brought up to do the likes o' that."[22] Work that she herself performed uncomplainingly seemed to bring on an outburst of emotion when she considered Mrs. Pinkerton doing it. She was aware that class lines were not eas-

20. The correspondence between these views and those of mid-nineteenth-century economists is noteworthy. The possibility that economic progress (the force responsible for social mobility) might slow to a halt was not far from the mind of Francis Wayland, author of the period's most popular text in political economy. "If the increase of capital be less rapid than that of the human race," he noted before making the point that neither capitalists nor workers could willfully alter the laws regulating salaries, "the price of wages will fall, distress in the working classes will ensue, and they must either emigrate or starve." Francis Wayland, *The Elements of Political Economy* (Boston, 1849), p. 303. See also Joseph Dorfman's discussion of Wayland in *The Economic Mind in American Civilization, 1606-1865,* 2 (New York, 1946): 763-64. European economists were equally distressed. John Stuart Mill, for example, spoke of "the impossibility of ultimately a-voiding the stationary state—this irresistible necessity that the stream of human industry should finally spread itself out into an apparently stagnant sea." Mill is quoted in Paul M. Sweezy, *The Theory of Capitalist Development* (New York, 1942), p. 92. Economic assumptions like these reinforced the fears of those alarmed by the mobility and striving they witnessed. In the nonexpanding economy they pictured, ambitious, aggressive activity would be especially disruptive of social order.

21. When there is movement, it is generally to permit someone denied his rightful station to regain it. See T. S. Arthur, *Lizzie Glenn: or, the Trials of a Seamstress* (Philadelphia, 1859).

22. Arthur, *Sparing to Spend,* p. 347.

ily crossed in either direction.

In other novels of Arthur's, the same process seems to be operating. The evil protagonists in *Riches Have Wings* (1847), *Two Merchants* (1843), and *Debtor and Creditor* (1852) all undergo character changes and return to the mercantile community in a reduced but similar style of living. One merchant ruined predictably by excessive love of money in *Riches Have Wings* is forced after his failure to move into a smaller house. His daughter describes one place they consider renting as follows:

> There is a snug little parlor below, beautifully papered, and having in it a pure white marble mantle; and quite a large chamber over that, and another of the same size in the third story. Back of these is a kitchen, dining room, and good sized chamber, with bath-house and dressing room. Take it all in all, it is exactly what we want—perfectly new, neat, genteel and comfortable; and very cheap.[22]

Because there is no room for the servant to sleep—though his daughters maintained that they could do without servants, the merchant refused to allow them to do "menial household drudgery"—another house with extra space but otherwise (we are led to assume) the same is ultimately selected. The family will still live in smaller and cheaper quarters, but quarters that are consistent with their earlier genteel existence. Their life-style is reduced in scale but not in kind. In the new house, family life—the hallmark of middle-class existence—is even enhanced. "As they shrunk closer together in this smaller house," wrote Arthur, "they felt more sensibly the warmth of each other's hearts."[24] Later, the servant is dismissed and extra articles of furniture are sold. But the change is made only to eliminate crowding; it is again a reduction in scale only.

This accommodation underscores Arthur's appeal. The reduction in scale that Townsend undertook made him more virtuous: the "heavenly riches" he received from realizing that worldly goods are unimportant were an essential benefit of his change in residence. He

23. Arthur, *Riches Have Wings,* p. 140.
24. *Ibid.,* p. 147.

could remain content without the income he formerly depended upon because his inner worth and his family's harmony were enhanced in the process. In a society that worried far more than it liked to admit about the possibility that economic growth might stagnate,[25] that it might not be able to expand fast enough to provide mercantile places for all those who sought them, the message that the virtuous life and a reduced standard of living were connected was especially welcome. The message both justified the order that established merchants craved—a faltering economy would be stabilized if fewer demands, either for better paying jobs or more goods, were made on it—and cushioned the failure of the unsuccessful. Arthur's message assured the latter that their humiliation would not include being declassed and allowed them to believe that their slowed temporal progress was productive of spiritual, if not monetary, currency.

25. See chapter 5 on Edward N. Tailer, Jr., and fn. 20, above.

8

Phrenology

For merchants who sorely needed to know which young men would be good risks both socially and commercially and for virtuous young men who wanted to advance themselves while staying within acceptable limits of behavior, the picture of social mobility drawn in advice-literature could be discouraging. Virtue, they were told, would be rewarded. But they also saw that it might be neglected or overlooked. Writers themselves occasionally saw how little comfort could be taken from their urgings that honesty and trust would assure both groups of fair dealing. Charles Butler, in his *American Gentlemen,* at one point admitted that in the "turbulent and confused" social scene, words and actions were often misunderstood and misrepresented. Innocence and integrity, no matter how earnestly manifested, could not possibly avoid being tarnished by the reproach, abuse, contempt, and hatred of others that were certain to "hurt our interest and impede our advancement in life."[1] His hope that things might be otherwise was, as we have seen,[2] indeed feeble. Honest

1. Charles Butler, *The American Gentleman* (Philadelphia, 1836), p. 22.
2. See chapter 6.

men, men who expected to be dealt with fairly, could do nothing but take their chances:

> It is then the part of wisdom first to do everything in our power to preserve an irreproachable character and then to let our happiness depend chiefly on the approbation of our own conscience and on the advancement of our interest in a world where liars shall not be believed and where slanderers shall receive countenance from none.[3]

If liars were believed, if slanderers received attention there was apparently little the man of character could do to safeguard either his interests or the course of his advancement.

An apprentice system based on personal contact and recommendation had worked to the benefit of both merchants and young men when demand for entry into the commercial profession was relatively low. But when the enormous growth of the young population and the beginnings of industralization forced a redistribution of the labor force, the credentials of applicants were no longer easy to determine or verify. Merchants found that they did not have a reliable way to sift the young men they could use from those who hoped to use them. And, as the numbers looking for jobs in cities increased, young men found that they had no way of distinguishing themselves from others or of knowing whether they were wasting valuable time in the vocation they had chosen. Fortunately there were men, promoting a new science of man, who offered some hope to both groups.

In the 1840s and 1850s, the science of phrenology underwent an enormous growth in popularity. Americans had been familiar with the writings of Franz Joseph Gall, the originator of the theory of brain structure, and his popularizers, Johann Gasper Spurzheim and George Combe, since the early 1820s.[4] But it was not until two brothers, Orson and Lorenzo Fowler, started lecturing and giving character readings, it was not until the two New Englanders turned phrenology into an applied science, that it began to draw a public beyond the narrow following of doctors, professors, and ministers

---

3. Butler *The American Gentleman*, p. 23.
4. John D. Davies, *Phrenology, Fad and Science: A Nineteenth Century Crusade* (New Haven, Conn., 1955), p. 14.

that had first attended it. Audiences were less interested in the principles of the science—that the mind was composed of distinct faculties, each located in different parts of the brain, and that the development of these mental faculties corresponded to the size and shape of the cranium (pp. 4-5)—than with its practical application to aspects of their daily life and health at home and at work (p. 33). Orson Fowler was himself amazed at the reception traveling phrenologists often received, especially in rural districts. "They flock in from their mountains and their valleys for ten miles in all directions," he said, "and fill up any meeting-house that can be found. It is really astonishing, how much, not of interest merely, but of real enthusiasm, they evince, especially in reference to the bearings and applications of phrenology" (p. 35).

Urban crowds were just as enthusiastic. A recent historian of the movement tells us that a course of forty lectures in Boston in 1843 sometimes had audiences up to 3,000; in Philadelphia a group of 500 attended a series of twenty lectures; and in New York, Clinton Hall, also the home of the Mercantile Library Association, had a number of rooms devoted solely to phrenology and its associated sciences (p. 34). It was also in New York that the Fowlers decided to set up shop. Their offices on Nassau Street functioned as a lecture booking service, publishing house, phrenological museum, and character reading salon (p. 47). Character readings were also done by mail if a daguerreotype was enclosed with the four dollar fee. In addition to the services provided to the public directly, Fowlers and Wells (as the firm was called when S. R. Wells, who had joined the brothers as an assistant in 1843, was taken in as a partner after marrying Orson and Lorenzo's sister Charlotte) also became the wholesale suppliers of a growing body of itinerant phrenologists eager to profit from the spreading popularity of the science. Books, charts, and exhibits were all in demand. A set of forty plaster casts of such distinguished figures as John Quincy Adams, Sir Walter Scott, and Aaron Burr cost twenty-five dollars. Human skulls "imported from the battlefield" were five to ten dollars apiece and those of "rare races" over thirty dollars. A model of the brain with removable parts cost more than twenty dollars. For those more interested in the allied science of physiology, Fowlers and Wells supplied life-size anatomical drawings and wired skeletons. Galvanic machines, breast pumps, and other mechanical devices eventually led to the establishment of a special patent division to assist inventors (p. 52). The firm also began—for a price, of course—training courses for those who wanted to enter the profession and spread the benefits of phrenology (and not incidentally the further need for the services of Fowlers and Wells).

The most lucrative aspect of the firm was probably its publishing business. It distributed an almost never-ending spate of books and periodicals written or edited by other phrenologists and those in allied fields. The firm, according to Davies, claimed to have the largest mail-order business of any in New York City (p. 56).

To give their efforts a greater veneer of respectability, they also began the *American Phrenological Journal,* aping the older and respectable Edinburgh publication. But imitation of the venerable Scottish quarterly was as unsuccessful as had been earlier American efforts to discuss the science "philosophically"—it was well received, but did not sell. The Fowlers quickly got the point; the *Journal* soon began advertising itself as a unique publication exhibiting phrenology "in its *application* to home education, domestic government, self-culture, selection of pursuits, choice of apprentices, clerks, partners in business or companions for life."[5] By the mid-1850s, its circulation had grown to a phenomenal 50,000; power presses and electrotype were introduced to speed production and commercial advertisers clamored for space.[6] In the hands of the Fowlers, phrenology was changed from an experimental science to a product for sale; it passed from an esoteric behaviorism to big business.

From the efforts Fowlers and Wells made to cultivate it, from the amount of attention directed to it, it appears that the partners considered the mercantile community to offer great possibilities as a market for phrenological wares. As the capsule catalogue of concerns printed in the *Journal* (see above) indicated, Fowlers and Wells were well aware that the interest of their fellow merchants might be considerable. It is possible that the firm's own experience as part of the

5. *American Phrenological Journal* (hereafter cited as *APJ*) 27 (1858): iv. (italics mine)
6. Davies, *Phrenology.* p. 58. Like most of the above material taken from Davies's book, no documentation is provided.

mercantile community, as well as its strategic geographic position in its midst on Nassau Street, made it particularly sensitive to the needs of both merchant and clerk. On numerous occasions, for example, articles appeared in the *Journal* denouncing the "vagabonds" and "counterfeits" who, pretending to be representatives of the Fowlers, their students, or the brothers themselves, travelled "from bar-room to bar-room, into shops and stores, and offer[ed] their *(professional)* services for a shilling."[7] The "cheats" invariably wore calico shirts or other "fantastic" articles, looked seedy and dirty with breath smelling of bad rum and "execrable" tobacco. After warning its readers to beware of the thieves and quacks impersonating members of a dignified calling, the *Journal* added: "who would not wonder if there were no betrayers of truth and traitors to professional character in every other profession and science, including Phrenology with the rest" (25 [1857]: 59).

Such worries about preserving the integrity of their own profession may have led them to perceive the desperation and helplessness that accompanied the efforts of other merchants who tried to maintain the purity and high quality of their ranks. Whatever the source of their intelligence, Fowlers and Wells were quick to see the role they might play in helping their fellow businessmen. Articles and letters extolling the phrenologists' value to businessmen filled the pages of the *APJ*.

One letter from an Ohio businessman told how he had benefited from his study of phrenology. Phrenology, he said, gave him the ability "to judge the character of those who were in my employment, and with those I had occasion to transact business." After being examined by one of the Fowlers, he bought Orson Fowler's *Phrenology,* Combe's *Lectures,* and other related books, and tutored himself so that he "could estimate character by the form of the head."

> Thus, for instance, I would encourage and cultivate a modest young man, whom I perceived possessed talent and high moral worth, and qualify him as soon as possible to take a responsible place in my business. One whose head indicated arrogance and

7. *APJ* 25 (1857): 59.

ambition beyond his talent and integrity—who had a desire for responsible positions beyond what he was able to fill, I could understand him, and refrain from giving him power that he could not
wield honestly or well. (25 [1857]: 28)

Here was an answer to problems that often seemed insoluble.

Phrenology promised a method that converted the vagaries of
selection into an exact science. In the uncertain times of the 1840s
and 1850s, selection was often made on the basis of judgments of
appearance and the trappings of good breeding; valuable personnel
were secured largely by chance. But now, with the use of calipers
and compass, chance could be eliminated. Relations between young
men and their employers could be regularized and, in the sense that
each would have some clearer idea of what to expect from the other,
institutionalized. Phrenology, by compartmentalizing the mind and
developing a technique for its examination, made its intricacies and
idiosyncrasies accessible. By dividing the mind into units corresponding to a specific physical area, phrenology partially eroded the notion
that it was inscrutable or impossible to understand. Although men
like the Ohioan may once have felt largely helpless in choosing a
young employee, realizing there was little they could determine about
how he would perform on the job, they now had a guide to performance. Young men who were previously considered unknown quan-
tities, often irrational and uncontrollable, would now become predictable. With the use of phrenology, some idea of what to expect from
them could be obtained.[8] Merchants now had, as the Fowlers put it
in the *APJ*, an infallible method for discovering whom to trust and
whom not to. In addition, they said, those who manage men "now
had a way of approaching them," they now had a way to determine
"what chords to touch and the like" (9 [1847]: 19). Not only, it appeared, did phrenology guide merchants to the talented and worthy,
it also proposed to give them the key to their manipulation once on
the job.

If the promises seemed excessive, there is evidence that merchants

8. Writers of advice-books quickly incorporated the new advances into
their later works. William A. Alcott, in his *Familiar Letters to Young Men*
(Buffalo, 1849), included chapters on the advantages of phrenology and its
related sciences, physiology and physiognomy.

looked to phrenology with equally excessive expectations. Help wanted ads began appearing in the daily press requiring applicants to obtain phrenological examinations. One placed by Jonathan Leonard in the New York *Weekly Tribune* and reprinted in the *APJ* for 1847 was particularly revealing of the uses to which merchants may have hoped to put phrenology. The advertisement read:

> Apprentice Wanted.—Four able bodied young men, from sixteen to eighteen years of age, can have an opportunity, by applying to the subscriber, of learning the art of Moulding in Sand for Iron Castings. They will be required to serve four years and board in my own family. They must pass a phrenological examination, and be approved by Messrs. Fowler and Wells, 131 Nassau Street, N.Y. My business is believed to be a healthy one. They will be allowed the privilege of access to a good library, the reading of at least six weekly newspapers and attendance on a lyceum. The common wages for journeymen in this business are from $16 to $35 per month. (9 [1847]: 263)[9]

The elements combined in the advertisement are noteworthy. Leonard sought apprentices, but apparently was unable to secure them from young men he knew or from young men his former assistants knew. That he turned to phrenology as insurance of reliability suggests he had no other way to determine the capability of possible applicants. And that he sought four young men at once suggests that the apprentice system's internal springs of perpetuation and preparation of talent were drying up. This is also indicated by Leonard's need to assure applicants that they will not be shackled to the limited resources of education in his family, as was formerly the case for an apprentice. He recognized that young men accepting a position with him might harbor plans of their own for self-improvement and that it was wise to give the impression that such ambitions would be indulged, not denied. The method by which Leonard sought apprentices implied that the system was changing from the institution it once had been; certainly it no longer performed all the functions once attributed to it. Phrenology, which offered the hope of filling the vacuum left by a declining apprenticeship system, was being called upon to recruit tal-

---

9. For another example see Davies, *Phrenology,* p. 50.

ent for the system its very existence testified was less and less viable.

Besides his acknowledgment that phrenology provided a method to resolve the dilemma of selecting new employees, the Ohio businessman who had written to the Fowlers in 1855 also revealed what was to him and possibly to many others an equally significant use of phrenology. The phrenological examination he had undergone on first landing in New York as an immigrant years ago, he reported, set him on the course he was to follow for the rest of his life. He was advised to go into "some large business, because I had mechanical talent and practical intellect, combined with force of character and perseverance, which would enable me to succeed." This the writer did, and reported his success to his benefactors. "I owe my success to Phrenology," he wrote them. "It has assured me that I might hope for success on a large scale, and it has ever been at my elbow, as it were, whispering, 'go forward, be not afraid' " (25 [1857]: 23).

The problems merchants faced were complemented by the ones confronting aspiring clerks. If merchants sought devices to determine which of the many applicants for positions were worthy risks likely to repay their investment in time and money, so young men seeking those positions were eager for some indication that, if patient and hardworking in a chosen field, they could expect to be repaid with recognition and promotion. And just as the merchant took scant comfort in the reliability of the available agencies to help him find the assistants he sought, so young men could hardly rest assured that they would be noticed and rewarded for the fine qualities they hoped would advance them. Indeed, what if the trade they hoped to succeed in did not even value the qualities they possessed? The time and effort one might be wasting could be incalculable. Yet, until phrenology held out hope there seemed to be no way of discovering what one's abilities were and hence no way of knowing whether one was engaged in the work for which he was fitted. Once, when the day was occupied with long hours of routine farm work, young men had little need to reflect about such matters. But later, freed from that work and seeking urban situations, such information became crucial. Time was critical. Knowledge that prevented false starts gave a man an edge in competition with countless others.

That the problem was real enough is suggested not only by the novels picturing young men stumbling blindly from one vocation to another, wasting away years at tasks they later realized they were never fitted for,[10] but also by the biographies of many prominent men whose lives were marked by indecision about their capabilities and who later rejected years of training to assume careers they earlier never conceived as possible alternatives.[11]

Given such uncertainty, there is little wonder that the "science" of phrenology, which offered a panacea for just these problems, did a great business. Its attraction for one uncertain Southerner is revealed by the letter accompanying his renewal of the *Journal*. The writer acknowledged his debt to the science. "Until I was about twenty-two years old," he confessed, "I had never been able to decide what I should follow as a business." It was about this time that he began reading Combe and Fowler. His greatest inclination, he said, was to follow the watch trade. But his father was poor and could not spare him from home to learn the trade, so he studied at home when he could without instruction. When phrenology found him, he "was at a loss to know what to do."

> Not knowing myself, I did not know what I *could* do. I thought it impossible for me to follow the jeweler's trade without having served an apprenticeship. But this science told me I *could* succeed. So I concentrated all my attention to this one thing, for which I had a natural inclination from a boy, and now, at the age of thirty-two, I flatter myself there are few better workmen in the state where I reside. (25 [1857]: 57)

The Fowlers, recognizing how widespread were the problems faced by their correspondent, made a direct effort to provide the practical guidance they felt men in similar straits needed. Along with the publication of expository works on the nature of the science, they also brought out the *New Illustrated Self-Instructor in Phrenology and Physiology*. The volume was primarily a manual by which one

10. See, for example, Bayard Taylor, *John Godfrey's Fortunes* (New York, 1865).
11. See, for example, accounts of the lives of college president Mark Hopkins, journalist Matthew Hale Smith, and educator Thomas Gallaudet.

could determine his own character and abilities. A chart in the beginning of the book listed the faculties into which the recognizable areas of the cranium were divided. To the right of the list were columns in which the intensity or power of each faculty could be indicated. As the head of a subject was examined (this the authors hoped would most often be done by a trained phrenologist, though the book also provided detailed rules for finding the organs and faculties of the brain if one wished to do without an examiner), a mark was placed in the column denoting the relative strength of each faculty—seven gradations ranging from very large to very small—of the subject. In each column a number referred to the page in the text for a discussion of the faculty. Each discussion consisted of seven sections, corresponding to the seven columns on the chart. After being examined, a subject would have simply to turn to the page relating to the marking on the chart and read a description of what was supposed to be his own character. If the reader was unsure of the application of the data, two further columns gave additional directions. These were marked "restrain" and "cultivate," and like the other seven categories included numbers referring to the text, where one was told how either to impede or develop the particular trait involved. If they desired still further information, readers could refer to the discussions in some of the Fowlers' other books, to which most passages were keyed.[12]

Most readers, the Fowlers assumed, would not go beyond the *Self-Instructor*. By consulting the book, in addition to a professional examination, they could find the intelligence they sought. Where they had once been uncertain of their natures, unsure about what they might be suited for, now they could be confident. Their characters and abilities, revealed in neat, printed paragraphs in plain black and white, would no longer be obscure to them.

The book was clearly intended to provide vocational guidance. Its last page, in summary form, presented a phrenological description of the qualities needed "for particular pursuits" such as law, medicine, church, journalism, mechanics, and commerce. At the end of the

12. O. S. and L. N. Fowler, *New Illustrated Self-Instructor in Phrenology and Physiology*. . . (New York, 1859), viii, 167-75.

paragraph describing the faculties necessary for mercantile success, the Fowlers added a characteristic plug: "Why is *one* young man a better salesman than another?" Phrenology, responded the brothers, "answers this by pointing out the constitutional differences and showing who is, and who is not, adapted to mercantile life. You had better consult it."[13]

Edgar A. Hopkins was one of the many young men who decided to do just that. On December 18, 1868, he went to see Orson Fowler for a cranial reading.[14] Fowler, in the comments he wrote on the front end paper of the *Self-Instructor* he presented to Hopkins, tried to be honest with the young man. Hopkins was shy and sensitive to criticism. He had better choose a wife who complimented him often, he wrote, since he could not stand to be scolded. Hopkins also lacked hope and self-confidence. He had little faith that he could succeed. Apparently referring to the business career Hopkins hoped to undertake, Fowler warned that he was far too kind and trusting; to succeed he would have to be more selfish. But all in all, Fowler felt that Hopkins would reach his goal. He did possess sound judgment, great powers of observation, and good common sense. With those qualities to lead him, he would do well. Fowler told Hopkins that he would succeed as a coal dealer.

The chart the phrenologist marked for Hopkins supported this conclusion. Edgar had his faults, of course. He was too benevolent, too dependent on praise, too self-deprecating and lacking in self-respect. But on the whole the diagnosis was encouraging. Hopkins possessed "large" acquisitiveness, exactly the right amount for business success. It meant that he was one of those who "buy closely and make the most of everything; are industrious, economical, and vigorously employ all means to accumulate property."[15] He was also found to have large faculties of cautiousness and constructiveness; the two,

13. *Ibid.*, p. 176.

14. There is no way of knowing where the meeting took place. Fowler's comments about the examination are found in the copy of the *Self-Instructor*, now in the possession of Stephen Nissenbaum, Department of History, University of Massachusetts, that he presented to Hopkins.

15. Fowler and Fowler, *Self-Instructor*, p. 101. "Very large" acquisitiveness made a man too eager for riches and thereby doomed him to illicit dealing and eventual ruin. *Idem*, p. 100.

when found with acquisitiveness, denoted a provident nature and one "incline[d] to make money by engaging in some mechanical branch of business."[16] The coal business ought to suit perfectly.

Interestingly, in each of the three cases we have examined—the Ohio businessman, the southern jeweler, and Edgar Hopkins—the exposure to phrenology did not seem to reveal resources and talents largely unknown to the young men. Rather, its value appeared to be the impetus it provided in getting them started. The thrust of the enthusiasm of the first two about the science, for example, was not vocational guidance but a more general encouragement to go ahead and do what the young men already wanted to. The Ohioan took away from his encounter with phrenology the assurance to "go forward," the Southerner the confidence that he could succeed at the trade he was "naturally inclined" to follow, and Hopkins the confirmation that his character did actually fit him for the work he had already chosen.

It may have been this kind of "go forward" exhortation that has led historians to see phrenology as a doctrine of "extreme individualism [which] emphasized each man's individual endowment and set of capacities, by means of which he could lift himself . . . ."[17] But the kind of encouragement to personal advancement that phrenologists like Fowlers and Wells urged had important qualifications. It was not the encouragement to reach as high and as far as one thought possible, as the mythology of the self-made man decreed. That myth implied a view of social change and mobility far too reckless of established practices to gain a recommendation from the Fowlers and their brother-in-law, Samuel R. Wells. They had not positive and certain identification of character, become an agent presiding over the demise of a long-established system of chaneling. They did not realize that the popularity phrenology was experiencing was due in large part to the inability of an apprenticeship system to deal with the demographic changes of the 1840s and 1850s. Time and again, in the *Journal* and advice-books they wrote for young men, they exhibited a seeming unawareness of the social changes re-

16. *Ibid.,* p. 101.
17. Davies, *Phrenology,* p. 166.

sponsible for their success. In their reasons for exhorting young men to stay in the country and not seek employment in New York, for example, they showed a curious gap in understanding. They knew, apparently, that the pressure for city positions was greater than ever before, yet the knowledge had no effect on the picture of employment practices they often drew. In one article they revealed an awareness of the "vast amount of work [as] there is to in a city, and such an innumerable number of situations to be filled." At the same time, they pictured hiring practices as if they occurred in a static environment. One reason strangers would find it difficult to find employment, the writer of the article said, was that a vacant place in a shop or store would be filled by acquaintances of those already working there. Employers preferred someone who came endorsed by "an old hand," and it was not uncommon, he noted, for a person leaving a situation to recommend a successor—"some relative, perhaps, or old friend." Only rarely did an employer take on strangers without some employee or relative recommending the applicant. In this way better security for faithful service and more trustworthy conduct was obtained. Even though "the stranger might be the better man, as to talent, and worth, and faithfulness," the writer added, "still the employer, anxious to supply the want of help as soon as may be, prefers to take the one well recommended, *rather than to consume time and patience to try experiments with the man from the country.*"[18]

Supposedly—by the Fowlers' own advertisement—this was just what phrenology enabled merchants to avoid. Where men lacked a personal recommendation, a cranial reading could provide a knowledge of the applicant's character quickly and surely. Yet, in the above passage, the author spoke as if no such aid to businessmen was available or necessary: merchants could simply do what they had always done. They could select replacements from those recommended to them by family or friends. Phrenology had no role in the picture; the author had re-created a time when the utility of the new science did not yet exist.

Fowlers and Wells saw phrenology as a tool adding precision to social arrangements that already functioned adequately. Phrenology was seen as a contributor to existing social stability, not a way of undermining it. Attention to its principles would provide the merchant and aspiring clerk with greater certainty that those seeking one another would meet instead of passing one another by. Although its literature often had a tone of self-improvement about it which gave the impression of encouraging young men to tackle their futures unabashedly the actual thrust of the phrenology purveyed by the firm was more conservative. Phrenology was a way to create order, not add to chaos. Although it offered hope to young men by holding out the prospect that satisfying work could be found the hope was related to the interests of the business community. Men of trade recognized that a contented work force—one settled in a broad spectrum of situations for which its members were individually suited—would be far more stable than one that persisted in reaching for positions having the most prestige or pecuniary benefits.

Men who pursued the prestigious jobs would soon become discouraged and present an easy target for temptation. They would seize upon dishonest schemes that promised quick rewards. If men, said one article in the *APJ* extolling the value of phrenology in selecting a trade, "could be provided with the means of procuring a respectable and honest livelihood, nearly all of the crimes which disgrace humanity would be done away" (25 [1857]: 2). The writer's advice for safeguarding the young—it is certain he also had in mind safeguarding their elders from the ravages of a discouraged, discontent youth—was plain. "Give your son," he said to his older readers, "a business or trade by which he can gain an honorable maintenance and a respectable place in society" (25 [1857]: 2). As with other writers of the time, it was assumed that young men possessed-—whether it was a better situation or, as in this case, a useful trade—what they were *given,* not what they earned by themselves through diligent and ambitious but, potentially disorganizing striving.[19] Young men were advised to be cautious and accepting of their lot as long as it provided them with an income—if modest, at least "tolerably sure." "Be not in haste," advised Samuel Wells, echoing much of the material appearing at this time in Hunt's *Merchants Magazine,* "to leave these honorable and comparatively easy positions [in the mechanic's shop or on the farm] for the harassing and brain-

18. *APJ* 25 (1857): 34. (italics mine)

wearing cares of the trader, for the chance . . . of a more rapid accumulation.''[20] Wells went on to deny that his remarks were meant to discourage the young man who felt that his "true mission" was to be a merchant (expressions like "irristibly [sic] impelled," "called by an authority [one] is not at liberty to question" appear in his discussion of the professions)[21] as if that alone were in the criterion for certain knowledge of one's vocation. He did not, after all, want to discourage those who *actually were* suited for mercantile pursuits, just those who were more likely suited for something else. It was better to spread the competition out.

Nelson Sizer, the long-time manager of Fowlers and Wells's Philadelphia office, in a book of vocational guidance published in 1876, was convinced that all men could have "enough to do of the right kind of business . . . if every man were in his true sphere."[22] He was dismayed that nearly every young man "with any pretention to talent" thought he had to be a lawyer, doctor, minister, or merchant. Most men were actually better adapted to farming or mechanical trades (p. 12). And since all men were not possessed of the same culture or ability, many had to

> be content to perform the simpler operations of labor, and happy is the man who has the wisdom and honestly [sic] to accept cheerfully the pursuit in which he can serve the world and himself best, whether it be according to the world's estimate, high or low. To be a good and faithful doer and to secure success in the doing should be the great object of effort. (p. 16)[23]

Phrenology, then, recommended itself to businessmen and other community leaders (most notably educators) for reasons other than its promise to end the worry about finding qualified successors. It provided them with comforting assurances that the social system would

19. See "The Quiet Man's Philosophy," *APJ*, 26 (1857): 67; also Nelson Sizer. *Choice of Pursuits: or, What to Do, and Why, Describing Seventy-Five Trades and Professions, and the Talents and Temperaments Required for Each* . . . (New York, 1876), pp. 121-24.

20. [Samuel Roberts Wells], *How to do Business: A Pocket Manual of Practical Affairs and Guide to Success in Life* . . . (New York, 1857), p. 55.

21. *Ibid.*, p. 83.

22. Sizer, *Choice of Pursuits*, p. 12.

23. See also pp. 41-42.

not be endangered, and at the same time allowed those eager to rise to believe that the system was expanding to accommodate them. Phrenology became popular because it could be all things to all people. It seemed to promise success to the aspiring, and did so without jeopardizing established social relations. It offered movement to those seeking it, but assured those jealous of their positions that such movement need not be upward. Mobility would be horizontal not vertical; young men could hope to move to positions in which they would be happier and men in power could champion their cause without feeling threatened. Advancement would occur in the same way that other writers pictured it. But now the process of selection would be less casual and fortuitous. Phrenologists like Wells and the Fowlers did not see phrenology as a system to replace other, however meager, devices to channel young men into careers proper to their talents; they saw it as another device adding precision and exactitude to the sources of guidance, like advice-books, that already existed.

Indeed, they often made their own contributions to this literature. Samuel Wells, for example, wrote as complete a guide to etiquette as was written in the period.[24] Its content, being in general similar to other books of its kind, is less significant than its appearance. Phrenology was not seen, as we might reasonably expect if we accepted the interpretation of its equalitarian and individualistic tendencies, as making the study of etiquette and rules of social conduct superfluous. Why need one in possession of knowledge about his own talents and future course of activity bother about his outward appearance? Why, at any rate, did those advocating the benefits of phrenological science bother about it? The reason is that phrenology did not stand alone in the selection process. Its study was only one among a number of items, such as conduct and experience, that determined social movement. While the recognition of personal ability and talent was important, it alone, as we have seen, did not determine mobility. Community leaders selected additions to their ranks not only by professional competence, but by such marks of class consciousness as good breeding and manners.

24. [Samuel Roberts Wells], *How to Behave: A Pocket Manual of Republican Etiquette, and Guide to Correct Personal Habits* . . . (New York, 1857).

9

The Founding of the YMCA

The number of merchants who put their trust in phrenology was probably small. But the extent of their interest is less important than their willingness to explore phrenology's merits in the first place. It is this that suggests their feeling of helplessness in confronting changes in their society. It suggests their feeling that available alternative solutions had dangerously narrowed. Fowlers and Wells sensed this desperation and directed, with some success, energy and time to demonstrate phrenology's value to them. The phrenologists knew that merchants were generally conservative and slow-going about developments that entailed innovations in social practice. Yet somehow they recognized an underlying despair that would provoke men of trade to respond to their promotional efforts. Some merchants, they must have realized, would be willing to examine any claim that offered the hope of restoring regularity to the world they inhabited.

The expansion of the trading community required merchants to secure employees for a variety of purposes. A minority, as before, were needed to occupy positions of trust and responsibility. But far greater numbers now had to be recruited for more limited tasks. The older generation recognized that they faced a dual problem. They had to recruit and control a growing workforce and refurbish a business and social elite. In both areas they felt that young men of virtue and high character were essential. The pressure of numbers had overloaded a traditional system of selection characterized by extended contact and personal knowledge. Once, merchants felt, judgments about new employees could be made slowly and carefully—talent could be evaluated, conduct supervised, and values nurtured. But with the appearance of inexperienced and unannounced newcomers like William Hoffman and the restlessness of well-connected youths like Edward Tailer, this system faltered. As we have seen, community leaders drew little comfort from their survey of the institutional forces that could stabilize the social arrangements that seemed threatened.

These forces were both too fragile and too amorphous to present clear directives for the organization of social conduct. This feeling of formlessness led community leaders to hope that young men would develop what David Riesman has called a "psychological gyroscope"[1]—an internal regulator that might govern conduct by internalizing patterns once determined by external, social agencies.

Yet, this faith that young men could forge the internal strength they would need resulted more from a paucity of alternatives than from a confidence in individual will. When they could, community leaders continued to believe that an institutional remedy offered the best chance of success. Connecting an individual to social organizations with fixed standards of personal behavior offered far greater assurances of social control than did relying on an individual's powers of self-discipline alone. If the density of society's organizational network could be increased, the influence of one or more of its components had a greater likelihood of touching the unattached young men in cities who had broken free from the controls of home, church, and local community. The mid-nineteenth century can be called an individualistic and anti-institutional age, not because faith in

1. See David Riesman with Nathan Glazer and Reuel Denney, *The Lonely Crowd*. abridged paperback ed. (New Haven, 1961), p. 45.

individual will was high, but because a changing society with momentarily loosened institutional controls could not conceive any other object or force to provide the glue of social cohesion. It talked about "society [as] the shadow of the single men behind it,"[2] not because, as writers like Stanley Elkins and George Frederickson have said, it opposed or ignored institutional ties,[3] but because it could not imagine any other force holding society together.

Merchants and other community leaders, instead of turning their backs on institutional agencies for regulating conduct, sought such agencies whenever possible. When it appeared that an established institution like the Mercantile Library Association or a new one of traditional design like the Young Men's Christian Association—both founded by young men for reasons narrower than those for which it was valued by an older generation—might serve their purposes, they eagerly offered their help. An examination of the founding of the YMCA will help clarify the social motivations underlying this support.

George H. Petrie, a twenty-four-year-old merchant from New York, was enthusiastic about what he had seen in London during an extended stay abroad in 1851. Like many in England for business and vacation purposes, he spent a good deal of time at the Great Exhibition then taking place in that Victorian marvel of prefabrication, the Crystal Palace. On display were the triumphs of the age presented by more than thirteen thousand exhibitors.[4] What most impressed Petrie was his discovery of a small but growing organization originally founded to "improve the spiritual condition of young men

2. The quotation is from a letter from George William Curtis to Brook Farmer John S. Dwight, dated March 3, 1844. Curtis, here arguing that Brook Farm could not provide the meaning Dwight seeks for his life, was himself deeply attracted to the community. The letter is excerpted in Henry W. Sams, ed., *Autobiography of Brook Farm* (Englewood Cliffs, N.J., 1958), pp. 106-8. Other evidence of Curtis's attraction can be found in Edith Roelker Curtis, *A Season in Utopia: The Story of Brook Farm* (New York, 1971).

3. See Stanley Elkins, *Slavery* (Chicago, 1959), pp. 33, 147-57 and George Frederickson, *The Inner Civil War* (New York, 1965), chapter 1.

4. Asa Briggs, *Victorian People* (Chicago, 1955), p. 38.

engaged in the drapery and other trades."[5] Having casually accepted one of the invitational tracts being distributed at the exposition by the organization—it called itself the London Young Men's Christian Association—young Petrie was soon making repeated visits to its modest headquarters. Here in rooms made over into library, lounge, and classroom he attended Bible classes and devotional meetings and became acquainted with founder George Williams and his associates. By the time the young importer returned home in the fall of 1851, he was so steeped in the evangelical purposes of the British organization that he was determined to begin a similar one in New York.

Soon after he took up his duties at the offices of the family firm, J. and A. Petrie, of 27 William Street, he called a meeting at his home. At this first gathering only three listeners—Oliver P. Woodford, Milton St. John, and H. K. Bull—showed up. All of them, like Petrie, were young merchants whose fathers had established businesses.[6] During a number of subsequent meetings, however, the support of a few respected pastors and merchants was enlisted and the young men were able to set up a tentative organization. Again meeting at Petrie's home, an expanded group on April 21, 1852, adopted a resolution stating that those assembled thought it desirable to form an association "consisting of members of evangelical churches in this city to be called the New York Young Men's Christian Association." Cordially, they invited other young men to join them.[7]

By the end of May, preparations—including the drawing up of a proposed constitution—for a large public gathering were completed. On the twenty—eighth, in the lecture room of the Mercer Street Pres-

5. Terry Donoghue, *An Event on Mercer Street: A Brief History of the Young Men's Christian Association of the City of New York* ([New York]: Privately Printed, [1953]), p. 16.

6. See New York City business directories for the year 1851 and Cleveland E. Dodge, *"Y.M.C.A."—A Century at New York (1852-1952): An Address at New York* (New York, 1953), p. 10.

7. See George H. Petrie, "Narrative of Incidents in the Formation of the N.Y. Y.M.C.A.," undated copy of manuscript in YMCA Historical Library, New York City; Donoghue, *Event on Mercer Street,* p. 21, and New York Young Men's Christian Association, *First Annual Report* (New York, 1853), p. 18.

byterian Church, the Reverend Isaac Ferris, one of the group's early supporters, welcomed an assembly of three hundred young men.[8]

Ferris's enthusiasm for the new organization was evident. He fully subscribed to its religious purposes; that it might "win to evangelical truth, some youth of high tone, whose training has been in error" seemed to him the highest of goals. He felt, in fact, that groups of young men might be more likely than professional clergymen to succeed at this evangelical task. Where the churches may have failed (he was not yet ready to admit that the question was completely closed), "you will be able," he told his audience, "to meet [the nonprofessor's] sense of a social want; you will be his natural counsellors when he may become the subject of religious impressions, and his guide when the pastor may know nothing of his case."[9] By providing congenial rooms where young men unwilling to discuss their religious inclinations with staid, somber men a generation or more distant from them might congregate, the members of the YMCA would be in a unique position to recognize and turn such sentiments into evanelical directions when they appeared.[10]

In addition to this religious work, the atmosphere of security and familiarity such an organization of young men created could more easily break down the isolation and disorientation that confronted a young provincial on his arrival in the city. New York, as Ferris saw it, was a "moral maelstrom" for even the most virtuous. It was a

8. Donoghue, *Event on Mercer Street*, p. 21.

9. Isaac Ferris, *Address Delivered at a Meeting of Young Men, Convened for the Formation of the Young Men's Christian Association, Held in the Lecture Room of the Mercer-St. Presbyterian Church, May 28, 1852*. (New York, 1852).

10. As an example of how this process might work, Ferris recounted a story about a boy brought to Christ through an association with young Christians. The story was obviously all the more appealing as the youth was claimed from the ranks of Catholicism. With evident delight, Ferris told about an Irish boy brought by the New York Bishop to the Harper Brothers to learn the publishing trade. "He was placed in the midst of lads of his own age—some older, some younger—some piously inclined, others mere church goers. Frequent, earnest and continued was their interchange of views in their daily association." The result was more than Ferris hoped for. "That Irish lad," he said, "became a Christian young man—at length a minister of the Gospel." *Ibid.*, p. 11.

cold, cheerless place, one where a young man thrown "perhaps into the midst of scenes foreign to all [his] former tastes and feelings" soon found himself led "now by ridicule, and then by persuasion to all manner of indulgences, step by step until the end is reached." When this occurred, reclamation was virtually impossible. The youth would literally vanish into the bowels of the city's netherworld and would never be heard from again (p. 12). In contrast, Ferris recalled the time when a boy who came to the city to be a clerk or an apprentice found his home among his employer's own family. His home and place of work were the same. "But now," Ferris lamented, "it is sadly altered. The lad is left on the wide world—he is surrounded by the mercenary and the callous, and is happy if he escapes unhurt" (p. 12). What the youth needed and what the Association now provided was a group of young Christians who could "rallye around the young stranger and save him from the snares of this wicked city" (p. 11). Many who would otherwise become lost, swallowed by the temptations of the card and billiard player, could find attachments that, in effect, "shall keep up the home feeling associated in his mind with the sweetest recollections." The YMCA became a sanctuary or surrogate family, shielding newcomers from the evils of a hostile environment that might retard their progress toward Christ.

Positively, the institution brought men closer to religion by acting as an incubator of Christian character. Thrown together at YMCA gatherings, each man, felt Ferris, would emulate the example of the others in a way certain to encourage "new energy and animation." Presumably, as each man tried to outdo the next in piety, intelligence and virtue, "character," the catch-all term for the personal qualities most valued in the early nineteenth century, would be developed and strengthened (p. 8).

At the close of his address, Ferris offered a final suggestion to the newcomer eager for friendship. Although he had hailed the YMCA because it seemed able to do what the churches were failing to do—evangelize unattached youth heading for the nation's urban centers—he did not expect the minister's role as guardian of the community's virtue to be bypassed altogether. He therefore hoped that each young man upon arrival in the city would make his way to any New York pastor, introduce himself, and present a letter from the local minister back home. "I can answer for all my brethren—we should love to be the friend of such" (p. 12). The letter from a recognized figure of authority would apparently assure the pastor that the boy had roots and an identity someplace; with this knowledge he was willing to invite him to put down roots in a new community. These ties might not hold, but at least the community would know who had been making the attempt—it would have a way of keeping track of the numbers that had arrived and the length of time they had remained.

After the Reverend sat down, 173 of the 300 young men present joined the new organization.[11]

One month later, a final constitution was formally adopted. In a preface to the document's first public presentation, the founders announced that their efforts were a direct response to spiritual and evangelical needs existing in the larger cities. Their objects, they said, were

> no less than the prevention of the ruin, physical and spiritual, which overtakes so large a portion of the multitude of young men constantly arriving in our city destitute of christian associates and connections, also the promotion of christian fellowship among our members and, to sum up all, the formation of the whole body of our young men into a vast harmonious band, working with all their might in the cause of Christ.[12]

Active membership, the constitution stipulated, was open to any man under forty years old who was a member in good standing of an evangelical church. Any man of "good moral character" not a church member could become an associate member, entitled to the same privileges except voting and eligibility for office.

The duties of members were explicitly defined. They called upon members to seek out newcomers moving into their neighborhoods and, by helping them find suitable living quarters and employment,

11. Donoghue, *Event on Mercer Street,* p. 21
12. *Constitution of the New-York Young Men's Christian Association. Organized June, 1852.* (New York, 1852), p. 7.

by introducing them to other members and the privileges of the YMCA, by encouraging them to worship at nearby churches, "endeavor to bring them under moral and religious influences." Native New Yorkers were not to be overlooked, either; members were told to "labor to induce *all* suitable young men of their acquaintance" to join the Association. The YMCA, in short, enjoined members to uncover all young men unattached to or unaffiliated with their organization. Whether or not they were lonely, whether or not they were in danger of falling into sin, they were encouraged to renounce their solitary lives by, as the by-laws put it, "connecting themselves" with an organization dedicated to the "promotion of evangelical religion among the young men of this city." (p. 10).

To aid in attracting young men, the constitution established committees to develop library facilities, to select and furnish accommodations for the Association, to distribute information to the public, and to provide a series of lectures and sermons. Another committee significantly was to compile statistics that "shall endeavor to ascertain how many young men are communicants in the several evangelical churches in this city; the number of young men who attend divine worship, and also the number of those who desecrate the Sabbath. . . ." (pp. 16-17). Evangelical recruitment apparently required a careful survey of the field. If possible communicants were not to go overlooked or neglected, a rigorous accounting would have to be kept.

During the summer of 1852, with a formal constitution written and officers secured, the Association's first headquarters were established in two rooms on the third floor of the Stuyvesant Institute (the name of the old New York City Lyceum) at 659 Broadway. At a cost of about nine hundred dollars, the rooms were furnished to serve as both a reading room and meeting place.[13] On September 20 the YMCA opened its doors to the public. Daniel Lord, a prominent member of the New York Bar, was invited to make the dedicatory address.

In much the same fashion as Ferris, Lord detailed what he took to

13. Donoghue, *Event on Mercer Street,* p. 23.

be the objects of the Association. He too was concerned about "how the stranger youth [is] armed to meet [New York's] attack of worldly excitement and sensual allurements." Unlike life in his home town, where he was a familiar figure, unlike "that little circle where he had a character, well known, well prized by him who had it, and by those who knew it," a young man now found everyone absorbed in his own interests with little time to bother with a newcomer.

This was especially true of his place of business. Soon after the young arrival finds a position, said Lord, he discovers "that the business of his employer is too weighty, his time too much absorbed in it, for him to bestow care or sympathy on his humble assistant." While the employer had "the deepest pecuniary interest" in the youth's morals and social habits, he had no other choice but to trust that meager wages would moderate his clerk's life style and that police vigilance and fear of criminal prosecution would discipline his principles.[14]

His social relations were equally isolating. Instead of a community of neighbors, the young man found himself in a cold and friendless environment. "You may die in your boarding house," said Lord, "and scarcely any but your landlady, the doctor, and perhaps the parson know it." In such a setting Lord hoped young men of the YMCA would assure the newcomer that there were people concerned about him. By meeting and surrounding him with social kindness, he could be drawn "to the elevating and preserving influence of Christian society and intercourse." In doing so, Association members would be serving their society well; they would be "giv[ing] a direction to your age, by infusing principles into those who will soon control its movements" (p. 9).

Lord next turned to the young arrival's search for employment and leisure-time activities. YMCA members, said Lord, could help him find both. He had few doubts about the "inestimable value [of] the services of thsoe who, themselves young, and alive to the opportunities presented to their own class. . .will seek to discover where

14. Daniel Lord, *Address Delivered on the Opening of the Rooms of the New York Young Men's Christian Association, September 20, 1852* (New York, 1852), p. 9.

these [men] may be most useful, to whom they will be appreciated'' (p. 10). Regarding hours of relaxation, Lord assumed that members would quickly open their homes to the newcomer. Again like Ferris, Lord could remember the time when employers provided homes for their young apprentices within their own families. But today, with the progress of society, the expansion of commerce, and the luxury of increased wealth, the old system, Lord felt, had changed. Fortunately there was a way that some of its amenities could still be retained. "May not this want of a home," he asked, "be, in a degree at least, supplied? Can you not, finding your associate worthy of your friendship, take him into the society, the families of your friends?'' Lord granted that the provincial background of the country boy, especially the "awkwardness of unpolished manners,'' might occasion some embarrassing moments. But he hoped that this would not deter his listeners from extending the offer of hospitality to them. Manners were a kind of veneer that could be acquired quickly enough anyway. That the rural emigrant was a "hard-thinking, earnest, serious man'' was surely more important than his "ungainly person and inelegant attire'' (p. 13).

In his speech, Lord covered all the topics expected of a speaker addressing such a gathering. He conjured up the images of lonely young men becoming the innocent prey of those who would exploit them. He talked about the obligations members had to prevent this disaster and bring the young man to Christ. And, near the end of the address, he spent an acceptable amount of time talking about the YMCA's contribution to religion. But, although he touched all the conventional bases of YMCA speech-making, Lord's emphases had shifted from those of the Association's founders.

His discussion of the organization's religious motives, for example, sounded as if they came from one schooled by Norman Vincent Peale rather than Charles Grandison Finney. Instead of mentioning the enthusiastic Christianity at the heart of the YMCA, Lord spoke only of the "ethical'' functions and "practical'' value of religion. In everyday life religion would remind us of the "steady purpose of doing good'' (p. 14). The YMCA's real importance was secular. Lord continually subordinated the religious aims of the Association to social aims of his own. Young Woodford, the first president of the organization, felt that the "ultimate object [of the YMCA] is the *conversion of young men*," and that members "must contend" against those Christians who, as "the agents of a potentate who claims to sit paramount over priests and kings," were "enemies of the best interest of mankind."[15] Lord, on the other hand, congratulated the organization for presenting "a catholic religion. . .disregarding. . .distinctions of sect" and for refraining from turning religious teaching "into a proselyting experiment." Worried about efforts that would stir up debate and possibly alienate prospective members, Lord hoped that lecturers invited by the Association would confine themselves to "such common principles of faith as admit of a common effort" (p. 15).

Characteristically, whenever Lord talked about values and energies that had religious sources, he emphasized their social consequences. The YMCA was important, not because it would train up a body of evangelical Christians, but because it would train up a body of men prepared to take over the temporal affairs of the older generation of community leaders. As he saw it, the success of the YMCA

> will raise up a body of active and influential men on the verge of middle life who shall be the supporters of every public enterprise and the creators of many a private charity. The principles of temperance, moderation, industry, and perseverance which flow from religion acted out, seldom fail to lead to influence and fortune. . . . You can turn your eyes to not a few among our merchants and men of wealth who are examples of social virtue and religion. Soon will you stand in their places and from you will be expected those devotions of wealth to purposes of usefullness [*sic*] which make wealth an honor. (p. 17)

Lord was convinced that no matter how many philanthropic enterprises his listeners might undertake in their later years, nothing would provide greater satisfaction "than the remembrance of some stranger youth whom you took by the hand in this association, for whom you found a home, for whom you found employment. . ." (p. 17). To Lord, the YMCA appeared to be a prime source of po-

15. *First Annual Report of the New York Young Men's Christian Association, presented May 16, 1853.* . .(New York, 1853), pp. 11-12.

tential leaders; it was an avenue by which new talent could be conducted to positions of social as well as commercial responsibility.
Unaware, perhaps, how great were the demands he was making of
the YMCA, Lord looked to the Association for the community's future men of influence and fortune''; he looked to it for men who
would occupy high social position as well as high pecuniary standing. For him, as for a man like Joseph Scoville, the two categories
were still complementary. It is possible that Lord as much as
Scoville hoped that the relationship could endure. The YMCA, he
may have felt, attracting as it did young men of good character, was
just the kind of institution that could help secure men with the qualifications to maintain that relationship intact. As the rhetoric
throughout Lord's speech suggested, young men would be chosen by
those who already possessed the combined qualities of influence and
fortune. Young men would be "taken by the hand" after, as he said
earlier in his talk, they had been "found worthy." What the young
man himself had to do to win favor found no place in his discussion.
His language—strewn as it is with passive verbs—suggests that a
young man need not play a very active role in his own advancement.
After he was "found worthy," others would find him a place to live
and work. *They* would introduce him into society; taken "by the
hand," he would be led along a path whose end was prominence in
the community.

Lord was not alone in his preoccupation with finding worthy
young men to replace present community leaders. There was little
doubt among many of the men invited to address the early meetings
of the YMCA that the young had to be prepared for weighty responsibilities.

To the Reverend George W. Bethune, speaking at the second annual gathering, the situation was especially grave. Young men were
coming to New York, he said, when the role they would be forced to
play would require qualities generally reserved for special periods of
crisis only. In looking out at his audience—sixteen hundred men
faced him—he was heartened, however. He took satisfaction in the
great power they represented. Yet, in conceptualizing this force, he
saw not an assembly of well-behaved young men attached to prosperous countinghouses, but a unit far more disciplined and control-

led. What Bethune envisioned as he surveyed the audience before him was an elite guard of trained soldiers ready to defend the city against forces massing to besiege it.

> Imagine [he said] that the enemy were threatening our city-—imagine our present peace and domestic concord broken; that we were liable to invasion from an intestine foe; that in another day we might be sure that an attack would be made upon our dwellings and upon our homes; and we were to see so many hundred young men, calm, resolute, armed, drilled and prepared for the fight, taking their position as the guardians of the city and the guardians of the people.[16]

Interestingly, Bethune placed the danger inside the community; it was an "intestine foe" that alarmed him. Somehow an enemy already *within* the gates would *invade* the city. To him, the formulation was perhaps a logical way to deny the unwanted a legitimate place within the community. In order to be an invader, the enemy, no matter how much he actually formed part of the community, had to be external to it. He never named the enemy directly, but it seemed that Bethune was thinking about "the foreign elements" in New York. It was to prevent them from gaining control of New York that he urged support of the nascent YMCA. He clearly saw the Association as a counter-force to this other group made up of "the lowest order of people." Bethune assumed that those among the group seated before him would take their places among the "middling classes," that minority of the population who, by virtue of their moral and intellectual force, would inherit the rule of New York City (p. 42). Bethune could take no easy comfort from this, however. Too many of them were woefully unprepared for the obligations they would have to assume.

Unlike the practice of the Ancients, who carefully taught their young "a patient submission to age" (especially the Romans, whose young men were purposely kept back), young men in the United States were pushed forward and forced to enter business and other

16. George W. Bethune, "Address," *Second Annual Report of the New York Young Men's Christian Association, Presented May 15, 1854. . .* (New York, 1854), p. 40.

forms of employment before they were barely out of grade school (p. 41).[17] Their education, cut short by premature entry into the adult world, was only partially complete. Though many could read and write, he continued, most had no experience in that "which forms the mind for thought, which gives to the mind habits of labor, patience, determination, and a firm, deliberate resolution" (p. 41). In short, they lacked the kind of education necessary for the building of character. Yet, without character they would certainly be unequal to the dangers and temptations ahead of them.

Young men lacked this kind of education, explained the minister, because "they come here too young to have gained it. They enter their activities and become too busy to gain it. They are forced to become men before they cease to be boys" (p. 41). The only hope he saw was for young men to educate themselves after settling in the city. Unfortunately, the pressures of city life made it unlikely that self-education would be undertaken by the new arrivals. If they were going to have it, they had to be *"encouraged* to self-education"; they needed *"faithful interference"* in their behalf. But like Ferris, Bethune sensed a lack of communication between generations. Older counselors of his own age group would be viewed, he felt, only with suspicion. Bethune quoted an imaginary "ardent, rosy" youth who refused both to "listen to the prosy garrulity of age" and to be brought "into an assemblage of people with whom I have no sympathy and who have no sympathy with me" (p. 41; italics mine). The YMCA, on the other hand, whose members were young men themselves, might succeed in "leading" others away from disaster.

After covering the usual ground about the YMCA's offering a sanctuary from the temptations of vice, Bethune enlarged upon the danger of neglecting the education of the city's newcomers. As we have seen, Bethune assumed that it was a minority of middle-class citizens who ruled New York City. Now he pointed to the racial character of the governing group. Despite the large proportion of immigrant population (Bethune was quick to acknowledge, however, that "all our fahters were once strangers in this land"), the minister,

17. Bethune's passive phrasing—"before he is brought into active life"—is, like Lord's, significant. He saw men as entering active life not on their own initiative but at the behest of others.

to loud applause, marveled at the beauty of seeing how," after all this infusion of foreign admixture, the Anglo-Saxon element pervade[s] and rules it." To be sure, he admitted, the majority of the young men coming to New York were American born. But, he added in characteristic tones, if they were not, "there is so much the more reason that they should be taken up and adopted, for then if they are not American born, they may be American bred and sir, those men will rule your city." In his enthusiasm, Bethune now addressed a different audience. His remarks now seemed directed to the men in whose possession present control reposed. "When our heads are in the grave," he asked them, "how shall [the young men] rule this city?" (p. 43).

By way of providing an answer, Bethune reminded them of the liberality with which they continued, since its founding in 1820, to support the Mercantile Library Association. Surely, he suggested, the YMCA was equally, if not more deserving of assistance. The MLA supplied the young clerk with book knowledge only. The YMCA, offering many of the same privileges (such as a library and facilities for social meetings), had the added advantage of resting on a religious base. The message, he hoped, was clear. Book knowledge "will not save the young man from the natural corruption of his human heart" or "enable him to overcome the world, to resist the Devil, to triumph over his own flesh." To do all this, religion was essential. He was certain that community leaders would therefore do "for the religion of their young men what they would not hesitate to do for their intellectual advantage." Trying to show that men who believed in the Gospel surely ought to assist the YMCA, he continued:

Do men believe that the redemption of the soul is precious? Do men believe that it is through the grace of the spirit of God alone that the heart is purified and the world is overcome? Do men believe that honesty, and truth, and fidelity and honor and temperance and purity, and all those graces which adorn life, and make a man trustworthy, come from the religion of Christ? (p. 44)

If they did, as he knew the elder merchants in his audience must, he expected their support. To make sure, he had chosen the words quoted above carefully. From questions dealing abstractly with the conditions for grace and the redemption of souls, he had quickly switched to one about earthly virtue and character. Specificially, he singled out the virtues conferred by the religious life that would most appeal to listeners who were the employers of sometime disobedient workers. If Christianity could make his clerks and mechanics honest, faithful, temperate, pure, and trustworthy, what merchant could turn his back on an institution dedicated to bringing young men to Christ? As if his point was not sufficiently clear, Bethune answered this last question by baldly appealing to the self-interest of his more prominent listeners:

> If they do so believe I ask them for their own sakes, *as a principle of insurance to their interests, to make their servants—I mean those who are in their employ*—faithful to their duty, and to secure to them [the employers] larger gains in greater certainty. I ask them for these reasons to help these young men who are endeavoring to bring their youthful brothers unto God. (p. 44; italics mine)

Then, to return to his starting point and also to conclude on a more appropriate note, he added, "I ask them to do this for higher reasons. I ask them to do this in the name of Him who saves their souls" (p. 44).

The New York YMCA, like its counterparts in other cities, continued to grow in the years following 1854, the year Bethune addressed its members. Their numbers increased and their activities and services expanded. Unlike earlier young men's organizations, short-lived creations of the revivals of the 1820s and 1830s, the Associations of the 1850s were soon numerous and wealthy enough to start a viable national apparatus.[18] Partially responsible for the longevity of the later organizations was the base of support they were able to maintain among community leaders. Businessmen, especially, continued to support the YMCA, even after revival fervor dissipated itself. Many of them looked to the YMCA, just as they looked to institutions like the MLA, for reasons different from its founders'. Except possibly for the address of the Reverend Ferris, whose remarks

18. See C. Howard Hopkins, *History of the YMCA in North America* (New York, 1951).

themselves had significant social implications, the evangelical emphases of the young founders were shunted aside by such community elders as Lord and Bethune.[19] These men were concerned with a variety of problems occasioned by the growing numbers of young arrivals. They were concerned with accommodating these young men, with finding places for them in the social and occupational structure of a rapidly changing city. To those who looked to the YMCA, membership in the higher echelons of the mercantile community was the vehicle for social leadership. In a nonhereditary society where occupational station largely determined social position, recruitment for the former, as the speeches of Lord and Bethune indicate, suggested induction into the latter. Joseph Scoville's insistence, in chapter 4, that merchants comprised a hereditary class may have been another way of expressing the hope that the mercantile profession would continue, as it had done in the past—especially in New York—to serve as the agent for supplying a social aristocracy. If access to mercantile positions could not be controlled, then it might also become impossible to control access to the social positions associated with them. Given this concern, they were as much interested in the character of the inductee—though this was important for purely business reasons as well—as in his commercial prowess.

Yet, the way some of the speakers formulated the role of the YMCA as the link between virtue and power suggests that they recognized that the argument had other uses. Connecting membership in the YMCA with the development of "the principles of temperance, moderation, industry, and perseverance which flow from religion acted out [and which] seldom fail to lead to influence and fortune,"[20] supporters like Lord and Bethune were speaking not only to members who, because of their special qualities, found themselves being groomed for elite roles. They were also speaking at the same time to others who were to remain more modestly situated as clerks, bookkeepers, and salesmen. The Christian virtues that were said to

19. At the second anniversary gathering, for example, all four speakers, three of whom were ministers, dealt with the Association exclusively as a social institution.
20. See above.

mediate the way to prominence were also those that would create a patient and tractable force of reliable employees.

Bethune especially, as we have seen, seems to have realized how a special version of the view of the YMCA as a training ground for an elite could be turned into an argument for support of the YMCA as the training ground for a docile workforce. At the start of his speech he is addressing his young listeners as potential social leaders. The kind of leadership is never precisely defined, but he seems to be talking about roles of political domination. By the end of his remarks, however, he is addressing the older generation as employers. He moves easily from one concern to the other, without feeling any need to separate the different appeals he is making. The YMCA could mediate the movement of newcomers into both areas. To maximize the value of the Association, it was perhaps better to ignore the distinctions between the two areas than to make them explicit. The clerk was offered the belief that his efforts, if wisely directed, would lead to prominence; the merchants were offered the hope that those efforts, if properly channeled, would pose little threat to their control. The precise way in which organizations like the YMCA would serve the interests of both groups can be seen by looking at two other organizational responses to urban newcomers, the Association for the Suppression of Gambling and the Mercantile Library Association.

10

Institutions: Reservoirs of Character

In May 1850, a group of New Yorkers met to consider ways to eliminate gambling in the city. They believed that no existing organization could hope to combat the problem and planned to establish one that could. The group's first act was to commission J. H. Green to undertake a systematic study of the evil in New York. His efforts disclosed "the gigantic proportions of the abomination" and convinced the men who commissioned him of the "breadth and depth of that social ruin of which [that] business is naturally the parent." They concluded that only an organization thorough and efficient enough to "detect the hidden workings of darkness" would be able to "check the farther progress of this widespread evil and reclaim the domain it had already subjugated."[1] In addition to the businessmen

1. *First Annual Report of the New York Association for the Suppression of Gambling* (New York, 1851), p. 21. (Hereafter referred to as *ASG.*)

and ministers who agreed to serve on the board of directors of the new organization were Albert Gilbert, the clerk of the Board of Education, Joseph M'Keon, Superintendent of Common Schools, Horace Greeley, editor of the New York *Tribune,* and, interestingly, Lorenzo Fowler, the phrenologist.

A year later on May 9, 1851, the New York Association for the Suppression of Gambling held its first anniversary meeting. The annual report provides a fairly complete account of the proceedings. The Reverend Isaac Ferris, who was one of the first to address the fledgling YMCA organization, delivered the opening prayer. Then the president, R. N. Havens, rose to address the gathering. Havens, an elderly merchant, had retired as early as 1815 from active commercial life. Since then, he had been a trustee of the Public School Society, the New York Sunday School Union, and the Mariner's Church. He had also served for more than twenty-five years as an elder in Gardiner Spring's Brick Presbyterian Church. In 1825 he chartered the Howard Insurance Company and, as its president until his death in 1854 at the age of eighty-one, directed its growth. Scoville, reviewing his career, commented that no merchant in the city was more highly esteemed.[2]

In his address Havens wasted no time in levity or in celebration of the group's first anniversary. He had something troubling to discuss; he was not simply discharging an obligation as the presiding officer of the Association's annual festivities. The meeting was not self-congratulatory. Instead of being welcomed for the public service it hoped to perform, the ASG had been attacked and reviled. Havens, in his speech, sought to defend the young organization against its detractors and offered in effect a justification for its existence. The Association, like other benevolent groups, had been founded, he said, to influence the course of public morals. This could be done, as was generally agreed, by "influencing or controlling" the actions and habits of individuals.[3]

Most of the Association's proposed efforts to bring about the

2. Walter Barrett, clerk [Joseph A. Scoville], *The Old Merchants of New York,* 5 vols. (New York, 1885), 1: 361.

3. *ASG,* p. 5.

changes they deemed essential caused little stir. The distribution of
tracts, lobbying for desired legislation, and the delivery of lectures
aroused no objection—probably, Havens imagined, because "their
very common[n]ess preclude[s] the possibility of arousing any indignation against us on this account" (p. 5).

But there was one aspect of the organization—an aspect that radi-
cally separated the ASG from the other benevolent organizations, it
seemed, at least in form, so closely to resemble—that did provoke
comment, or rather "abuse" as Havens put it. This was the "Intelligence Agency," which turned out to be the heart of the organization. Its functions, he felt, were sensible and reasonable; he was surprised that it had been stigmatized as a "spy-system." The Agency
proposed to keep a register, compiled by a paid staff member, of all
the gambling-houses, lottery, and policy offices in New York. In addition, the organization intended, through its agent, to record "in a
private book" the names of those who habitually frequented gambling halls. The people involved would be warned against continuing
their immoral conduct. But if they failed to respond, if "admonition
. . . failed to reclaim them," the Association would then turn over
whatever information it had to subscribers (the rates for subscription
were graded according to ability to pay) who requested information
about those in their employ or confidence (p. 6). According to Havens, critics attacked the proposal as an infringement on individual
rights. They charged that the Association could be deceived in its observations; that without knowing all the mitigating and justifying circumstances of an action it could easily misinterpret what its inves-
tigators thought they saw. The resulting damage to individual reputations could be irreparable. Each man's responsibility was to his
Maker Alone, they argued; it was only He who had the right to judge
His creatures' actions (pp. 6-7).

Havens, however, was convinced that the "scrutiny and observation" of the character and conduct of others was both morally and
tactically correct. He was indignant at those who criticized him. The
public, in approving the other work of the Association, agreed that
there were moral evils that needed correction. But as soon as the
group actually went ahead and placed "the finger on the sore spot of
personal deportment, there is an extraordinary nervousness

awakened'' (p. 5). All men, he continued, were inseparably linked to those around them by their respective interests; evil-doing therefore sent its baleful influence through the whole indeterminable line of human relations and dependencies. The man who gambled away what was even legally his own could inflict ruin and misery on others "to indefinite extent." The only way to safeguard one's interests against the follies or wrongs of others, said the old merchant, was by "constant watch and observation of their character as manifested in their conduct." This was, in fact, exactly what each man, as best he could, was doing all the time. Instinctively and rightly, men were quick to blame those who, by neglecting this duty, caused themselves, their families, or their creditors to be injured. How many times, he asked, had his listeners heard reproaches such as, "Why did you give your confidence to this man? Proper inquiry would have convinced you of his unworthiness." The rightness of this question seemed self-evident and Havens assumed that it demonstrated the rightness of his general position:

> And now it is to be observed, that what is right in itself, a man may employ another to do for him—excepting matters, of mere personal duty. So, also, what is right for each of a hundred to do personally (with the same exception), it is right for the hundred to do collectively. If this line of argument be correct, where is the wrong in any body of men associating for their mutual protection against the frauds, the vices or the crimes of others? And it is for this very thing that human governments, with the divine sanction are instituted. (p. 8)

Since it was right for men to make inquiries about those working for them in positions of trust, it was right for them to delegate others to make the same inquiries. And if this was correct, it was also permissible for men having reason to make the same kind of inquiries to band together to have the inquiries made for all of them. The Association was simply the institutionalization of a process that the individual merchant performed automatically about each of his employees. Shouldn't the creation of one body to perform activities they all undertook singly have been greeted more enthusiastically? Didn't the Association's proposal simply represent a logical extension of a generally accepted premise? To both questions the answer, as Havens saw it, appeared to be yes; the indifferent response from the mercantile community bewildered him.

The structure of the institution in itself hardly seemed pernicious. The process he appeared to be defining amounted to nothing more than the decision of individual men to join into a single unit; the institution was nothing more than the sum of these individuals. Governments, he hinted, were exactly the same kind of creations, except on a larger scale. Furthermore, the aims to which the group was pledged were ones that had been reiterated time and again in the press and in the popular literature of the day. They were hardly controversial. The organization's chief aim was to save the young from temptation. "We shall stand *sentinels* at the threshold," said Havens, "to prevent if we can the entrance of the 'simple ones' into the haunts of the destroyer" (p. 9; italics mine). Using a common illustration, Havens pictured the Association as a watchtower or lighthouse near a dangerous reef. As had C. L. Brace in his example, he pictured a situation that presented no guidelines or landmarks to alert the young "navigator" to an approaching vessel. Hidden rocks and the absence of warning breakers made the passage treacherous. Cautious as well as bold young men often made a shipwreck of everything—property, friends, character, body, and soul—that they possessed (p. 9). Was it wrong for the keepers of the lighthouse to caution those who had entrusted valued interests to young men, steering, in their infatuation, once and again, directly for these rocks? In doing so, Havens said that the Association was acting in a way in which mankind, by its universal consent and practice, recognized as right. It would never consider promoting a good end by improper means. Havens, still unable to fathom the Association's poor public reception, asked in conclusion, "Who will say that this act of friendliness both toward the deluded mariner and his friends, *the voice of the monitor* shall be silenced, and his light shall be turned into darkness?" (p. 9; italics mine).

After Havens finished, Lucien Burleigh, the corresponding secretary, read the annual report. In general it sounded much like Havens's address (it is possible that Havens as president of the ASG had authored it), although it lacked some of his defensiveness. The report tried to account for the growth of vice. It noted the wealth, numbers, power, and moral recklessness of the enemy, the "frigid indifference" of the city authorities to enforce existing statutes, and the opposition of the city delegation in the State Assembly to additional laws (pp. 22-27). Clearly, the founders may have reasoned (further convincing them of the need for organization), it was not worth while to look to political "representatives" for help.

The bulk of the report focused even more sharply than had Haven's address on the young men who often fell prey to the gambler's come-on. The population of the nation's larger villages was rapidly increasing, the report noted, and the influx consisted largely of young men unsettled in character, inexperienced, and too often lacking in "just parental instruction and a deep-toned sense of obligation."

> Removed from the eye and conscious watch-care and restraint of parents, friends, and neighbors they easily yield to the pressure of circumstances, associate themselves on their natural affinities of temper and depravity, pass beyond those restraints which once reached and held them, and soon become, according to their degree of tact and cunning, deceivers or dupes. (p. 28)

In the city it appeared that a young man was subject to none of the inhibiting forces or restraining influences that surrounded him at home. The result could be seen in the many incidents of theft from trusting employers that the Association had compiled. One example, taken from a memo sent to the Massachusetts legislature by an organization of Boston merchants, the Association for the Suppression of Lottery and other Gambling, reveals some of the thinking behind the founding of New York's ASG. A "young" clerk (aged thirty-five) of established integrity and ability had for the last ten years been bookkeeper and treasurer of an important local firm. He had recently been discovered to "have sunk under the temptation of gaming by lotteries." The life of the young man, the report emphasized, had been irreproachable. But in just eight months he had consumed all his own means and nearly $18,000 of his employer's money (p. 31). The emphasis on the past irreproachability of the man's character, the concern "that young men of untarnished public reputation are in the habit of visiting gambling houses" (p. 34), is central to understanding the Association's purposes. In addition to the desire to save young men from the "dark depths of a gambler's ruin," merchants, as we have seen, were looking for a solution to a problem that involves them directly as employers and as the guardians of a social elite. They needed trustworthy subordinates and tractable replacements. Yet, as their emphasis on examples like the above demonstrates, the feeling that they were without even remotely reliable ways of determining who was deserving of confidence was disturbing. Equally upsetting was the fear that one might be completely fooled by external appearance. There might be no indication at all that a man of acknowledged virtue harbored evil impulses within him. Not even the character of someone thirty-five years old could be considered safe from their incursions. The young man whose reputation was unblemished and whose character and ability had placed him in a position of great trust could one day be revealed to have been secretly gambling or engaged in other destructive activities that might silently, in the worst of merchant nightmares, be taking his unknowing employer to financial ruin.

In its most significant sense, the Association for the Suppression of Gambling was intended, in the most direct way possible, to provide the information that its leaders felt was available in no other way. As Havens's choice of metaphors suggests, the ASG was the *only* institution lighting the way for the bewildered navigator; there were no other agencies marking the route or pointing out the safe passages. Similarly, to the merchant jealous of his profits, the horizon must have appeared lacking in agencies to help him decide among the many petitioners for jobs and to help him communicate to them the behavior and character expected of them. How could he distinguish between young arrivals with similar past histories, of similar appearance and financial resources? For all the confidence of certain advice-book writers that character could be read at a glance, merchants rightly had their suspicions. They were all too aware that good manners and even public reputations could be feigned. Ackland, the merchant in T. S. Arthur's novel *Sparing to Spend,* who seemed to read Lofton's virtue almost intuitively, had, after all, first taken in the deceitful Pinkerton as a partner without realizing the ruin to which the liaison had almost brought him.[4]

To some merchants, the creation of the Association's Intelligence Agency must have seemed like a way out of the darkness; accurate knowledge could be secured and accurate determinations about the moral worth of employees could be made. Convinced of its value, the directors appealed to the public for support that would enable the ASG to take "its appropriate place among the moral and beneficial agencies of the day." The directors were convinced that when merchants, mechanics, and manufacturers, as well as the public generally, saw where their true interests lay, they would willingly pay to support an organization "proposing to check, counteract and finally sup[p]ress the secret robberies" that the evils of gambling fostered. The appeal closing the annual report, however, was less than hopeful. "It is for the public to say," the author repeated, "whether our organization shall be a strong and efficient instrumentality or drag out for a few months a lingering existence, and, dying, become the mock of its exulting foes."[5]

The words of the closing appeal were apparently prophetic. The Association does not seem to have achieved the "public esteem" it sought. No evidence of its continued existence, beyond the first annual report has been found. Perhaps its early demise was due to its barely guarded appeal to the self-interest of the merchant community. It did not take a very deep inspection of the Association's language to reveal that it was more concerned with the losses sustained by merchants than with the losses in character and virtue sustained by young men. To a merchant community that often prided itself on its philanthropic impulses, on its charitable contributions and efforts on behalf of the victims of urban life, the aims of the ASG may have been too transparently self-seeking for it to gain admission "among the moral and beneficial agencies of the day." Sentiments like the Reverend John Pierpont's, which recommended the Association almost purely as an agency for the protection and insurance of property against the depredations of merchants' clerks and sons, may have offended as many potential supporters as it attracted (p. 14).

4. See chapter 7.
5. *ASG,* p. 35.

But even though the Association was so short-lived, so hard put to generate public support, the very fact that merchants and other community leaders were willing to turn to methods that, despite their protestations to the contrary, were *not* recognized as right by "the universal consent and practice of mankind" points up the critical nature of the situation they felt they were facing. That an organization should propose methods so close to the fringe of public acceptance demonstrates the desperation some men experienced in confronting a problem common to the entire mercantile community. In so baring its intentions, it makes the solutions and institutional arrangements that did gain wide currency in the community more intelligible than they might otherwise be; it helps us to understand the appeal of other organizations that could be used, perhaps less efficiently, to perform similar functions with greater discretion.

When the New York Mercantile Library Association began operation in 1820, its purposes were limited to the founding of a "literary institution;" its founders' sole object was to establish a library to aid the "dissemination of knowledge and the cultivation of intellect."[6] These young men, themselves clerks, urged all other clerks in the city to join. The Association got off to a slow start. The second annual report noted with disappointment the "absolute neglect" the MLA had received from the great body of New York merchants; except for one or two of the institution's early patrons, they had not been visited all year by a single one (pp. 11-12). Not even the cabinet of specimens in "Minerology and Conchology" that they had set up to encourage membership had seemed to help (p. 10).

The report's author noted that the Mechanics Library and Scientific Institution, founded at the same time as the MLA, was flourishing; it had over two thousand members and had alerady been able to erect its own building. The young founders of the MLA had expected to increase at least as rapidly in numbers and support. Experience, the report said, had proven this hope futile; they would have to act for themselves and not rely on the patronage and countenance of the older merchants (pp. 13, 18-19). Yet, the next year, with little

6. *Annual Reports of the Board of Direction of the Mercantile Library Association of the City of New York, from 1821 to 1838* (New York, 1868), p. 3.

change in the organization's fortunes, they were still appealing to established merchants for help. Although they did not wish to offend possible benefactors, the report could not refrain from pointing out the continued coldness they received. It was not so much pecuniary aid they sought. Rather, they hoped that merchants would occasionally visit their premises and use their influence to persuade their clerks to join (p. 19). By the end of 1825, the founders were finally beginning to sound a bit hopeful. Membership had begun to rise and a successful appeal for more books had been made. This time the Board had more slyly approached its quarry:

> Conscious that the subordinate stations which we occupy, and the little weight of character which unobtrusive youth can carry with them, would render these applications in no great degree successful, recourse was had to more mature years and the more elevated standing of our honorary members for aid; and the Board have it to acknowledge, with heartfelt gratitude, that the solicited patronage was promptly extended even beyond our most fond expectations. (p. 23)

The pose the writer assumed, that of a humble, submissive petitioner to the mighty is revealing. If it does not tell us much about the way young men actually saw themselves, it does tell us something about how they felt an older generation of merchants expected them to appear. The writer clearly felt it necessary to play such a role to curry the favor the organization sought.

So quickly did they now begin to grow that, by the sixth annual report, the directors could look back as if it had been three decades instead of three years to the "language of despondency and almost despair" that characterized the third report (p. 31). The library collection, they could now proudly report, had increased one-third over the past year, and the volume of books borrowed daily had also sharply increased. And, if any of their employers and patrons still had doubts about the "tendency" of the institution, they were invited to visit the rooms and see for themselves the decorum that prevailed and the behavior and character of those present. "They will see," the report stated confidently

none who are frequenters of the dram-shop, none who seek the

society of the vicious and profane, and few, if any, who are devoted to the theatre. They will meet those who give satisfaction to
their employers; those who, while they devote their leisure hours
to the acquisitions of knowledge, perform the duties of the store
or counting-house with diligence and activity, and are anxious to
establish a reputation on which they are to rely principally in their
pursuit of fortune. (p. 35)

With that invitation, the Association began an appeal that was to
dominate the future of the institution. The directors seemed to learn
quickly that an appeal for support based on moral grounds was more
likely to succeed than one based on purely education grounds. An
appeal to the importance of general information to the merchant provoked far less response than one recommending the institution as an
agency that helped maintain order and decorum and helped instill
these qualities in its subscribers. Increasingly, after the sixth annual
report, the Association was advertised in this light. The purposes of
the organization were now altered to read "the *dissemination of correct principles* and the *moral cultivation* of the clerks of this city . . .
a subject in which every merchant has a deep interest" (p. 41; italics
mine), and not the "dissemination of knowledge and the cultivation
of intellect" as stated in the first annual report. It was of great importance to the city's merchants, an increasingly typical passage
noted, that the men they employed should not only perform their
routine transactions satisfactorily but should try to excel at them and
thereby merit promotion. The kind of men who would do this, the
kind of men merchants needed, were those of correct principles,
principles, it was assumed, that they had cultivated through their association with the MLA. The reason, they explained, sounding like
the ASG, was plain. The merchant placed his property to some extent in the hands of his clerks. "If he finds his salesman disposed to
prevaricate to serve his employer's interest, will he not do as much
to serve his own? If he can be induced to do an act which he knows
to be morally wrong to please his employer, is there any security that
he will not do as much to serve himself?" (p. 41).

With this appeal, the directors of the MLA struck the chord to
which merchants would respond most readily. In helping the MLA,
they would be helping themselves. And, if merchants were convinced

that the kinds of young men they needed could be found at the MLA, clerks had every reason to become members. It was the duty of the present membership, the seventh report stated, to seek out those unattached young men and convince them of the organization's benefits. The writer of the report began his charge to members generally, abstractly. "A regard for the respectability of the mercantile character, for the reputation of our city," he said, "should stimulate us to exertion." But he soon left no doubt that it was career considerations that he had in mind:

> We now act a subordinate part in the drama of life; but doubtless there are some among us who may be called, when our employers retire from the busy scenes of life to occupy the places which they now fill. . . . How solicitous then should each individual be to store his mind with that knowledge which alone can render him respected, and enable him to exert a beneficial influence on the society in which he is destined to move. (pp. 42-43)

For our purposes, it is not important to determine whether the writer's expectation was justified, whether and to what extent clerks could expect to move into vacated mercantile places. What should be noted is the writer's recognition of the way in which the process of mobility was conceived: a young man was to patiently acquire the qualities that would "render him respected" and wait until called. Even if clerks did not internalize this message, their understanding of it would probably set boundaries within which their ambition would be expressed.

By the next meeting, the Board could report that over $20,000 had been pledged by the mercantile community for a new building. The Association, though still not reaching the membership it sought, considered its period of infancy and initial struggle over (p. 49). It had, the author felt, convinced the public of its worth. By January 1831, the report again noted the gradual progress of the Library; members were more punctual about payment of dues and the stock of books was increased to the point where the author was confident that the MLA "proffer[ed] to the young men of this city greater advantages for acquiring useful knowledge than any other [library] to which they can have access." But his pride came primarily from another source.

The success of the institution had become "fully identified with the character of the young men of this city." "Who of our members," he asked, "who profit by its advantages, will not look back when a few years have rolled away, and exult that they were members. . .?" (p. 54). The author's greatest satisfaction came from the increasing interest in the organization's welfare manifested by a large number of the most respectable merchants in the city. No doubt, he happily wrote, it "must exert a very salutary influence in stimulating those of our members who are ambitious of acquiring a solid reputation." He continued:

> It is becoming a practice of merchants to look to the Library as a test of character of a clerk applying for a situation. Is he a member of the Mercantile Library? Does he employ his leisure in profiting by its advantages; and what is the character of his reading? Is it light and frivolous, or does he delight in books that will increase his stock of information, tend to elevate his character, and extend his influence? If these questions can be answered in the affirmative, there is confidence indulged that he is not only free from vicious habits, but that he also possesses one of the most effectual securities against the temptations of vicious companions and vicious indulgences. (p. 54)

In later reports they proudly advertised, as if they had just realized it, a truth that they had known for some time. The Association's "beneficial influence on the character of its members," they said, "begins to be seen and appreciated." The Board recorded "with pleasure" that they did not know of an instance where a member of the Library "who had read with any attention, or promptly discharged his dues [had] defrauded his employer or abused his confidence" (p. 63). This effect on the morals of the city's clerks was the source of greatest pride to the Board. It now saw itself as a significant agency of social change. Before, and several years after, the founding of the MLA, the young men of New York, said the twelfth report, showed only slight interest in intellectual pursuits. Their leisure was wasted in unprofitable amusements which, they said, too often injured both body and mind. Highly gratified, they noted that within a few years "a wide and favorable change has occurred in the tastes and amusements which formerly prevailed among them." The time wasted in idle leisure had been replaced by a desire "for mutual improvement and ambition to distinguish themselves as useful members of society" (p. 80).

Later annual reports continued to be strewn with self-congratulatory praise. Time and again they would ask rhetorically, now assured of their importance and value, what would result if they did not exist. The answer was obvious: "Places of amusement thronged (as was sagely predicted by some at our onset), morals destroyed, and reputation with them, and many a merchant would now be compelled to mourn the loss of a much valued clerk" (p. 113). Compared to earlier difficulties, problems of finances and resources now seemed slight. The Association still complained about inadequate funds and insufficient numbers, but generally was more than satisfied with the support it had received and the position it had assumed (p. 86). By 1834 it considered itself secure enough to confidently declare that the MLA was "one of the few exceptions to the multitude of associations which start up around us, and after a short-lived pursuit of unattainable objects, perish and pass to forgetfulness [*sic*]" (p. 84).

So much of a fixture in the mercantile community had it in fact become that the Association came to be used as a meeting place for clerks looking for work and merchants seeking workers. It found itself becoming a clearing house for job contacts. The Board, perhaps realizing how natural such a function was for an organization of its professed aims, encouraged the liaisons. In September 1835, the directors opened a register for members seeking positions, and by advertisements in the daily press, urged merchants needing assistants to consult it. The service, which was free, gratified the directors. Many clerks had obtained positions and, to the credit of the membership, they noted proudly, "We have had more applicatoins from merchants than from clerks" (p. 112).

In view of this, the Board of Directors once again addressed the young men who had still failed to join. Membership in the MLA was not incidental, but central to their interests. There were about 10,000 clerks in New York, the Board estimated in its twenty-fourth annual report (1845). But only 2,000 had availed themselves of the "unrivalled" advantages of the institution. This, the report said, certainly spoke poorly for the intelligence of "Young New York"—especially since it cost a mere two dollars a year to enjoy all of the organization's privileges. The young directors made their meaning plain in the next sentence: "We should consider it an important item in the credentials of character, in a young man applying to us for a clerkship, to know that he was a member of the Mercantile Library Association."[7]

The venerable Philip Hone, who had chaired virtually every annual meeting of the MLA since its inception, thought no less of the Association's importance. One of its earliest supporters, he saw clearly—as clearly as the young men themselves—the role it had come to play. As a man who had spent years trying to guard mercantile traditions of honor and integrity against the "new" men, he knew that the MLA's functions were extremely valuable to the community. In one short paragraph in a long speech to the Boston MLA on the traditions and history of the mercantile profession, he made these functions explicit. Associations like the MLA were essential in providing the talent that would preserve the relations he valued so highly.

> An institution of this nature is, to society, like an eddy in one of those rivers of the southern Continent in which gold dust is found. It brings within its vortex, *and concentrating in one spot,* gives a value to the scattered particles of the precious metal; whilst others, beyond the reach of its influence, rendered worthless from the want of the benefits of association, *lie unnoticed* on the shoals, or amid the quick-sands of the stream, or *are swept away, and lost in the undiscriminating ocean.*[8]

Both Hone and the Board appeared to see the MLA as the way to institutionalize the process of advancement that we have discussed in past chapters. Both saw mobility as taking place in the same way that men like Scoville, Arthur, and the Fowlers had viewed it. Pro-

---

7. *Hunt's Merchants' Magazine* 12 (1845): 393.
8. Philip Hone, *An Address Delivered Before the Mercantile Library Association, at the Odeon in Boston, October 3, 1843* (Boston, 1843), p. 20. (italics mine)

motion was the result of one's selection by another, more highly placed. Virtue, once displayed and recognized, was rewarded by the elevation to a new position of esteem and repute. The MLA, as Hone and the Board saw it, was the institution through which these changes could take place. It served as the gathering place where young men of character could be noticed, where they could be spotted by established merchants seeking reliable, responsible assistants. In *Sparing to Spend*, selection was haphazard—one always had to be "ready." Every insignificant detail had to be carefully attended to, because it was impossible to know when or how selection would take place. One simply had to be "available"—but Arthur never located "availability" in any specific temporal or spatial setting. The MLA was such a setting. It was a concrete institution where young men and merchants could come together for the mutual advantage of both. It was the institutional lodestone drawing clerks of a certain kind and the merchants seeking their services to a definite location where the two groups (primarily, it was assumed, through efforts initiated by the merchants) could meet. In this sense, the MLA was truly like an eddy. It brought together in one place young men who, as Hone said, might otherwise and regretfully lie unnoticed or be overlooked. But Hone's choice of the figure is significant for another reason. In the sense that an eddy runs against the main current, often being tucked away in an enclosed pocket of water, Hone's usage may reveal his feeling that such institutions, though desirable, were all too uncommon features on the social landscape. This scarcity only increased their value and perhaps explains the efforts of men to increase the density of the institutional fabric, a density that would maximize the encounters between those merchants and clerks whose interests naturally coincided.

The support the YMCA received when it was founded in 1852 was also motivated by such reasoning. What kind of institution, merchants may have thought, could better gather the kind of young men they were seeking if not one both devoted to evangelical principles and principally membered by aspiring young clerks? The process by which it performed this service was, as articulated by Charles Tracy in his address to the YMCA's second anniversary meeting, notably similar to Philip Hone's statement of the MLA's working:

A young man comes here who is a respecter of religion, or a sincere follower in its ways: he goes in and out of a church with a crowd: he visits another church in another crowd: *he is not noticed: his powers of usefulness, his good will to do good to others are unknown. Months go by when an accident reveals him, and he is at once in the way of usefulness and improvement,* or mayhap, the want of active duties and fraternal sympathy, with the unceasing pressure of business, has left nothing worth revealing. *To such this Society is a ready friend, taking him in at the outset into the circle of its friendships, and guiding him to ample fields of usefulness and improvement.*[9]

Like Hone, Tracy was aware how easy it was to be overlooked in a city like New York and how dependent on chance were those seeking the services of virtuous youths. Like the MLA, the YMCA could "reveal" these young men and expose them to the notice of others at the "outset."

It was not, therefore, surprising to see the young organization taking upon itself brokerage functions similar to the services the MLA had begun twenty-two years earlier. In 1857 the New York YMCA placed a notice in the New York *Independent,* one of the city's denominational newspapers, to announce that the newly formed "Employment Committee" was ready to accept applications from merchants and other businessmen needing clerks. A register of young men desiring employment would be kept, the Association assuring employers that this was "a most desirable medium" for obtaining worthy and capable assistants. The YMCA realized that "merchants often wish some guaranty of the moral character of young men who seek employment in their stores," that "young men of principle are expecially in demand." To help secure such help, the Association, said the announcement, had "undertaken to act as a committee of inquiry between merchants and clerks, consulting the best interests of each."[10] The YMCA presumably was to become another clearing house of character, another mediator coordinating the efforts of the

9. Charles Tracy, "Address," *Second Annual Report of the New York Young Men's Christian Association, Presented May 15, 1854. . .* (New York, 1854), pp. 47-48. (italics mine)

10. *Hunt's Merchants' Magazine* 36 (1857): 773.

two groups whose interests it hoped to serve.

In 1887 a merchant looking back on his early years in New York wrote about the value the YMCA had for him. "I was a stranger," the man remarked, "just from New England, come to take a clerk-ship in a dry goods house." He was boarding at the Cortlandt Street Hotel, in a small, cold room on the top floor. New York was strange and forbidding. "I was lonely in the midst of crowds," he said. "At night from Canal Street down Broadway was a dangerous place. . . . What new and strange temptations were around me and among them the voice of the siren."

In this environment the YMCA "was a new world," where friends welcomed him "and have remained true to this day." Most significant for our purposes, however, is the way he expressed the reason he most valued the friendships he made. He singled it out for special emphasis.

> I made there [at the YMCA] acquaintances who were of service to me in many ways; men whom I should probably never have met but for my connecting there; *one gentleman, for instance, sought me out, and desired my services at a salary more that double that I was receiving.* . . . Certainly my career was influenced by it in a marked manner.[11]

Just as the writer drew on convention to picture New York's night life, he also drew on convention to express its influence on his career. In bringing men like the correspondent above together with other "gentlemen," the YMCA and the MLA were not acting much differently from the Association for the Suppression of Gambling. In the way they defined the role that their institution was to play, each showed marked similarities to the other. The ASG monitored character, as did the MLA and YMCA. The only difference was that it performed this function using more direct methods and at a later stage in the process. The YMCA and MLA hoped that they were funneling the right kind of young men to merchants needing their services; the ASG, investigating the clerks once on the job, made sure that this was so.

11. New York Young Men's Christian Association, *Thirty-Fourth Annual Report* (New York, 1887), p. 27. (italics mine)

But despite tactical differences, all three had the same goals. The monitoring and screening functions were meant to contain, if not control, the conduct of the city's young men. The institutions did not want to force certain programmed responses from young men, but to provide a framework within which individual initiative, nonaggressive as it was, would operate. This role, as a collecting agency, as a reservoir for valuable human commodities, was the kind of channeling that merchants and other community leaders had in mind. If the indiscretion of the ASG (it was the only one of the three organizations founded by community leaders themselves) made its endorsement morally repugnant to many potential supporters, the YMCA and MLA served the same purpose with only a slightly greater chance of error. All three acted as regulating mechanisms controlling the flow and helter-skelter movement of upwardly mobile young men. In doing so, they reduced the pressure and consequent disorder that might accompany an unprecedented number of young men aggressively pursuing their careers.

The young men who left settled farm lives to come to the cities were considered the most ambitious, most aggressive, and most willing to take risks;[12] the society they were entering was pictured as being most willing to reward these qualities.[13] While pursuing a living in a business career had unquestioned advantages for building character—where else were the qualities of perseverance and diligence, for example, so necessary to success?—many writers and speakers sadly recognized the grave dangers it posed as well. It was just as evident to Charles Tracy as it had been to T. S. Arthur that large parts of the business world considered "the making of wealth the great end of life." All too easily the love of business was supplanted by a love of acquiring money. Luckily, institutions like the MLA and the YMCA could be "interposed" between the "seducing spirit of gain" and the best instincts of youth to counter this trend. An "ill-regulated mind" could easily be "exercised out of proportion in business pursuits" and find its benevolent sympathies crowded

12. See the speech of Daniel Lord, the remarks of Charles Tracy to the second YMCA anniversary meeting, and the ASG First Annual Report.
13. See almost any of T. S. Arthur's business novels.

out. A man, said Tracy, then became simply a machine, "a die-press for coining gold." In language that reminds us of the way the careers of young men like Edward Tailer were discussed, he noted the example

> of those who have started fairly, with the prestige of birth, the right bias of education and alliances and yet have dropped one good point of character or habit after another, lightening themselves for the hotter pursuit of wealth, until at last when accumulated fortune is a burden, and age is heavy and sight dim, they have no heart left for anything but clutching money with a dying grasp.

The YMCA was valuable to men like these, felt Tracy, because it "lift[ed] a barrier" to prevent this waste of nobler tastes and impulses.[14]

In doing so, the YMCA and other institutions like it became an eddy in yet another sense—a force exerted against the main current, a force acting to conserve impulses that would quickly be stripped away in the harsh business world. Many supporters of these organizations saw that this was where temptation primarily came from, not from amusements, no matter how dangerous. "It would be a great error," said Tracy, "to lose sight of this fatal snare of business, and to suppose that the theatre and the gambling house were the main things to guard against" (p. 47). Institutions like the MLA and YMCA that could turn a young man away from the immoral and unscrupulous behavior of his contemporaries, that "call[ed] the young man to higher themes," and that in effect taught him how he ought to behave to attract notice and gain recognition, were highly prized. In a sense the MLA and YMCA served as rest zones from a fast-moving and fast-dealing world. Like the nineteenth-century conception of the family for which these organizations often saw themselves a surrogate, they were meant to serve as oases where a young man could go, not to escape the business world, but to find a temporary respite from its pressures and hopefully to recharge the spiritual reserves that would give him strength to withstand its rigors. In addi-

---

14. Charles Tracy, "Address," p. 47.

tion, the YMCA, supporters hoped, would temper the avaricious drive of young men entering business life. But an oasis, after all, only enabled the young men who renewed themselves at its margins to gather their energies for the competition ahead. Tracy and Bethune, if they noticed at all, were probably untroubled by the apparent contradiction. They wished not to end the competition, but only to mute its most disorganizing tendencies. If the young men who stopped at the YMCA for sustenance took away with them standards of conduct that would direct their drive for success into manageable channels, if it made them recognize that social mobility was considered a reward for respect, for deference, it would be serving them well. Available positions had to go to someone; it was better that they go to young men who understood the desirability of restraint rather than to those who chafed at its suggestion.

In this sense, many older members of the business community realized that institutions like the YMCA and MLA were more valuable in helping them control the movement and aspirations of young men they did not know than in helping them control the movement and aspirations of those they did. The latter could still be admitted to mercantile and social positions informally; it was in dealing with the former that new measures were required. Because an apprenticelike system proved unable to perform either new or traditional recruitment functions—the pressure of processing newcomers produced tensions, as in the case of Edward Tailer, that made it less workable for placing better-connected youths as well—alternatives were sought. It was particularly necessary to find ways of securing a reliable work force of young men to fill new positions in expanding businesses. Few of these young men would gain access to higher mercantile positions and few would gain more than perfunctory recognition from employers for a job well done. For most, contact would increasingly be with personnel managers and salaried superiors, not with employers seeking prospective business or social partners.

The uses to which merchants put the YMCA and MLA pointed ahead to these developments. Although these organizations offered newcomers companionship and "home feeling," they never replaced, if indeed they ever expected to, the sundered ties of a more stable society. To the extent that these institutions seemed to honor the same manners and virtues of the communities young people had left, they can be seen as agencies that reinforced, rather than shattered, the continuity of their experience. But emphasis on the uses to which the voicing of familiar counsel was put suggests a different conclusion.

By disseminating and providing an institutional base for the moral advice widespread in this period, and by connecting this advice with a specific notion of vocational mobility, the YMCA and MLA became part of the search for new ways to accommodate changes in business and social life, not a way to deny them. In taking on brokerage functions in particular, they participated in bringing merchants and clerks together for business purposes alone. Away from the countinghouse, the lives of employer and worker no longer touched; if they were to meet, new avenues of contact would have to be specially created. Older, once reliable, ways of contact could not be depended upon and the search for new ways led community leaders tentatively to the YMCA and MLA. In time they would be abandoned. But for a while they were all that a group of desperate men could turn to.

Especially in a society viewed as growing too suddenly to have developed the regulating mechanisms of more settled environments, in a society groping for solutions to problems they never expected to face, in a society where young men were pictured as unattached and irrational, institutions holding out the promise of performing the feats of control and regulation were gratefully supported. Until such time as growing urban areas proliferated specific forms to deal with these unanticipated problems, organizations close at hand would be commandeered to carry out services traditionally handled by many different small-town institutions. With the development in the coming decades of more impersonal and less customary institutions, the services performed by church, family, and apprenticeship would find more permanent institutional homes than those provided in the 1850s by the YMCA, MLA, and ASG. The significance of these organizations lies not in the length of time they performed these services, but in the way they mediated a change in institutional practice. Functions once performed by familiar business and kinship units would come to be performed by distantly monitored schools, impersonal universities and corporations, and "scientific" charity organizations. The moment when merchants and other community leaders turned to institutions like the YMCA, MLA, and ASG marked the beginning of this transformation of social life.

Selected Bibliography

1. PRIMARY SOURCES

Alcott, William A. *Familiar Letters to Young Men*. Buffalo, 1849.

[Alcott, William A.] *The Young Man's Guide*. 3rd ed. Boston, 1834.

Alexander, James W. *The Merchant's Clerk. Cheered and Counselled*. New York, 1856.

American Phrenological Journal. Vols. 3-27. New York, 1840-1857.

Arthur, T. S. *Advice to Young Men on their Duties and Conduct in Life*. Boston, 1848.

———. *Lizzie Glenn: or, the Trials of a Seamstress*. Philadelphia, 1859.

———. *Making Haste to be Rich: or, the Temptation and Fall*. New York, 1855.

———. *Retiring from Business*. New York, 1848.

———. *Riches Have Wings: or, a Tale for the Rich and Poor*. New York, 1847.

———. *Sparing to Spend: or, the Loftons and Pinkertons*. Philadelphia, 1853.

———. *True Riches*. New York, 1852.

Barrett, Walter. [Joseph A. Scoville.] *The Old Merchants of New York*. 5 vols. New York, 1885.

Belden, E. Porter. *New York: Past, Present and Future*. . . New York, 1849.

Bethune, George W. "Address." *Second Annual Report of the New York Young Men's Christian Association, Presented May 15, 1854*. . . New York, 1854.

Brace, Charles Loring. *Short Sermons to News Boys*. New York, 1866.

Browne, Junius Henri. *The Great Metropolis*. Hartford, Conn., 1869.

Buntline, Ned. [E. Z. C. Judson.] *The Mysteries and Miseries of New York*. New York, 1849.

Butler, Charles. *The American Gentleman*. Philadelphia, 1836.

Chapin, E. H. *Humanity in the City*. New York, 1854.

Clarke, John. *Discourses to Young Persons*. Boston, 1804.

Constitution of the New-York Young Men's Christian Association. Organized June, 1852. New York, 1852.

Dickens, Charles. *American Notes*. New York, 1961.

Dodge, D. Stuart. *Memorials of William E. Dodge*. New York, 1887.

Dodge, William E. *Old New York*. New York, 1880.

Early Letters of Mark Hopkins. New York, 1929.

The Eno Collection of New York City Views. 5 vols. Prints Division, New York Public Library.

Ferris, Isaac. *Address Delivered at a Meeting of Young Men, Convened for the Formation of the Young Men's Christian Association, Held in the Lecture Room of the Mercer-St. Presbyterian Church, May 28, 1852*. New York, 1852.

[Foster, G. G.] *New York in Slices by an Experienced Carver*. New York, 1849.

Fowler, Orson S. and Lorenzo N. *New Illustrated Self-Instructor in Phrenology and Physiology*. . . New York, 1859.

Hardie, James *A census of the new Buildings Erected in this city, in the year 1824*. New York 1825.

———. *The Description of the City of New York*. . .New York, 1827

Hartley, Robert M. Papers, Archives, Community Service Society, New York.

Hawes, Joel. *Lectures to Young Men on the Formation of Character*. . . Hartford, 1828.

———. *Lectures to Young Men on the Formation of Character*.

Originally Addressed to the Young Men of Hartford and New Haven. . . With Two Additional Lectures Not-Before Published. Boston, 1856.

Hoffman, William. Diary. New-York Historical Society. Manuscript Division.

Hone, Philip. *An Address Delivered Before the Mercantile Library Association, at the Odeon in Boston, October 3, 1843.* Boston, 1843.

———. *The Diary of Philip Hone, 1828-1851.* Edited by Allan Nevins. New York, 1936.

Hunt, Freeman. *Lives of American Merchants.* 2 vols. New York, 1858.

———. *Worth and Wealth: A Collection of Maxims, Morals and Miscellanies for Merchants and Men of Business.* New York, 1856.

Hunt's Merchants' Magazine. Vols. 1-41. New York, 1839-1859.

Lord. Daniel. *Address Delivered on the Opening of the New-York Young Men's Christian Association, September 20, 1852.* New York, 1852.

McCabe, James D., Jr. *Great Fortunes, and How They Were Made; or, the Struggles and Triumphs of Our Self-Made Men.* New York, 1871.

———. *Lights and Shadows of New York Life.* Philadelphia, 1872.

Martin, Edward Winslow. [James D. McCabe, Jr.] *The Secrets of the Great City.* Philadelphia, 1868.

New York Association for Improving the Condition of the Poor. *Annual Reports, 1848-1860.*

New York Association for the Suppression of Gambling. *First Annual Report.* New York, 1851.

New-York Magdalen Society. *First Annual Report of the Executive Committee.* New York, 1831.

New York Mercantile Library Assocation. *Annual Reports of the Board of Direction, from 1821 to 1838.* New York, 1868.

———. *Nineteenth Annual Report. . .* New York, 1840.

New York Trade Agency. Confidential Reports on Business Concerns, 1851. New-York Historical Society, Manuscript Division.

New York Young Men's Christian Association. *Thirty-Fourth Annual Report.* New York, 1887.

Petrie, George H. "Narrative of Incidents in the Formation of the N.Y. Y.M.C.A." Undated copy of manuscript in YMCA Historical Library, New York City.

Porter, Kenneth W. *The Jacksons and the Lees*. 2 vols. Cambridge, Mass., 1937.

[Prime, Samuel I.] *Life in New York*. New York, 1847.

Ross, Joel H. *What I Saw in New York; or, a Bird's Eye View of City Life*. Auburn, N.Y., 1852.

Scoville, Joseph A. *The Adventures of Clarence Bolton; or, Life in New York*. New York, n.d.

Sedgwick, Catherine Maria. *The Poor Rich Man and the Rich Poor Man*. New York, 1836.

Sizer, Nelson. *Choice of Pursuits: or, What to Do, and Why, Describing Seventy-Five Trades and Professions, and the Talents and Temperaments Required for Each. . .* New York, 1876.

Smith, Elizabeth Oakes. *The Newsboy*. New York, 1854.

Still, Bayrd. *Mirror for Gotham: New York as Seen by Contemporaries from Dtuch Days to the Present*. New York, 1956.

Strong, George Templeton. *The Diary of George Templeton Strong. 1835-1875*. Edited by Allan Nevins and M.H. Thomas. 4 vols. New York, 1953.

Tailer, Edward Neufville, Jr. Diary. New-York Historical Society. Manuscript Division.

Taylor, Bayard. *John Godfrey's Fortunes*. New York, 1865.

The Old Brewery and the New Mission House at the Five Points. By the Ladies of the Mission. New York, 1854.

The Young Merchant. Boston, 1840.

Thomas, F. W. *Clinton Bradshaw*. Philadelphia, 1835.

Tracy, Charles. "Address." *Second Annual Report of the New York Young Men's Christian Association, Presented May 15, 1854. . . .* New York, 1854.

Van Doren, William Howard. *Mercantile Morals: or, Thoughts for Young Men Entering Mercantile Life*. New York, 1852.

Washburn, Emory. *Anniversary Address to the Boston Young Men's Christian Union*. Boston, 1856.

Waterbury, Jared Bell. *Considerations for Young Men*. New York, 1832.

Wayland, Francis. *The Elements of Political Economy*. Boston, 1849.

[Wells, Samuel Roberts.] *How to Behave: A Pocket Manual of Republican Etiquette, and Guide to Correct Personal Habits. . .* New York, 1857.

————. *How to Do Business: A Pocket Manual of Practical Affairs and Guide to Success in Life. . . .* New York, 1857

Wise, Daniel. *The Young Man's Counsellor: or, Sketches and Illustrations of the Duties and Dangers of Young Men.* New York, 1854.

2. SECONDARY SOURCES

Albion, Robert Greenhalgh. *The Rise of New York Port, 1815-1860.* New York, 1939.

Becker, Dorothy G. "The Visitor to the New York City Poor, 1843-1920: The Role and Contribution of Volunteer Visitors of the New York Association for Improving the Condition of the Poor, State Charities Aid Association and New York Charity Organization Society." Ph.D. dissertation, School of Social Work, Columbia University, 1960.

Briggs, Asa. *Victorian Cities.* London, 1963.

————. *Victorian People.* Chicago, 1955.

Brown, Henry Collins. *Old New York: Yesterday and Today.* New York, 1922.

Carman, Harry James. *The Street Surface Railway Franchises of New York City.* New York, 1919.

Curtis, Edith Roelker. *A Season in Utopia: The Story of Brook Farm.* New York. 1971.

Davies, John D. *Phrenology, Fad and Science: A Nineteenth Century Crusade.* New Haven, 1955.

Dodge, D. Stuart. *Memorials of William E. Dodge.* New York, 1887.

Donoghue, Terry. *An Event on Mercer Street: A Brief History of the Young Men's Christian Association of the City of New York.* New York, 1953.

Dorfman, Joseph. *The Economic Mind in American Civilization, 1606-1865.* 2 vols. New York, 1946.

Elkins, Stanley M. *Slavery*. Chicago, 1959.

Ernst, Robert. *Immigrant Life in New York City. 1825-1863*. New York, 1949.

Foner, Eric. *Free Soil, Free Labor, Free Men*. New York, 1970.

Frederickson, George. *The Inner Civil War*. New York, 1965.

Harlow, Alvin. *Old Bowery Days*. New York, 1931.

Harris, Neil. *The Artist in American Society*. New York, 1966.

Hawley, Amos. *Human Ecology: A Theory of Community Structure*. New York, 1950.

Hopkins, C. Howard. *History of the YMCA in North America*. New York, 1951.

Katz, Michael. *The Irony of Early School Reform*. Cambridge, 1968.

Kouwenhoven, John A. *The Columbia Historical Portrait of New York*. Garden City, N.Y., 1953.

Lanier, Henry Wysham. *A Century of Banking in New York, 1822-1922*. New York, 1922.

Lees, Lynn H. "Patterns of Lower-Class Life: Irish Slum Communities in Nineteenth-Century London." *Nineteenth Century Cities*. Edited by Stephan Thernstrom and Richard Sennett. New Haven, 1969.

Levinson, Leonard Louis. *Wall Street, A Pictorial History*. New York, 1961.

Lowitt, Richard. *A Merchant Prince of the Nineteenth Century: William E. Dodge*. New York 1954.

Mack, Edward C. *Peter Cooper, Citizen of New York*. New York, 1949.

Meyers, Marvin. *The Jacksonian Persuasion*. Stanford, 1957.

Miller, Douglas T. *Jacksonian Aristocracy: Class and Democracy in New York. 1830-1860*. New York, 1967.

Nevins, Allan. "Arthur, Timothy Shay." *Dictionary of American Biography*. Vol. 1. New York, 1928. ·

Pessen, Edward. "The Egalitarian Myth and the American Social Reality: Wealth, Mobility, and Equality in the 'Era of the Common Man.'" *American Historical Review* 76, no. 4 (1971).

Peterson, A. Everett. "Hunt, Freeman." *Dictionary of American Biography*. vol. 9. New York, 1932.

Porter, Kenneth Wiggins. *The Jacksons and the Lees*. 2 vols. Cambridge, 1937.

Potter, James. "Demographic Factors in American Population Before 1860." Lecture to Economic History Workshop, University of Wisconsin, May 1965.

Riesman, David; Glazer, Nathan; and Denny, Reuel. *The Lonely Crowd*. Yale Paperbound. New Haven, 1961.

Romaine, Lawrence B. "Talk of the Town: New York City, January, 1825." *Bulletin of the New York Public Library* 63, no. 4 (1959).

Rothman, David J. *The Discovery of the Asylum*. Boston, 1971.

Sams, Henry W. *Autobiography of Brook Farm*. Englewood Cliffs, N.J., 1958.

Schlesinger, Arthur M. *Learning How to Behave*. New York, 1947.

Scott, Donald M. "Making It in Ante-Bellum America: Young Men and Their Careers, 1820-1860." Paper delivered to the Organization of American Historians, New Orleans, April 17, 1971.

Still, Bayrd. *Mirror for Gotham: New York as Seen by Contemporaries from Dutch Days to the Present*. New York, 1956.

Strauss, Anselm. *Images of the American City*. New York, 1961.

Stokes, I. N. Phelps. *The Iconography of Manhattan Island*. 5 vols. New York, 1915-28.

Sweezy, Paul M. *The Theory of Capitalist Development*. New York, 1942.

Taylor, George Rogers. "The Beginnings of Mass Transportation in Urban America: Part I." *Smithsonian Journal of History* 1, no. 2 (1966).

———. "The Beginnings of Mass Transportation in Urban America: Part II." *Smithsonian Journal of History* 1, no. 3 (1966).

Taylor, William R. *Cavalier and Yankee*. New York, 1961.

Walzer, Michael. *The Revolution of the Saints*. London, 1966.

Weitenkampf, Frank. *The Eno Collection of New York City Views*. New York, 1925.

Whiteside, William B. "The Boston YMCA and Community Need: A Century's Evolution, 1851-1951." Ph.D. dissertation, Harvard University, 1951.

Wyllie, Irvin G. *The Self-Made Man in America: The Myth of Rags to Riches*. New York, 1966.

Yasuba, Yasukichi. *Birth Rates of the White Population in the United States, 1800-1860*. Baltimore, Md., 1962.

Index

Advice literature, 147-63; on social mobility, 98-105, 118, 128-29, 137, 150-51, 200-209; development of, to 1830s, 147; on character development, 157-59, 161-62; on value of experience, 159-60; and social control, 179-80

Albion, Robert G.: on social background of merchants, 71-72

Alcott, William A.: *Young Man's Guide,* 151-53, 155-56; *Familiar Letters to Young Men,* 156, 215n

Alexander, J. W., 152

Ambition: attitudes toward, 68, 103-4, 118, 127-28, 129-30, 133, 134, 203.

American Phrenological Journal, 213

Apprenticeship: and early mercantile practice, 12-13, 74-75; in New York City art world, 76-78; breakdown of, 12-15, 83-105, 163-78, 211

Arthur, Timothy Shay: on ambition, 68, 203; *True Riches,* 68; on reputation, 162-63; biography of, 188-89; *Retiring from Business,* 188-96; on business activity and social stability, 193-96; on etiquette, 196-98; *Making Haste to be Rich,* 200-201, 205; *Sparing to Spend,* 201-9; and views

on social stasis, 207-9; *Riches Have Wings,* 208-9; on social mobility, 204-9; *Advice to Young Men,* 163, 196-98

Association for Improving the Condition of the Poor (New York), 46

Association for the Suppression of Gambling (New York), 244-51; and surveillance of young men, 246-50; and social stability, 249-51; and recruitment of workforce, 249-52; lack of support for, 251-52

Barrett, Walter. *See* Scoville, Joseph A.

Belden, E. Porter: and scale model of New York City, 40

Bellows, J. N.: on business education, 176-78

Bethune, Rev. George W.: on political leadership, 237-38, 329-40; on social education of young men, 238-39; on recruitment of workforce, 240-43

Biography: as vicarious experience, 160-61

Broadway, 31, 42-43

Browne, Junius Henri: on poor, 51-53; on "fashionable classes," 57-58

Buntline, Ned. *See* Judson, E. Z. C.

Business Activity: and insanity, 101-2, 198, 200; and social stability, 193-96; and dishonesty, 199, 262-63

Business novels: of Joseph A. Scoville, 98-105; of Timothy Shay Arthur, 68, 188-96, 200-201, 201-9

Business schools: appearance of, 173-76

Butler, Charles: *The American Gentleman*, 162, 210-11.

Chapin, E. H.: on the poor, 54

Character: development of, urged, 157-59, 161-62; and social stability, 161-162; in Timothy Shay Arthur's novels, 202, 205-6; and Mercantile Library Association, 256

Cities. *See* New York (City); Urban Change

Clarke, Rev. John, 150

Clerks: defined as young men, 168-69; duties of, 111-15, 117-18, 124-36 changing experience of, 163-78

Coles, John B., 87

Constitution of Man (George Combe), 131

Curtis, George William, 228n

Country Boy, ideal of, 93-96

Davies, John D., 213, 221

Dickens, Charles, 47, 60-62

Dodge, David Low, 69, 70

Dodge, D. Stuart, 81

Dodge, William E., 67-82, 106n; career of, 69-71, 78-79; and social breakdown, 79-82

Economic stagnation: fears of, 125-26, 207n, 209

Elkins, Stanley, 228

Employer-employee relations: changing nature of, 163-78; and appearance of business schools, 173-76; and changes in business education, 176-78; and changing view of young men, 178

Etiquette: and social stability, 196-98

Fanshaw, Millikin and Townsend, 138-41.

"Fashionable Classes"; as social problem, 47, 56-58

Ferris, Rev. Isaac, 230-33, 245

Five Points, 23, 57-58

Five Points Mission, 64-67

Fowler, Lorenzo, 245

Fowler, Orson and Lorenzo, 109, 211

Fowlers and Wells, 211-13, 226

Fowler's Phrenological Cabinet, 108

Frederickson, George, 228

Gilbert, Albert, 245

Greeley, Horace, 245

Guidebooks (New York City): and class divisions, 46-48; and depiction of vice, 48-49; as advice to newcomers, 48-51; and representation of the poor, 51-54; as way to conceptualize social change, 46-64; and picture of the slum, 55-56; and poverty, 59-61; and view of the city, 59-63; and view of "fashionable classes," 56-58, 63

Hardie, James: census of new buildings, 26-30; *Description of New York*, 48

Hartley, Robert M., 46n

Havens, R. N.: career of, 245; defends Association for the Suppression of Gambling, 245-48

Hawes, Joel: *Lectures to Young Men*, 148-51

Hawley, Amos, 30

Hoffman, Williams, 106-21; career of, 107-18; seeks employment, 108-11, 115-17; and lack of experience, 108-9; as clerk, 111-15, 117-18; on California fever, 115; reflects on career, 118: on ambition, 118; as diarist, 119-20; patterns of advancement, 118-20

Hone, Philip: career of, 34-35; on urban growth, 36-38; on social change, 38-39; on social divisions, 46; on value of Mercantile Library Association, 258-59
Hopkins, Harry, 76-78
Hopkins, Mark, 76, 218n
Hunt, Freeman: career of, 164; advice on value of experience, 159-60; on mercantile prestige, 184-86
Hunt's Merchants' Magazine, 164

Immigrants, 32, 33. *See also* Poor, as pictured in guidebooks
Individualism, 221, 228
Institutional breakdown, 12-14; and evangelical religion, 79-82; in writings of Joseph A. Scoville, 92-93, 98, 105; in writings of T. S. Arthur, 188-96, 201-9; and phrenology, 211, 215-16, 221-25; and YMCA, 226-28, 242-43; and Association for the Suppression of Gambling, 244-51; and Mercantile Library Association, 258-59; and role of benevolent organizations, 259-66

Judson, E. Z. C. [pseud. Ned Buntline], 51

Lee, Henry, 74-75
Little, Alden and Company, 124-36 passim., 140
Lord, Daniel: on problems of young men, 233-35; on practical religion, 235-36; on social role of YMCA, 236-37

M'Keon, Joseph, 245
Mercantile Library Association, 252-59; early purposes of, 252-53; appeal to merchants, 254-57; appeal to young men, 256-58; as employment bureau, 257; and social mobility, 258-61; as social oasis, 263-64

Merchant Prince: ideal of, 86-88, 180-81
Merchants: social problems of, 11-16; and sensitivity to change, 35; and tradition, 67-69, 83-89; background and training of, 72-75; and social control, 210-11, 226-28; and recruitment of workforce, 13, 120-21, 221-25, 240-43, 261-66; as members of honorable profession, 180, 181-85; and feelings. of social decline, 184-87; and interest in phrenology, 214-17; and support of YMCA, 241-43; and support of Mercantile Library Association, 254-57; and support of benevolent organizations, 261-66
Merrill, Nelson, 166-67
Mill, John Stuart: on economic stagnation, 207n
Mott, Dr. Valentine, 123

Nevins, Allan, 38
New England Society in the City of New York, 72
New Illustrated Self-Instructor in Phrenology and Physiology, 218-20
New York Association for the Suppression of Gambling. *See* Association for the Suppression of Gambling
New York (City): growth of, 25-34; visual representations of, 40-44; as dangerous to young men, 230-31; as pictured in guidebooks, 48-51. *See also* Guidebooks (New York City)
New York Magdalen Society, 172n
New York Mercantile Library Association. *See* Mercantile Library Association
New York Trade Agency, 173n
New York Young Men's Christian Association. *See* Young Men's Christian Association

Old Brewery, The, 61

Osbrey, John, 138, 142-43

Petrie, George H., 228-29

Phelps, Anson G., 71, 72-73

Phrenology, 108-9, 131, 210-25; growth of, in 1840s, 210-13; merchant interest in, 213-17; and career guidance, 217-21; social functions of, 221-25

Poor, 33; and social change, 46-47; as pictured in guidebooks, 51-54

Prime, Samuel I.: and reaction to social change, 55-57

Reputation, 162-63

Riesman, David, 227

Romaine, Lawrence, 28

Ross, Joel: view of the poor, 49, 59-60

Rothman, David J.: *Discovery of the Asylum*, 17-18

Scott, Donald M., 199

Scoville, Joseph A. [pseud. Walter Barrett], 72, 83-105, 172n; career of, 84-85; on generational divisions, 83-84, 95-97; as author of *Old Merchants of New York*, 85-86; and mercantile tradition, 86-89; and view of social change, 89-90; and view of younger generation, 83-84, 90-93; on self-made man, 93-96; on social education of young men, 96-97, 98-105; *Clarence Bolton*, 98-105; on social mobility, 104-5

Sedgwick, Catherine Maria, 63-64

Self-Made Man, 93-96

Sizer, Nelson, 224

Smith, Elizabeth Oakes: *The Newsboy*, 55, 63

Social change: New Yorkers' view of, 45-48

Social control: and advice literature, 179-80; and phrenology, 221-25; and benevolent organizations, 240-43, 249-52, 258-61

Social mobility: attitudes toward, 67-69, 98-105, 118, 129-30, 200-209, 249-52, 258-61

Social stability: and writings of Joseph A. Scoville, 98-105; and character development, 161-62, 205-6; and ideal of Merchant Prince, 179-80; and T. S. Arthur's novels, 188-96, 201-9; and YMCA, 226-28, 240-43; and benevolent organizations, 258-61

Sparing to Spend (Timothy Shay Arthur), 201-9, 250, 259

Suffern, Thomas, 142

Tailer, Edward N., Jr., 121-43, 227, 263; advancement pattern of, 120-21, 129-30, 142-43; chooses a career, 122-24; on California fever, 124-25; on physical training and fear of economic collapse, 125-26; on self-defense training, 131; seeks employment, 124, 138-39, 141; and ambition, 127-28, 129-30, 132-34; interest in phrenology, 131; impatience as clerk, 129-36

Tappan, Arthur: on surveillance of work-force, 172n

Taylor, William R., 157n

Tracy, Charles, 259-60, 262-63

Urban change: James Hardie on, 26-30; Philip Hone on, 36-38; visual representations of, 40-44; use of Dickens to conceptualize, 47, 60-62

Van Doren, William H., 153

Wall Street, 31, 41-42

Waterbury, Jared Bell, 153-55

Wayland, Francis, 207n

Wells, Samuel R., 212, 221, 225

Whitney, Stephen, 90-91

Wise, Daniel, 157-58

Workforce: channeling of, 13-14,

217-25; recruitment of, 226-27, 242-43, 265-66

Work: changing nature of, 163-78

Young men: viewed as social problem, 13-14, 67-69, 83-84, 90-93, 151-56, 190-91, 230-31, 262-63; advice offered to, 157-61; defined as clerks, 168-69; and changing employer-employee relations, 178; and YMCA, 226-43

Young Men's Christian Association (New York), 226-43; origins of, 228-30; and recruitment of workforce, 226-27, 240-43; merchant support of, 226, 241-43; as surrogate family, 231, 264-65; first constitution of, 232-33; and recruitment of social and political leaders, 236-39; and social control, 259-61; as social oasis, 263-64

Young Merchant, The, 159